Roadkill on the Three-chord Highway

Roadkill on the Three-chord Highway

ART AND TRASH IN AMERICAN POPULAR MUSIC

COLIN ESCOTT

ROUTLEDGE
NEW YORK · LONDON

Published in 2002 by
Routledge
29 West 35th Street
New York, NY 10001

Published in Great Britain by
Routledge
11 New Fetter Lane
London EC4P 4EE

Copyright © 2002 by Colin Escott
Routledge is an imprint of the Taylor & Francis Group.

Printed in the United States of America on acid-free paper.

Cataloging-in-Publication Data is available from the Library of Congress.

ISBN 0–415–93782–5—ISBN 0–415–93783–3 (pbk.)

Contents

Introduction

On October 4, 1934, the Boswell Sisters recorded "Rock and Roll." One month later, it became the first record with *rock 'n' roll* in the title to dent the charts. These are trivia-obsessed times, so you might need to know that. The Boswells were the Spice Girls of their day, except they didn't dance because Connee Boswell's legs were partially paralyzed (she at least sang on pitch without studio gizmos). The Boswells aren't the key that unlocks the secret history of rock 'n' roll, though. "Rock and Roll" was just a goofy novelty record.

Only gradually did it become clear that there was no such key. There were just trails. Follow them back and then back some more. The Everly Brothers borrowed the sound of the Louvin Brothers. The Louvins sang an old murder ballad called "The Knoxville Girl," and if you dig around you'll find that the Blue Sky Boys recorded a spookier version twenty years earlier, in 1937, and that the first recorded version dated all the way back to the dawn of the country record business in 1924. Dig around some more and you'll find that the song came over from England as "The Wexford Girl," but what's really interesting is that "The Wexford Girl" isn't really "The Knoxville Girl." Something happened in the darkness and isolation of Appalachia, something indefinable. It happened before the recording machine and it happened in the little hollers and valleys. The American experience warped and transformed the immigrants, changing their music as it changed them. "The Knoxville Girl" is eerier and darker then "The Wexford Girl," despite the fact that "The Wexford Girl" is more explicit.

Likewise, blues and jazz are not African musics. You can point to some rhythms, drones, dances, or "primitive" instruments that seem to come from the Caribbean and thence from Africa, but west Africa doesn't really explain the blues. There are missing links we'll never understand. It was only in the 1920s that record companies began their unwitting documentation of American ethnic music. If there had been a record company in New Orleans in the 1880s and 1890s, perhaps we would understand how the freed slaves and Creoles took the instruments left behind by the Confederate marching bands and began improvising, thus creating jazz. If someone with portable recording equipment had traveled through Mississippi in the nineteenth century, we might figure out how the blues developed from field chants. There are tantalizing little accounts, like one from W. C. Handy, that point to a strange unheard music, quite dissimilar from anything we know as "blues." In 1903, Handy was traveling through Cleveland, Mississippi, leading a brass band when a trio of musicians comprising bass, guitar, and mandolin played a blues for him. "They struck up one of those over-and-over strains," Handy wrote later. "It seemed to have no very clear beginning, and no ending at all. . . . On and on it went, a kind of stuff that has long been associated with cane rows and levee camps." Handy took out a pencil and jotted down some of what he'd heard. Later, waiting for a train in Tutwiler, Mississippi, he listened to a shabbily dressed man play a slide guitar and sing a mournful song. It's a compelling image: two black men alone on a deserted railroad platform at nightfall; one a schooled musician, the other down-at-heel and relatively unskilled. But the schooled musician realized that the unschooled musician knew something he didn't. The tragedy of the music business is that it captured moments like that, then recorded over them.

This book is about earlier times and forgotten stuff. I had other, probably more entertaining, ideas. I intended to go to friends at record labels, asking for the most outrageous superstar stories, the kind of stories that get traded around the bar when record company folk get together. I was going to call it *Tales from Mount Hubris*. But instead I was drawn back to talking about the untalked about.

Rock music started taking itself seriously in the 1960s, and now that we have a little more perspective we can see that some interesting stuff happened as the books and docs started appearing. For one thing, it wasn't enough to sound the part; you had to *look* the part. This was almost as true before MTV as after. It was probably for that reason that poor old Bill

Haley was written out of the story. The Haley-less history of rock was so complete by the time PBS aired a multipart history of rock (with accompanying book) that the poor guy barely rated a footnote. He didn't belong in the designer history of rock 'n' roll because he didn't look cool, and the Pennsylvania polka bars where he started didn't have the same eye candy appeal as Beale Street after dark. But Bill Haley had figured out rock 'n' roll by 1952. In May of the following year he scored the first rock 'n' roll hit, "Crazy, Man, Crazy." Percy Faith's "Theme From Moulin Rouge" had just supplanted Patti Page's "Doggie in the Window" as the Number 1 record when "Crazy Man, Crazy" charted. It would be another year before Elvis Presley made his first record. "Crazy, Man, Crazy" wasn't R&B, wasn't country, wasn't pop. It was rock 'n' roll, and Bill Haley was there first. I wish I had something new and substantive to add to Haley's story, but I don't. I've just always felt sorry for him, dying neglected and mad on the Mexican border, and I've felt drawn to those similarly mad and neglected.

These little pieces run the gamut of forgotten ones, like West Coast country singers overlooked in the Nashville-centric history of country music, and the tragically unhip, like Jim Reeves and Perry Como. And it's only fitting that we conclude with Vernon Oxford, who came to Nashville thinking that it was his celestial city, only to find he was too country for country—a hell of a fate.

Colin Escott
Nashville

PART I

The Smoother Side of Town

CHAPTER 1

Roy Orbison

STARLIGHT LIT MY LONESOMENESS

F. Scott Fitzgerald surely couldn't have written "There are no second acts in American lives" if he'd witnessed Roy Orbison's astonishing rebirth. Most rock stars die dreaming of the Big Comeback, but Roy Orbison died in the middle of one.

Through all the upturns and downturns, Orbison seemed to maintain a Zen-like calm. When interviewers spoke to him during the last months of his life, he was polite and deferential, taking his renewed success in stride. Eighteen years earlier, in 1970, when Orbison was a negative equity pop star, Martin Hawkins and I spoke to him backstage at a pitifully small theater in an English coastal town. If he was wondering what ghastly turn of fate had brought him to a half-empty house in a dreary off-season English seaside resort, it didn't show. He was polite, deferential, and willing to talk for ages to two neophyte journalists with no credentials whatsoever.

Roy Orbison was a true enigma. Born in Texas, he recorded in Nashville and lived most of his life there, yet wasn't a country artist. Not only was there no "country" in his music, there was almost no "southernness." His greatest recordings are curiously timeless and placeless. He was the lonely blue boy out on the weekend: got a car—no date. Equally intriguing is the fact that his signature hit "Only the Lonely" wasn't a progression from earlier singles. It's almost as if the nine previous records were by another Roy Orbison.

These days, if a record bores or irritates you, it does so for at least four

Roy Orbison, c. 1960. Courtesy Bear Family Archive.

or five minutes. Roy Orbison came from a different era. He understood compression. He'd relate a short story or imprint his mood on you in two-and-a-half minutes. The great Roy Orbison records were perfect pop symphonettes. Bruce Springsteen especially admired the little introductions that "synthesized everything down so perfectly." Two-and-a-half minutes later came the Kleenex Klimax. Not a surplus word or note.

Roy Orbison was a star, yet not. His biggest hits came during the early and mid-1960s pretty-boy era, but there were no stories in *16* magazine. "My dream date with Roy Orbison"?—not likely. "Roy's Pet Peeves"?—who cared? He was the career outsider. "Only the lonely know the way I feel" after all.

Orbison's music was very much his own, setting him apart in that era. He wrote most of the songs and effectively coproduced his sessions, which made him a prophet of sorts. Within a few years, the Beatles, the Rolling Stones, and the Beach Boys, among many others, would be clamoring for that same level of artistic control. Orbison stretched the boundaries and unsettled the imagination. What or where was a Blue Bayou? Nowhere I'd been. Sometimes, he was almost surreal. "In Dreams" was a deliciously poetic record that seem to drift out of the shadows: "A candy colored clown they call the sandman tiptoes to my room every night. . . . " Very different; delivered in *that* voice, very weird. Even the name Roy Orbison had a touch of unreality. Do you know anyone else called "Orbison"?

Two biographers couldn't quite come to terms with the fact that Roy Orbison's life was, by rock star standards, untainted by perversion or paranoia. This little piece tries to unravel the music more than the man, although, of course, the two are inextricable. Roy Orbison's great records were far outnumbered by middling-to-bad records, but for four years he was the most innovative artist in popular music. How did he suddenly elevate himself to greatness in 1960? Why did it all dissolve so fast? Why was he playing a half-empty auditorium in an off-season British coastal resort just five years after topping all the charts in 1965?

Willie Nelson and Texas mythologists would be hard-pressed to find romance in the part of west Texas where Roy Orbison grew up. It's as desolate as anywhere in the world. There seem to be just two colors: light tan and brown. No one seems to know where the Orbisons came from or how they ended up there. Local history files in North Carolina carry references to Orbisons as far back as the 1750s, but we know little of Roy's immediate forebears. His father, Orbie Lee, was born in Texas on January 8, 1913, and his mother, Nadine Schultz Orbison, was born on July 25, 1914. Orbie was a rigger, holding down a hard job in a brutally inhospitable climate. Roy was born in Vernon, Texas, on April 23, 1936, but Orbie Lee and Nadine moved to Fort Worth to work in the defense plants shortly after the United States entered the Second World War. It was there that Roy acquired his first guitar. Orbie taught him some chords, and took him to see Ernest Tubb playing on the back of a flatbed truck.

The story of Roy's earlier years has been pieced together in the biographies, so there's little need to recap much of it here. Very briefly, he was sent back to Vernon in 1942 because of a polio epidemic in Fort Worth. While there, he made his first radio appearance on KVWC (a delightful acronym for Keep Vernon Women Clean). He performed every Saturday for a while, bicycling down to the station. After the war, the Orbisons moved to the Permian Oil Basin. Roy was an albino with chronically poor eyesight. He wasn't good-looking; he had no money; and he lived in a town called Wink. "Football, oilfields, oil, grease, and sand," was how he later characterized that part of west Texas; he rarely if ever went back. Wink tried to claim him as its own, but Orbison was having none of it. He felt an apartness from an early age. "You know," he said later, "I wrote 'Only the Lonely' in west Texas." The implication was obvious.

Roy began to dye his sandy hair black at an early age, and heard something in his voice that promised deliverance from a bleakly predictable future. As he said later, "I didn't think it was a good voice, but I thought it was a voice you would remember if you heard it again." Talking about music with David Booth, he said, "My first music was country. I grew up with country radio in Texas. The first singer I heard on the radio who really slayed me was Lefty Frizzell. He had this technique which involved sliding syllables together that really blew me away." Roy and Orbie went to see Lefty. They pulled into the parking lot and saw a car sticking out ten feet farther than all other cars. It was Lefty's Cadillac, and its image seared itself into Roy's brain. You could drive out of Wink in that Cadillac; drive out and never look back. When Roy signed a buddy's high school yearbook it was as "Roy 'Lefty Frizzell' Orbison," and when he joined the Traveling Wilburys toward the end of his life it was as Lefty Wilbury. For all that, Lefty Frizzell doesn't explain Roy Orbison, not in the way that Lefty explains, say, Merle Haggard.

Around 1949, Roy's buddy, Billy Pat Ellis, borrowed the high school drum kit, and he and Roy put together a band, the Wink Westerners. They appeared on KERB in Kermit, Texas, and the character of their music can be judged by their name and the Roy Rogers bandanas tied jauntily around their necks. "We played whatever was hot," recalled mandolinist James Morrow. "Lefty Frizzell, Slim Whitman, Webb Pierce . . . we did a lot of their numbers. We also played a lot of Glenn Miller–styled songs, like 'Stardust' and 'Moonlight Serenade,' which we adapted for string instruments. I played the electric mandolin and later the saxophone. I fed the mandolin through an Echoplex amp so it sounded like an organ sometimes." Morrow's electric mandolin had an eerie sound that complemented Roy's voice, but there were many bands as good or unusual as the Wink Westerners—and many better.

In his 1954 high school yearbook, Roy spelled out his ambitions: "To lead a western band / Is his after school wish / And of course to marry / A beautiful dish." And he did, and he did. In the fall of 1954, he went to North Texas State College in Denton, and subsequently transferred to Odessa Junior College for his second year. He studied geology in Denton, preparing to follow his father into the oilfields if all else failed, but, after flunking his first year exams, he switched to English and history.

The Wink Westerners became the Teen Kings, and the explanation for the name change is simple: Elvis. Those yellow Sun records from Memphis turned Roy Orbison's head around. It's hard to date the epiphany because Elvis all but lived in mid- and west Texas in 1955, and he was on the Louisiana Hayride, which blanketed Texas, every week. "I was at the University of North Texas," Roy recalled, "and my father wrote me a letter. He said he had seen a concert with Elvis Presley and it was terrible. He said this greasy-haired kid came out and stole the show. Anyway, Elvis came to town and about four hundred of us showed up. It had to be late summer because everyone had gotten on trains and gone to Abilene to see a football game. Elvis came out and I thought I saw him spit onto the stage. As he walked out, he just went Puhhh. It was him, Scotty Moore, Bill Black, Floyd Cramer, and my old drummer. The show was pretty good. He sang a lot of other people's songs." Elvis was in Odessa in February 1955, but Roy would have been in Denton at the time, so perhaps this was the show that Orbie saw. Then Elvis was at the Big "D" Jamboree (within driving distance of Denton) in April 1955 and back in west Texas in June, August, September, and October 1955. Roy could have been at any or all of those dates.

Frat party days. Left to right: Jack Kennelly, Johnny Wilson, Roy, Billy Pat Ellis, James Morrow. Courtesy Bear Family Archive.

The Teen Kings won a talent contest sponsored by the Pioneer Furniture company in Midland, and the prize was a television appearance. Roy persuaded Pioneer to sponsor a Friday night show on KMID-TV and a Saturday afternoon show on KOSA-TV Odessa. Television was a novelty in west Texas, but Roy was amazed how many more people turned up at their gigs once they started announcing them on television: another epiphany.

Roy returned from Denton with an original song, "Ooby Dooby." He'd learned it from two fellow students, Wade Moore and Dick Penner, who had written it in fifteen minutes on the flat roof of the frat house at North Texas State. Roy had seen them perform it onstage at a free concert. "They sang this song and the people went crazy," he remembered. So he sang it too. It appears as though Roy first recorded it at some point in late 1955 or early 1956 during a demo session, possibly at Jim Beck's studio in Dallas. Beck scouted acts for Columbia Records' head of country A&R, Don Law, although Roy remembered that the audition was held by someone called "Green." It's possible that he was thinking of RCA's roving A&R man, Charlie Grean. Roy was friends with Charline Arthur, a female rockabilly singer of uncertain sexual orientation, who recorded in Dallas for RCA, so it's possible that she arranged an audition with Grean.

Columbia's Don Law had signed Lefty Frizzell, but saw no merit in Roy "Lefty Frizzell" Orbison. He gave the acetate to one of his contracted artists, though, and the otherwise forgotten Sid King recorded "Ooby Dooby" on March 5, 1956. One day earlier, Roy Orbison cut the song at Norman Petty's studio in Clovis, New Mexico, together with "Trying to Get to You." It became the first release on Je-Wel Records. (Je-Wel was a rough acronym for JEan Oliver and WELdon Rogers.) The Je-Wel story isn't really relevant to our story, and doesn't explain where "Only the Lonely" came from, but it's a fascinating little sidebar that says something about the usually well-disguised Orbison ambition.

Je-Wel was underwritten by Jean Oliver's oil executive father, Chester. "We had this TV show on Channel 2 in Midland," Weldon Rogers told Kevin Coffey.

> Just before we came on for thirty minutes there was a young band on for thirty minutes. It was Roy Orbison and the Teen Kings. So, anyway, we had a session set—we were going to do a session at Norman Petty's—and the gentleman that went in with me on this deal, Chester Oliver, said, "Did you listen to them boys in there?" I said, "Yeah, I listened to them." He said, "What do you think?" I said, "Well, they don't play my kind of music, but I tell you what, they are very, very good for the type of music they do. They're tops." He said, "Well, I was thinking we ought to go talk to this young man that's the head of the group—what's his name?" I said, "Orbison? Roy Orbison? He goes to college out at Odessa." He said, "Let's go talk to him to see if they'd be interested in recording. Do you think it'd sell?" I said, "Yep. It sure would." So we talked to him a night or so later, went over to his apartment in Odessa. . . . He said, "Well, I've been turned down by every record label there is . . . we've tried 'em all." I said, "Well, we'll put you on a label and if it

does what I think it will, you'll get a label deal—I plan on getting you a good deal on a label."

The Olivers lived in Seminole, Texas, sixty miles north of Odessa and 150 miles from Clovis. Roy's mandolin player, James Morrow, claimed at one point that he dated Jean Oliver and paid for the Clovis session. Roy once insisted that he paid for it, but in an interview with Glenn A. Baker he confirmed Rogers's account: "There were some people in Seminole, Texas who wanted me to make a record for them, so they paid for the time. It was the first custom session Norman Petty ever did." Within a year, Petty would be working with Buddy Holly and forging a little musical frontier in Clovis. In retrospect, Roy might have been well-advised to hang around.

"I was selling those records just as fast as I could peddle 'em," said Rogers.

> They were selling faster than I could get 'em pressed. Sid Wakefield out in Phoenix, Arizona pressed the record for me and did a good job. We were selling records galore. Cecil Holifield had a record shop in Odessa and a record shop in Midland. He was selling a lot of those records. I went back about a third time to take him a hundred. There was a music store in Lubbock that bought 'em 250 at a time—and a week later they called, "Hey, I'm out! I need some more." It was doing that well. Well, Cecil Holifield, it stirred him up. [He] picked up the phone down there and called Sam Phillips at Sun Records in Memphis. When I signed a contract with Roy Orbison, age did not enter my mind or Mr. Oliver's mind. We just took for granted that he was of age. Well, he wasn't. He was only nineteen. We didn't ask him. He didn't tell us. He signed the contract—but you know about how much that was worth. And that's what Cecil Holifield called Sam Phillips and told him: "I got some boys out that's got a record that's just selling like hotcakes and this old boy that signed him to a contract don't know that he's just nineteen. If you'll get them down there and record them, you can make a mint with this old boy." So Sam Phillips got in touch with Roy, said, "You boys come on down. Bring your father to sign the contract with you." In the meantime, they filed an injunction against me and Mr. Oliver in the district court in Odessa, an injunction to stop me from selling his records.

Roy more or less bears out Rogers's account. The Je-Wel record had probably been on the market no more than a few days or weeks when Sam Phillips approached Roy. "I took this recording from Clovis to Cecil Holifield," Roy told Baker. "He played it on the phone for Sam Phillips. Called Sam on the spur of the moment right there. Sam said, 'Can't hear anything. You'll have to send it to me.' He sent it and Sam called Mr. Holifield and Mr. Holifield called us and said, 'Can you be in Memphis in three days?' And I said, 'Yeah, we will.' I was under contract but I had the opportunity to be on Sun Records, so I asked my dad about it. 'What am I gonna do here?'" It was probably Phillips's idea, not Orbie Lee's, to ask if Roy had been twenty-one when he signed the contract, and it was almost certainly Phillips's idea to slap a cease-and-desist on Rogers and Oliver. A district judge ruled against Je-Wel, and then, according to Rogers, "The judge ordered me to give Roy all of the records that I had on hand . . . about fifty is all I had with me. So I gave 'em to him. Later on, I went back to Norman Petty's and I told Norman what happened. It made Norman [mad]—it hacked him off pretty good. He said, 'What exactly did that judge tell you?' I said, 'He told me that I had to turn over all the records that are on hand to Roy Orbison.' 'Did he tell you, "Do not press any more?"' I said, 'No, Norman, he didn't tell me that. There wasn't anything said about that.' 'You need quite a few of 'em, don't you?' I said, 'Yeah.' He reached over and got the phone, said, 'This call's on me.' He called Sid Wakefield in Phoenix and said, 'Press this Je-Wel 101—press five thousand up and send 'em to me just as soon as you can get 'em here.' So, anyway, we sold another five thousand records of that—except for about a dozen that I kept." This would certainly account for the fact that, although rare, Je-Wel 101 is available with several different label backgrounds and is nowhere near as hard to find as it would be if it had been on the market just a few weeks.

Roy Orbison on Sun Records is one of the great comic horror stories of the record business. Rarely was an artist so misunderstood, especially by someone who had such a sparkling track record, as did Sam Phillips. It seems as though Phillips's golden ear told him that he was onto something, but didn't tell him what it was. For Roy Orbison, Sun Records was the celestial city. He was standing where Elvis had stood. The idea of saying no to "Mr. Phillips" was unthinkable. Roy knew how many kids simply wanted the opportunity because he saw them lined up outside the studio, and saw the tapes arrive in the morning mail.

"My first reaction," Phillips recalled many years later, "was that 'Ooby Dooby' was a novelty type thing that resembled some of the novelty hits from the thirties and forties. I thought if we got a good cut on it, we could get some attention. Even more I was impressed with the inflection Roy brought to it. In fact, I think I was more impressed than Roy." This was an astute observation. Some say that rock 'n' roll was R&B under another name, yet songs like "Ooby Dooby" and "Be Bop-a-Lula" were closer in many ways to dumb old pop novelty songs like "Hoop-Dee-Doo" than to R&B or blues. R&B was adult music; rock 'n' roll was not. "Ooby Dooby" certainly wasn't.

Sensing that "Ooby Dooby" might break like "Blue Suede Shoes," Phillips moved fast, bringing the Teen Kings to Sun in late March or early April 1956 to rerecord the song. According to Weldon Rogers, Phillips called him during the session:

> After all of this, Sam Phillips had the nerve to call me one night at home when they were doing the session down there. [He] couldn't get the sound in his studio that Norman Petty had gotten. He told me, "This is Sam Phillips at Sun Records. Weldon, I understand you cut a record with Roy Orbison and the Teen Kings." And I said, "You ought to know about it." He said, "I hope there's no hard feelings. . . . By the way, do you still have the master for that?" "Yeah, I've got it." "I'm recording these boys down here and we can't get the sound that they had at Norman Petty's studio and I wonder if you would sell me that master?" I said, "Yeah, I'll be happy to sell it to you." "What would it take to buy it?" I just pulled a figure out of the air: "I'll take one thousand for it." "Oh my," he said. "You ain't got nothing like that much in it." I said, "It's not any of your business what I've got in it. You asked me what I'd sell it for. So I'll just keep it."

It's true that "Ooby Dooby" was a dumb song, making it all the more remarkable that one of the writers, Dick Penner, became a professor of English literature, but it was a remarkable little record nonetheless. There was fragility and tenderness in Roy's voice, and he had crafted a lyrical guitar solo that he repeated note-for-note on the Columbia audition, the Je-Wel recording, and the Sun recording. Phillips might not have known what to do with Roy Orbison, but he knew how to capture that guitar sound. And then there was the ending. What other rock record ends with five descending acoustic bass notes?

Roy and the Teen Kings, c. 1956. Courtesy Colin Escott.

Sid King's Columbia recording of "Ooby Dooby" was hitting the streets, so Phillips was in a hurry to get Roy's version released. Given the haste, it would have made sense to put "Trying to Get to You" on the flip side, but he told Roy that he had sold Elvis's version to RCA on the understanding that he wouldn't recut it. This, of course, was nonsense. Phillips hadn't released Elvis's version because he didn't own the music publishing, and wasn't about to release Roy's version for the same reason. Roy and his drummer, Billy Pat Ellis, offered a song they'd written—"Go! Go! Go!"—and the coupling was released in mid-May 1956.

The Teen Kings returned to west Texas after the session and heard nothing until Phillips called to tell them that the record was breaking in Memphis and other markets. Phillips had organized a booking agency, Stars Incorporated, with Presley's first manager, Bob Neal, and he placed the Teen Kings with Neal. Dropping out of school just weeks before final exams, the Teen Kings hit the road as part of a package show headlined by Johnny Cash, Carl Perkins, and Warren Smith. "We played all these unbelievable little towns," Roy remembered later. "We were trying to make stage shows out of one hit record, which is very difficult, so we jumped around on stage like a bunch of idiots." Warren Smith's drummer, Jimmie Lott, remembered that Roy wouldn't wear his glasses and would have to be led to the microphone like a blind blues singer. "We started in West Virginia or North Carolina," Roy remembered, "then wound up in Memphis." Elvis made a surprise appearance at the Memphis show, held at Overton Park Shell on June 1, 1956. This was as good as it got: on Elvis's label and sharing Elvis's stage.

"Ooby Dooby" reached Number 59 on *Billboard*'s Hot 100 and sold around 200,000 copies, but it would be the biggest hit that Roy would see for four years, and it would blind Phillips to the prospect of Roy recording anything but rockabilly. The follow-up, "You're My Baby"/"Rock House," was already too countrified and too late. "You're My Baby" was Johnny Cash's stab at rock 'n' roll. Originally titled "Little Woolly Booger," it was, he later admitted, "the worst thing I ever conceived in any field." "Rockhouse" was the themesong of Conway Twitty's group, the Rockhousers. Twitty, or Harold Jenkins as he then was, had auditioned at Sun and desperately wanted to be on the label. Phillips was sufficiently impressed with "Rockhouse" to acquire it for his publishing company, but sufficiently unimpressed with Twitty's hand-me-down Elvisisms to offer him a contract.

At some point during the fall of 1956, Roy split from the Teen Kings. The first hint of dissent came when "Go! Go! Go!" appeared with just Roy's name in the composer credit despite the fact that Billy Pat Ellis's name was on the contract. And then the record label credit ran as Roy Orbison—Teen Kings, when everyone but Roy was under the impression it would run as the Teen Kings. Then came the division of royalties and personal appearance fees. The group was meant to be a commonwealth, but someone, probably Bob Neal, whispered to Roy that he was the star.

"We split up in the studio," said James Morrow. "We had a commonwealth drawn up in which the royalties would be split five ways equally. It worked out that wasn't the way Bob Neal wanted it and evidently it wasn't the way Roy wanted it. We hadn't actually drawn up a legal document and that was where the disagreement arose. We went back and formed ourselves into another band." Billy Pat Ellis remembered that Roy and Sam Phillips had gone to Taylor's Café next door when the Teen Kings decided to load up and head back to Texas. Phillips, though, remembered sitting in his little office when Roy came in looking like death. "They were racking up their drums and walking out," he said. Jack Kennelly drove the communal Cadillac back to Wink, then looked out of his window one day to see the repo man taking it away.

Weldon Rogers now reenters the story. His affiliation with Orbison had two stings in the tail. He went to California in search of a recording contract and ended up at Imperial Records: "Lew Chudd [the president of Imperial], who [has] to be one of the most obnoxious human beings that I have ever met in my life, listened to the tapes that I had, and listened to the tape of 'Ooby-Dooby'/'Trying to Get to You.' 'That you singing that?' I said, 'Yeah.' 'Okay.' He signed me to a contract right there. I guess I was getting a little revenge. That's how I got on Imperial, thanks to Roy Orbison. So ol' Chudd, he wrote me out a check, said, 'You got some songs?' Of course, I said, 'Yeah, I've got some songs.' 'Well, do me a session and do me a good one. I don't want no stuff. Bring me back a good session.' 'I'll do the best I can.' 'You do better than that.'" The remaining Teen Kings now had something in common with Weldon Rogers: a grudge against Roy Orbison. They went to Petty's studio with Rogers in April 1957 and worked on what would be his only Imperial recording. They tackled "Trying to Get to You," but Rogers had nothing like Roy's range and it could well have been spite on Rogers's part that led him to ship Roy's version to Imperial.

Most of the surviving Teen Kings now admit that the only reason anyone has any interest in the group is because Roy Orbison was in it, but that was less apparent to them in 1956. They were peeved. Meanwhile, Roy hung around Memphis, trying to figure out the studio. Like many rock stars of the future, the studio was his natural habitat. He worked sessions for other artists, performed commercials and radio spots for Sam Phillips, and pitched one of his songs to Warren Smith. "I don't think people know how good a guitar player Roy was," noted Phillips. "He used the bass strings and played combination string stuff. He also had the best ear for a beat of anyone I recorded outside of Jerry Lee Lewis. If we had a session going, Roy would come in early and pick an awful lot just warming up and getting his fingers working. His timing would amaze me. He'd play lead and fill in with rhythm licks. I'd kid him and say, 'Roy, you're trying to get rid of the band and do it all yourself.' He just hated to lay his guitar down. He was either writing or developing a beat. He was totally preoccupied with making records." Roy became the only Sun artist to stay at Phillips's house. "Roy told me, 'We've been splitting our money, what little we've made,'" Phillips remembered. "'Basically I don't really have anything. I'd just love to stay in town.' 'Roy,' I said, 'No problem. Nobody around here's going to bed hungry. I don't usually invite my artists out to my house, I want to get away from you damn fools,' but I brought him to my house. This is when he brought Claudette in. I said, 'We can make room for her, too.' They weren't married at the time and they didn't sleep together. They stayed a long time."

Roy always insisted that Phillips derided the idea of ballads, but his third single, "Devil Doll"/"Sweet and Easy to Love," almost headed in that direction. If it had sold, Phillips might have seen the light. Taking his cue from Elvis and the Jordanaires, Roy brought in a vocal group, the Roses, from Texas. At someone's suggestion, the Roses sang "sweet and easy" as "sveedle 'n' eezy," as if Yiddish were their first language.

By Easter 1957, Roy was back in west Texas, cutting sessions at Norman Petty's studio and patching things up with the Teen Kings. He returned to Sun in October 1957. There were five days of sessions, and Phillips's logbook notes that he paid Roy's $20 tab at the Travelodge and gave him $35 to get home. By this point, Phillips was retreating from production and assigned Roy to engineer Jack Clement and music director Bill Justis. "I came to town to record," Roy recalled, "and [Jack] and Bill Justis teamed up to record me. I had two or three songs written, and they said, 'Let's go have a bite to eat.' As we were eating, Bill and Jack both said, 'Look, the material you brought is not quite up to par.' They said, 'We've got a couple of songs that we think are really right for you.' So we went back to the studio and I cut a couple of the worst recordings in the history of the world." This was no exaggeration. "Chickenhearted"/"I Like Love" was a ghastly record. Session guitarist Roland Janes remembers that Roy detested both songs, but wouldn't complain to either Clement or Justis. The situation, bad as it was, would have been worse if "Chickenhearted" had been a hit, because there would have been more in the same vein. Years later, when Roy was touring Australia with the Rolling Stones, the Stones challenged him to play the worst song he'd ever recorded. Even then, he couldn't bring himself to do "Chickenhearted," opting instead for "Ooby Dooby."

Sun was starting to leave a bad flavor in Roy's mouth. It was so obviously the place to be in April 1956, and so obviously *not* the place to be in October 1957. He'd had a taste of stardom, only to see it fade as fast as it had come, and he'd been kept on a steady diet of rock 'n' roll, ending ingloriously with "Chickenhearted." Several songs showed just how original Roy Orbison was, but they were squirreled away in little tape boxes. Perhaps the best was "This Kind of Love," which worked because it was a contradiction: a romantic rockabilly song. Then there was "A Cat Called Domino," a moody, atmospheric rocker that worked in all the ways that "Chickenhearted" didn't. If Roy's career as a rocker was going down in flames, then "A Cat Called Domino" was the one to go out on.

Roy often said that he was more or less out of the business for seven months, quite possibly the gap between the last known Sun session in January 1958 and his first trip to Nashville in July. Frustrated that his career was stuck in neutral, he admitted to being jealous of Buddy Holly's success. If he was thinking of staying in music, it was probably as a songwriter. Buddy Holly recorded two of his songs; Warren Smith scored a fleeting hit with another; and Jerry Lee Lewis sloppily refashioned "Go! Go! Go!" as "Down the Line." Then the Everly Brothers recorded "Claudette." Roy had almost quit performing when he borrowed $75 to go to Hammond, Indiana, to do a show with the Everlys. "Everyone was pitching songs to them," he recalled, "I wouldn't do that. I just said hello and headed for the door when they asked if I had any material. I said I had one song and played them 'Claudette.' They said, 'Write down the words, Roy,' so I tore off this cardboard box top and wrote down the words."

Roy had recorded two rough demos of "Claudette" at Sun, probably in January 1958. In a deposition taken in conjunction with his lawsuit against Acuff-Rose, he recalled that the Everlys' manager/publisher, Wesley Rose of Acuff-Rose, had sent him a contract for "Claudette" in care of Sun Records. "Sam Phillips got onto the phone," Roy said, "and it was a three-way conversation. I remember Sam saying that he wanted to get something out of it because I was his artist. [But] I wasn't signed as a songwriter to Sam Phillips. I remember Wesley Rose saying, 'Why do you want part of Roy's money?' And that impressed me. The next morning, I signed the contract for 'Claudette.'"

Phillips remembered it differently, insisting that he had the publishing on "Claudette" and was being asked to surrender it. If this were true, Phillips would have signed Roy to a music publishing deal at the same time he signed him to Sun, but that was almost certainly not the case. Roy had demoed songs at Norman Petty's studio, and Petty not only took half of the composer credit but all of the music publishing. The two Orbison songs that Buddy Holly recorded, "An Empty Cup" and "You've Got

Return to the Rockhouse. Roy with Sam Phillips, December 28, 1961. Courtesy Sally Wilbourn.

Love," would have been copublished by Phillips's Hi-Lo Music if Roy had been signed to an exclusive Hi-Lo contract. But they weren't, so Sam Phillips was bluffing.

"The next thing I know," said Phillips, "Roy came to me like a gentleman and said he had an opportunity to record for someone else if it was alright with me. Well, we had to sit down and have a little prayer meeting. I considered everything in my interests and hopefully in his and we worked out a deal on the songs which enabled him to do this." In all likelihood, the discussion played out in a far less friendly fashion, and the outcome suggests that Phillips had his own interests a little higher on the prayer sheet than Roy's. But then, if Phillips was prickly he had good reason. His world was crumbling. Within the space of a few weeks, he had lost Johnny Cash, then watched Jerry Lee Lewis's career self-destruct in England. During the three-way conversation with Rose, Phillips used the threat of dropping Roy from Sun, but when Roy seemed very interested in that option, Phillips decided to hold him to his contract. As part of the deal under which Roy eventually left Sun, he had to sign away the composer's royalties on all the Hi-Lo songs he had written, the most lucrative of which was "Down the Line (Go! Go! Go!)."

Talking to Joe Smith, Roy seemed to imply that Phillips had also shortchanged him on airplay royalties while he was at Sun. "I was in New Mexico," he said, "and I met a guy named Slim Willet who wrote 'Don't Let the Stars Get in Your Eyes.' He said, 'How's your BMI running?' I didn't know what he meant. He says, 'When they play your song on the air, they pay you.' I said, 'Bull.' Then he told me how much he made on 'Don't Let the Stars Get in Your Eyes.' I told Carl Perkins, 'They pay you to play those songs!' We floorboarded it all the way to Memphis to talk to Sam about it." In his autobiography, Perkins recalls just such a revelation, but says it was Jim Denny at Cedarwood Music who opened his eyes to BMI. The standard Sun/Hi-Lo music publishing contract made no mention of BMI, which could be because Phillips saw it as the songwriter's responsibility to register with BMI and collect the airplay royalties or because the BMI royalties vanished into a black hole at Sun. Talking later about his dealings with Sam Phillips, Roy said, "Sam taught me a lot about business and contracts . . . afterward." While Perkins, Cash, Lewis, and others came to look back fondly on their days at Sun, Roy never did. "Sam was pretty much full of himself," he told Joe Smith. "He seemed to know what he was doing, but, as it turned out, I don't think he did. But he lived his life the way he wanted."

Wesley Rose impressed Roy. While Sam Phillips was artistic, flamboyant, visionary, and strange, Rose was the exact opposite, an ascetic former accountant who found himself heading a music publishing company after his father, the legendary Fred Rose, died. Fred had written pop hits back in the 1920s, then written for Gene Autry before launching Acuff-Rose music publishers with Roy Acuff in 1942. In 1946, he'd discovered Hank Williams. That year, Wesley was brought in to bring some discipline to Fred's burgeoning empire, but Fred's death in 1954 left Wesley looking after the music and the books.

It had been a constant struggle to liberate money from Sun Records, but, with "Claudette" in the charts, Roy called his manager, Bob Neal, and requested that Bob call Acuff-Rose for an advance. "I said, 'How much do you think I could get?'" he recalled. "[Bob] said, 'What do you want?' I said 'I'd like to have five thousand dollars,' sort of jokingly. He said 'Okay.' He rang the next day, and five thousand dollars was in the mail. So I called Mr. Rose, and he said, 'Why don't you come to Nashville and let's have a chat.'" Roy drove from Texas to Nashville around July 1958 and signed with Acuff-Rose Publications and Acuff-Rose Artists Corporation. A few weeks earlier, Bob Neal had dissolved Stars Incorporated and cast his lot with Johnny Cash. As so often in the past, Wesley Rose played the Hank card. "He said I didn't have to read the contract because he would tear it up any time I was unhappy," Roy asserted. "He said Hank Williams never looked at a contract, he always just signed them."

Roy and Claudette moved to Nashville, and found a place on Eighth Avenue South, where Acuff-Rose was located and where there were a number of cheap motels and apartment houses. Roy's new Cadillac was parked out front, but he rarely had money to put gas in it. He sent out some tapes, one of which went to Chet Atkins at RCA Records. Not having a phone in his rooming house, he was forced to follow up from pay phones. Chet invited Roy to come see him, and signed him to a contract. Two of the RCA recordings, "Sweet and Innocent" and "Jolie," rivaled "Chickenhearted" for cranial-numbing stupidity. In all, there were seven RCA sides. Chet Atkins's ear was as golden as Sam Phillips's, yet he too missed the specialness in Roy Orbison. The simple acoustic joys of "Almost Eighteen" made it the only RCA side to almost hit the mark.

"Seems to Me," the flip side of Roy's first RCA single, was a Boudleaux Bryant song that sounded very much like an Everly Brothers reject. Just a year or so earlier, Boudleaux and his wife, Felice, had been starving in Nashville. They'd moved there from Georgia in 1950, and Felice remembered that when Boudleaux hung out at the Opry telling people that he was trying to make it as a songwriter, "they thought it was the dumbest thing they'd ever heard." Jimmy Dickens cut some of the Bryants' songs, as did Carl Smith and Eddy Arnold, but the Bryants were still scuffling when a song that had been rejected all over town, "Bye, Bye Love," was force-fed to the Everly Brothers. The Bryants were contracted to Acuff-Rose, and Wesley Rose had midwifed the Everlys' deal with Cadence Records on the understanding that Acuff-Rose songs would be used at every turn. The Bryants suddenly found that they were the only songwriters at Acuff-Rose who could deliver the sort of songs that the

Everlys needed, so they switched to teen playlets. Roy too would come to depend on them.

Roy and Claudette married in 1957 (Roy was 21; Claudette was 16) and Claudette had given birth to their first child, Roy DeWayne, shortly before the move to Nashville. Roy remembered that they only had one visitor all the while they were there—an insurance salesman. Claudette was often alone with a small child, and, at seventeen, was little more than a child herself. It's a measure of Roy's willingness to sacrifice everything for his career that he took Claudette away from her family to chase his dream. In late 1958, though, they moved back to Texas, living first with Roy's parents, then Claudette's parents. They were still in Texas when Roy's RCA deal fell apart in 1959. His total income that year was around $1700.

According to Nashville session bassist Bob Moore, Roy talked to him during the final RCA session. "He said RCA [was] not going to renew his contract," said Moore, who also insists that he was surreptitiously buying a stake in a new record label, Monument Records. "So I called Fred Foster, the owner of Monument, and said, 'You know what I heard today? RCA [is] letting Roy Orbison go. We should do something about that.' Fred took the bull by the horns and the next thing I knew we had Orbison signed." This account is born out by RCA's engineer, Bill Porter, who told John Rumble, "Bob Moore told Fred Foster that Orbison was being released and he thought maybe there was something that could be looked at there."

Fred Foster disagrees. He had been a Mercury Records promo man, and had produced the Eagles' original version of "Trying to Get to You" for the label (*these* Eagles were a D.C. area doo-wop group, not an embryonic version of *the* Eagles). He launched Monument Records on March 11, 1958, from the stockroom of J&F Wholesale Record Distributors in Baltimore, Maryland. At the time, he was managing the pop division of J&F, whose largest supplier was London Records. London was the industry's lame duck, relying on cheesy British acts like Mantovani, but it had an excellent distribution system. Marketing Director Walt Maguire decided to build a network of distributed labels, and offered Foster a deal. Foster took the name Monument from the Washington Monument, which he would see when he was flying home. He took $600 in savings, borrowed $300 from a local deejay, Buddy Deane, and another $300 from J&F, and launched his label. The first record was a hit. A local guitarist, Billy Grammer, who had lost his steady gig on the *Jimmy Dean Show* when it moved to New York, recorded an adaptation of an old folk song, "Gotta Travel On." It became a Number 4 hit early in 1959 and gave Foster much-needed encouragement and cash flow. Grammer's follow-up, a revival of Pee Wee King's "Bonaparte's Retreat," brought Foster into contact with Wesley Rose, who owned the music publishing rights to the song. Foster then remembered running into Wesley in Baltimore when Wesley accompanied his wife to Johns Hopkins University Medical Center for some tests. They talked, and Foster told Wesley to keep him in mind if he heard of any acts on offer.

Foster says that Wesley offered him the chance to sign Roy Orbison. "I remembered 'Ooby Dooby' and 'Rockhouse,'" recalled Foster. "They weren't the greatest records in the world, but Roy had a quality about him—tender, wistful—I thought I could work with. I'd also wanted to do a project with Wesley Rose, and this was an opportunity to kill two birds with one stone." Some people, Roy included, later insisted that Foster had confused "Ooby Dooby" with "Rock 'n' Roll Ruby" and thought he was getting another ex-Sun star, Warren Smith, but Foster vehemently denies this. Not much had been heard from Roy Orbison or Warren Smith since 1956, so confusing them would have been understandable. Ironically, Smith's career rebounded (as a country artist on Liberty) within months of Roy's resurgence.

The one person in the dark through all this was Roy Orbison. The last RCA session had yielded two songs, "Paper Boy" and "With the Bug," which Roy assumed would be his third RCA single. "Wesley Rose called me and said, 'I'm pulling you off of RCA and putting you on Monument,'" remembered Roy. "I said, 'What's Monument?' He said they just had a Number 1 hit with 'Gotta Travel On.' He said, 'Come fly in, we'll discuss it.' I flew into Nashville, went to Acuff-Rose, and [they] told me that I was late for my session. I said, 'I can't be. I don't have a session.' We got into a little station wagon and drove to the RCA studio. I walked in, I saw Fred Foster behind the controls and the engineer was Bill Porter. So I rerecorded the same two songs I had done with RCA, 'Paper Boy' and 'The Bug,' and after the session I got to meet Fred Foster. I also talked with Chet Atkins and Chet told me that he thought it would be a good move if I moved away from RCA because he couldn't get done what he wanted done in releasing songs and promoting artists." Chet always knew how to let them down easy.

After the session, Foster went out to eat with Roy, and Roy told him that he was preparing some songs back in Texas that were much better than "Paper Boy." This was what Foster needed to hear. The RCA sales and promo staff had already given "Paper Boy"/"With the Bug" the double thumbs down, and the sales of the Monument record, cut some six weeks after the RCA session, bore out their judgment. By this point, Roy was noodling around rock bottom. He was off RCA and on a label he hadn't heard of. It was the fall of 1959, and he hadn't had a hit as an artist since the summer of 1956. He had no bookings except hops and beerhalls in west Texas. The "Claudette" money had gone, and Acuff-Rose couldn't find any takers for his new songs.

Then came the slow turnaround.

Back in Texas, Roy had started writing with Joe Melson, leader of a group called the Cavaliers. "A mutual friend, Ray Rush, was dealing around in management," recalled Melson,

> and he loved my songwriting. I played him a song one night, and he said, "I want you to meet Roy Orbison." I think Ray wanted to show Roy that someone in the area could write songs besides him. I went to Odessa where Roy and Claudette lived with Claudette's mother. They had just released his first record on Monument, "Paper Boy." He loved my song, "Raindrops," and got a dub of it. When I was leaving, I said, "Roy, I really love your singing," and his whole face just brightened up. We became friends right then.
>
> One night I was at the drive-in, and Roy drove up. I got in his car and we had the normal musicians' conversation. Finally, he said what I wanted him to say. He said, "You write a pretty good song and I wrote a pretty good song. I believe if we put it together, we could write some great ones." I said, "Let's do it." I was studying rhythm 'n' blues and I was studying themes that were selling in the market. We'd ride around in the car and play the pop stations and try to write. We wrote some cute songs, but no quality. Then we were in adjoining motel rooms in Odessa, trying to write. I hit a melody line on the guitar and Roy really liked it. He said, "That's a real uptown melody. . . . Uptown . . . Uptown." We wrote "Uptown" that night. We moved from rock 'n' roll to class rock right then.

In his way, Melson was as out of place in west Texas as Roy. Hyperactive and slightly foppish, he nonetheless looked like an early 1960s pop star, which Roy did not. He and Roy drove to Nashville with their new songs, "Uptown" and "Pretty One." Foster flew in from Washington, and they spent three or four days going through songs and arrangements. Roy decided to ask for strings. It was the one thing he wanted more than anything in the world. Foster agreed, although by his account Wesley Rose questioned the expense, saying that Roy wasn't good-looking enough to have a big hit. "I thought, 'Boy, with friends like this, who needs enemies?'" recalled Foster, "but I just said, 'It's my money, Wes.'" If we're being picky, it was Roy's money because session costs were deducted from royalties, but Foster was the one who paid Anita Kerr to write the arrangement and then contracted three players from the Nashville Symphony. "We stood in the studio listening to the playbacks," said Melson, "and thought it was the most beautiful sound in the world." The song was built around a gently rocking Jimmy Reed shuffle, but the combination of Roy's newfound assurance and the full arrangement made it an almost wholly realized Roy Orbison record. Something was happening.

"Uptown" sold better than any Orbison record since "Ooby Dooby," peaking halfway up the Hot 100. Now Roy needed to build on that momentum. Both he and Melson take credit for "Only the Lonely," so it was probably a joint effort. Working apart a year earlier, the best they could come up with was formulaic numbers like "Raindrops" and "Almost Eighteen." Together, they found the courage to chase something different. "Only the Lonely" was different. Driving to Nashville, they detoured to Graceland with the idea of pitching it to Elvis. They figured that if Elvis took it, they could write another song before they reached Nashville. "We stopped by Elvis's house at six in the morning," Roy told Glenn Baker, "We'd driven to Memphis from Texas. We handed the guard a note telling him I was at the gate. I was going to hang around if it was too early, you know, and eventually sing this song, 'Only the Lonely,' hoping he would record it. He sent back a note and it said, 'Everybody's sleeping all over the place. Leaving for Nashville today. I'll see you there.' I thought, 'Well, he should have found out, you know, I've got a smash here.' Then I sang it for Phil Everly, and I got about halfway through, and Phil said, 'Well, I've been working on *this* song . . . ' So he wasn't blown away by it. Then I sang it for Fred Foster, and he said, 'Yeah, that's terrific.'"

Elvis, just out of the army, was indeed on his way to Nashville to record his comeback single. In fact, RCA had block-booked the studio and all the musicians that Roy wanted to use, forcing Roy and Joe to hang around town for a few days, fine-tuning "Only the Lonely." It was Foster's idea to graft on the vocal intro ("dum-dum-dum-dummy-doo-wah") from another song Roy and Joe had brought, "Come Back to Me, My Love." Once they got some studio time, Roy began probing the frightening potential of his voice. Joe led the Anita Kerr Singers on the vocal countermelody ("dum-dum-dum-dummy-doo-wah"), but Roy's voice was still quite thin and unaccustomed to anything more taxing than teen ballads. Fred Foster and Bill Porter placed him behind a coat rack laden with coats, which had the effect of isolating his voice from the other sounds in the studio. The RCA studio had a three-track recorder, which gave Porter the option of feeding Roy's vocal back upon itself in two tape loops, fattening it up before committing it to tape. If you listen to the song on CD, the slapback becomes apparent on the word "take," which becomes "take-ake-ake." Porter also rethought the standard Nashville mix, built around the rhythm section. Instead, he used Melson and the chorus as the platform, crowding them around the microphone for maximum intimacy, then built the mix around the vocal countermelody. The drums are almost inaudible. Bassist Bob Moore didn't like the way the song was heading, telling Roy it was out-of-meter and people couldn't dance to it. By this point, Roy had been brushed off by Elvis and been told obliquely by Phil Everly that his song was no good; now the bass player was telling him the kids couldn't dance to it. Anyone else would have blown a gasket. Roy just quietly persevered.

"Only the Lonely" was different. All the little hurts from west Texas poured out. Almost too dark and brooding, it was somehow universal. Roy later came to understand the song's power. "I didn't consciously think this," he told Roy Trakin, "but I realized that only the lonely know the way I feel. That's an exclusive statement, but the club is very big. I'm sure I was influenced by country music and by ballads I'd heard during the war, like 'Born to Lose' and 'No Letter Today.' I felt the need to share my loneliness, so everyone could share theirs. There was a lot of loneliness in west Texas where I grew up. We used to say it was the center of everything, five hundred miles from anything."

At some point in their short partnership, Roy and Melson began disregarding songwriting norms and drawing the specialness from each other. "We knew we had to give the public extra," Melson said. "You can't sell 'C,' 'D,' or 'F' songs in an 'A' market." Then there was the production. The Nashville standard was three songs in four hours. Foster was willing to spend all four hours on just one song, if it was *the* song. He was also willing to splash some money around at a session, calling for string arrangements and additional instruments. Coming from outside Nashville, he set his sights on a broader audience. He was willing to experiment if he thought it might lead somewhere. "I wanted exciting records," he said, "and Ray Charles was my standard for excitement." For his part, Roy began to explore the outer limits of his voice and figure out how to use its unique tonality.

The studio musicians were known as the A Team. Many outside Nashville thought them capable of no more than three chords, but they were surprisingly adaptable. Elvis used them throughout the 1960s on songs like "Little Sister," "Surrender," and "It's Now or Never." Bob Moore explains, "I was working weekends with Owen Bradley's society dance band. I knew more then three-chord country music, and so did most of the others. I led a rehearsal band on Sundays because some of the younger musicians wanted to practice. Bill Porter, who was a high school friend, engineered the sessions at RCA's Studio B. Forty or fifty musicians would come by, and the younger arrangers would bring arrangements. That's where the big sound came from. We were like a young prizefighter: hungry, lean, and wanting the recognition so bad you can taste it."

Immediately after "Only the Lonely" was released it started showing up strongly in some eastern markets, such as Boston and Baltimore. The momentum spread quickly. Roy went to New York with Foster to visit London Records. "We were in a theater watching a movie," Roy told Glenn Baker, "and Fred said, 'Let's go check the charts.' And I said, 'Well, I don't like to do that, but we will.' So we went downstairs to the [pay phone in the] men's toilet, and he called and we'd got Number 70 in one of the trade papers and Number 88 in the other. So we got really excited, and by the time we sat down to watch the movie, I told Fred, 'I don't really want to watch the movie any more,' and he said, 'I don't either.'" It peaked at Number 2 in *Billboard* during August 1960, and reached Number 1 in England in October.

Roy and Fred relocated to Nashville. Roy had become good friends with the Bryants (Boudleaux wrote the liner notes for Roy's early albums), and decided to join them in the north Nashville suburb of Hendersonville. He needed very little incentive to leave west Texas, despite the fact that he didn't have enough money to buy furnishings. The Bryants lent him some sheets and a rollaway bed.

Roy wrapped up his first album, *Lonely and Blue,* in September. The cover was Orbison-in-a-nutshell: the lonely blue boy out on the weekend, by himself at the drive-in. It included "Only the Lonely" and the two follow-ups, "Blue Angel" and "I'm Hurtin'." Both seemed to have the right ingredients, but stalled short of the top. "'Only the Lonely' went to two million," Roy said later. "'Blue Angel' was a million, and 'I'm Hurtin'' was 600,000. I said, 'I'm on my way out again.'" As 1961 dawned, he pondered his next move.

"Running Scared" is a classic of nerd triumphalism. The happy ending notwithstanding, it was the most paranoid song ever to hit the charts. The melodrama was played out to a bolero rhythm, reckoned to be the legacy of Roy's early days within earshot of Mexican radio stations. Not so according to Fred Foster: "I asked Roy if he had ever heard Ravel's 'Bolero,' and he said he hadn't, so I gave him an album with 'Bolero' on it, and asked him to write something around that rhythm. He took that record home, and loved it, but misread the time signature, which is 3/4. He heard it as 4/4, and wrote 'Running Scared' in 4/4." In an era when records were supposed to sink or swim on the basis of the first thirty seconds, Foster had the courage to begin with an intro so muted that anyone with the radio on low must have thought that the station had gone off the air. In the studio, someone—and both Melson and Foster take credit for this—suggested that the ending should be done full voice rather than falsetto. "He did it," recalled Foster, "and everybody looked around in amazement. Nobody had heard anything like it before. Bill Porter said, 'I don't believe I got that on tape.' I said, 'If you don't, it's all over for you.'"

Porter's problems stemmed from the song's dynamic range. As he explained to John Rumble, "Dynamic range is the difference between the very softest note and the very loudest. Operatic and classical music is known for having a very wide dynamic range. 'Running Scared' started off real soft, and built and built. I changed my balance concept three times trying to get the dynamics going. Harold Bradley starts out playing that acoustic guitar. Harold came in to play electric bass guitar [a six-stringed guitar tuned an octave below standard tuning]. After the intro, Harold puts the acoustic guitar down and walks about six feet. He picks up his electric, and he joins in on the song, but not at a place you would think. It's almost in the middle of a bar. He added much more depth on the low end. From the very beginning of the song to the end, there's a 25 dB [decibel] dynamic range. Classical music is about 40, so we were approaching that, which was unheard of for a commercial 45 release. If you get the sound too low, you get too much tape hiss, so you've got this small win-

Roy recording in the RCA Victor studio. Left to right: Hank Garland, Anita Kerr, Gil Wright (hidden), Dottie Dillard, Louis Nunley, Harold Bradley, Roy, James Wilkerson, Fred Foster. Courtesy Bear Family Archive.

dow you've to operate in. That's where the fun comes in. We had a few takes for Roy to get it right, and he's still out of tune on the master, but Fred said, 'That's it, we're gonna keep it.'"

Underscoring the fact that three people at the same event will remember it three different ways, Roy recalled an unintentional slight as the session's turning point: "Boudleaux Bryant suggested we use an augmented chord on the intro to 'Running Scared.' All thirty-two players didn't come in until the end of the song. When I hit that last note no one could hear it. Instead of coming out and asking me . . . or having me come in [to the control room] and telling me . . . someone just pushed the [talkback] button and said, 'We can't hear you on the ending. If you don't sing out a bit, we're gonna lose the record.' That embarrassed me and upset me, so I said, 'Run it by once again.' They did, and I really let go. I had to sing above all the people there."

Wesley Rose was also there, and he too had an agenda, insisting that Boudleaux Bryant's "Love Hurts" go on the flip side. He told Foster that he had no faith in "Running Scared." Talking later to Glenn Baker, Roy remembered, "They said, 'What's the release going to be?' and Boudleaux was standing there. He'd helped me with a little part of 'Running Scared.' He was such a kind man. I said, 'Well, I don't really . . . ' and Fred said, 'Well, I can tell you what it's going to be.' I started to punch him out because he had no right to make decisions like that. He said, 'It's going to be "Running Scared."'"

As Foster noted, he thought that putting "Love Hurts" on the flip side was "throwing away a great song, but I respected Wesley's judgment and I took both songs to Howard Miller, who was a top-rated deejay in Chicago, and asked him to spin them on the air, and let me know the response. I was in a cab on the way to the airport when I heard him on the radio saying, 'I'll have to call Fred Foster and tell him it's "Running Scared" one hundred to one.'" What no one knew was that Rose had a very specific reason for championing "Love Hurts." The Everly Brothers' five-year management deal with Acuff-Rose Artists Corporation, due to expire in May 1962, was terminated early, leading to a lawsuit and mutual recrimination. "Wesley took 'Love Hurts' that we recorded and had in the can," said Don Everly, "and he covered us with Roy Orbison. The arrangement was ours, and it was written for us. We couldn't release it as a single because we didn't know if Acuff-Rose would license it or not because we were in a lawsuit with them."

On June 5, 1961, "Running Scared" became Roy Orbison's first Number 1 hit, but was so indelibly associated with him that few have revived it since. "Love Hurts," on the other hand, has become a standard. The Everly Brothers eventually released their version; Emmylou Harris and Gram Parsons made an achingly perfect record out of it in 1974; the Scottish rock group Nazareth took it to the Top 10 in 1975; and Cher made it the title song of her 1991 collection. Had Rose not been so anxious to poke his finger in the Everly Brothers' faces, Roy could have had two hits instead of one.

"Running Scared" was followed by "Crying." Joe Melson and Roy had started it as a custom job for Don Gibson, once Acuff-Rose's star song-writer. Back in the 1950s, Gibson had written "Oh Lonesome Me," "Sweet Dreams," and "I Can't Stop Loving You" before he ran dry. The first draft of "Crying" was called "Once Again." "Then," said Roy, "we were singing along and Joe Melson said, 'Once again, I'm crying' and it occurred to me that we needed to switch straight away to 'Crying' and rewrite the song. Immediately, I thought of a past experience with a girlfriend and just retold it. I was worried about it because we had just come off 'Running Scared' and everyone said you shouldn't follow a ballad with a ballad."

"Crying" was recorded during an all-night session along with some album cuts and a rough-and-tumble blues song, "Candy Man." The latter was written by Fred Neil and Beverly Ross, surely the all-time unlikeliest songwriting partnership. Neil later wrote "Everybody's Talkin'" and stoned sixties folk anthems like "Cocaine" before disappearing to Florida to work with dolphins; he died in 2001 without ever telling his story. Beverly Ross was a career New York songwriter best known for "Lollipop" ("Lollipop, lollipop, oh lolly, lolly pop"). "Candy Man" wasn't an Acuff-Rose song, so Wesley Rose didn't like it, but as the session was held in the middle of the night, he probably wasn't there.

Once again, accounts differ. Foster remembered, "The demo of 'Candy Man' was in the style of 'What'd I Say,' which didn't fit at all. Charlie McCoy was my utility man. He'd played vibes on 'Crying,' and he said he could play harp if I wanted that old Jimmy Reed feel. I pulled the drums out into the middle of the studio, took all the sound deadening away so that [drummer Buddy Harman] was playing in everybody's microphone. Then we taped Buddy's wallet to the snare drum for the bluesy, thumpy sound."

Engineer Bill Porter confirms that the original demo of "Candy Man" was up-tempo, but takes credit for the muddy, bluesy sound. "I never heard the demo in the studio because I was doing something else," he says, "but I found it later. [Orbison's record] was a head arrangement they worked up and it was almost 180 degrees opposite from the original demo. Roy knew his music and some of the things he wanted to do. 'Candy Man' was a black-oriented song. I wanted to match the sound as much as I possibly could. I went into the bathroom and got some cloth towels. I asked Fred about it first. Said, 'I'm gonna make it sound deader.' I laid the towels across the drums. Buddy Harman hit it a couple of times and said, 'Damn,

I don't like this.' I said, 'Will you please try to work with it 'cause I think it'll get the sound we're talking about.'"

Roy later took credit for bringing the harmonica onto the song. By his account, McCoy wasn't even there at the outset. "I asked, 'Can anyone play a harmonica?' and John D. Loudermilk was there, and he said, 'I play a little bit, but not good enough for a record.' And they said, 'I know Charlie McCoy plays harmonica,' so we stopped the session, called him on the telephone and said, 'Charlie, you want to come down and play harmonica on this song?' He and Boots Randolph worked up the intro and the end pieces." Needless to say, Charlie McCoy, newly arrived in Nashville at that point, told it from another slant: "I'd done an Ann-Margret record, 'I Just Don't Understand,' and one of the guys on the session said, 'I really dig what you're doing. You want to do a session with Roy Orbison this week?'"

"Crying" eventually peaked at Number 2. Roy's second album (or third, if you count an inglorious mishmash of overdubbed Sun numbers titled *At the Rockhouse*) included both "Running Scared" and "Crying." It also included a Boudleaux Bryant song, "She Wears My Ring," which became a country chart-topper for Ray Price in 1968. Roy was starting to make a career out of throwing away great songs. He'd tried to give away "Only the Lonely," then put a Gene Pitney song, "Today's Teardrops," on the flip side of "Blue Angel," only to watch it become a hit for Rick Nelson. Wesley Rose had insisted on making a B-side out of "Love Hurts," and then "Candy Man" and "She Wears My Ring" were buried on B-sides and albums. And then, as if they'd painted targets on their feet, Roy and Joe gave one of their best songs, "I'm in a Blue, Blue Mood," to Conway Twitty.

Trying for a complete change of pace after the high psychodrama of "Running Scared" and "Crying," Roy's first single of 1962 was a jaunty rockabilly number, "Dream Baby." They kicked it off like a demo. It wasn't one of Roy's songs, but was published by Foster's Combine Music, so Foster liked it and Rose didn't. Songwriter Cindy Walker is one of the great, rarely told stories in country music. She wrote more than fifty songs for Bob Wills, and wrote hits for Jim Reeves, Webb Pierce, Ernest Tubb, Eddy Arnold, Bing Crosby, Stonewall Jackson, and many others. "Bubbles in My Beer," "You Don't Know Me," "In the Misty Moonlight," and the hauntingly desolate "Dusty Skies" were among her best work. Unlike most of Roy's hits, "Dream Baby" was heavily revived. Glen Campbell took it to the country Top 10 in 1971, as did Lacy J. Dalton in 1983. Even Smokey

Robinson and the Miracles recorded it. Roy's original reached Number 4. (Walker had long ago given up her aspiration to be a singer and rarely strayed far from her home in Mexia, Texas, but Fred Foster tempted her back into the studio to record an album, *Words and Music by Cindy Walker*, in 1964.)

Then came "The Crowd." Roy and Joe overreached on this one. It was a towering, Wagnerian ballad that almost no one remembers. Roy later concluded that it was "too fussy," and his writing partnership with Joe Melson dissolved around this time, although several of their joint efforts remained unreleased, notably "Blue Bayou." Neither Roy nor Joe talked in depth about the dissolution of their partnership. Joe was recording for Acuff-Rose's vanity label, Hickory, but was frustrated in his attempt to get his solo career off the ground. Clearly, he wanted to be more than " . . . and Joe Melson" in Roy Orbison's composer credits. He also felt that he had been largely responsible for finding the uniqueness in Roy Orbison, and he was probably right. "Even Roy admitted the fame wasn't divided equally," said Joe. "I'd helped him establish the artistry and style. We wrote songs for that voice. We made a stylist. In the writing room where nobody sees, we pieced each song together, phrase-by-phrase, step-by-step, all molded around his voice."

Now Roy was on his own. His first wholly self-composed single since the Sun days coupled "Leah" with "Working for the Man," neither of them especially memorable. "Working for the Man" was a blue-collar anthem, hinting at "Big Boss Man" and "Chain Gang." Roy later said that it stemmed from his summer in the oil patch before his transfer to Odessa. "I was working for El Paso Natural Gas in the daytime," he said, "cutting up steel and loading it into trucks and chopping weeds and painting water towers. That's where I got the idea for 'Working for the Man.' Our straw boss, Mr. Rose, wouldn't cut me any slack. I was working in the blazing heat—hard, hard labor—then I'd play at night. Some nights I'd be too tired to eat or even undress."

But then came Roy Orbison's defining moment as a songwriter. "In Dreams" was a masterpiece: a perfectly realized statement. The song came to Roy in semiwakefulness and played out in a dreamlike trance. "I was falling asleep," he said. "[I was] half-asleep and my thoughts were still racing when that whole introduction just came to me. I thought, 'Boy, that's good. I need to finish that.' I woke up the next morning. Twenty minutes later, I had the whole song written." Sensual, surreal, it ached with unfulfilled desire and longing. And it took Roy Orbison back to the Top 10 in 1963, peaking at Number 7.

"In Dreams" was followed by "Falling"/"Distant Drums." "Falling" seemed like a made-to-order hit from the out-of-tempo introduction to the towering finale, but it stalled just inside the Top 30. Once again, Roy threw away a terrific song on the flip side, "Distant Drums." Cindy Walker had written it, and in some ways it almost prefigured the Vietnam torment. She'd tried to interest Jim Reeves in recording it, but Reeves's producer, Chet Atkins, nixed the idea. Reeves made a demo, telling Walker, "I don't think you'll have any trouble getting a release on it now." Walker offered the music publishing to Foster's Combine Music if Roy would record it, and was probably disappointed to see it end up on a B-side. Months later, Reeves died, and his posthumously overdubbed demo became a Number 1 country hit in the United States and a Number 1 pop hit in England—a windfall for Fred Foster, and another lost opportunity for Roy Orbison.

Roy's big hit of 1963 was "Mean Woman Blues." Once again, the flip side, "Blue Bayou," was too good for a throwaway. Anyone without the *Rockhouse* album had no idea that Roy could shake it up as he did on "Mean Woman Blues." "We needed an uptempo song in the worst way," recalled Fred Foster, "and Roy didn't have anything suitable, so I asked him if there was anything he did live that went over well, and he said, 'Yeah, "Mean Woman Blues."'" Written by Claude DeMetrius (who had written some misogynistic blues songs for Louis Jordan back in the 1940s), "Mean Woman Blues" was a custom job for Elvis Presley's second movie, *Loving You*. In 1958, Jerry Lee Lewis refashioned what he could remember of it, and Roy's version was modeled after Jerry Lee's. Ironically, Roy had quit Sun because he didn't want to make records like this. "Blue Bayou" had been recorded back in 1961. It came to Joe Melson as he was driving through Arkansas on his way back to Texas. "They had swampy areas and I always thought of things in terms of color," he said. "Suddenly it hit me, 'Blue Bayou.'" Roy finished the song, setting it to a sensual heartbeat rhythm. Some fourteen years later, when he was all but invisible, Linda Ronstadt's revival shot to Number 3, rekindling interest in Roy's music. When asked, Roy dated the slow turnaround in his career to Ronstadt's record, despite the fact that her record missed the point. Ronstadt was full-voiced and brassy where Roy had been muted and strange.

Recognizing that he worked best with a partner, Roy began writing with fellow Texan, Bill Dees. "I met him when 'Crying' was big," Dees said later. "My group, the Five Bops, had a song that sold well around Amarillo, and we played a show with Roy. We got to talking and he found out I was writing. The next time he came to Texas, I crashed a party and he asked me if I was still writing. I said I was, and he said I should come up to the hotel room and play him what I had. I played him 'Borne on the Wind,' and that got him. I was down on my luck then, eating over at my folks' house, when Roy called and asked me to come to Nashville. I moved there and brought a partly finished song, 'It's Over.' Roy came back from a trip with an idea for the chord changes and a melody on the middle part, and we just whipped it out." In England, "Borne on the Wind" was released before "It's Over," but stalled at Number 15. "It's Over" went to Number 1 over there and Number 9 back home.

"It's Over" was from Roy's first session at Fred Foster's new studio. Back in 1961, Sam Phillips had purchased a studio in Nashville's Cumberland Lodge Building, planning to make a play for Nashville business. Instead of finding the world beating a path to his door, he found that parking was impossible and the Nashville pickers, unlike the Memphis pickers, demanded scale, so he sold the studio to Fred Foster in February 1964. Meanwhile, Bill Porter had been kicked out of RCA because he co-owned a music publishing company with Anita Kerr. After a brief stint at Columbia's Nashville studio, Foster hired him to take over the studio, so the old team was reunited in new surroundings.

The biggest hit to come from the Monument studio, indeed the biggest hit Roy would ever have, was "Oh, Pretty Woman." Roy and Bill Dees wrote it after Dees had seen Roy give Claudette some money to go shopping. Roy said, "A pretty woman doesn't need any money" (whatever *that* means), and he and Dees sat down and wrote the song. The first version had a negative ending: the girl wouldn't go out with him. Foster told them to go rewrite it. In the studio, Roy inserted a playful little growl between verses, copped from a Bob Hope movie. At some point during or after recording, there was a minor edit for the benefit of AM radio. The phrase "come with me" was thought to have sexual connotations, so it was changed to "come to me."

Foster said that there were only two takes on "Oh, Pretty Woman," but failed to mention that it took almost three hours to get to the point where they could do the first take. Roy had brought in his road drummer, Paul Garrison, to work in tandem with Nashville studio drummer Buddy Harman. Garrison was overplaying, and, knowing that Roy hated confrontation, Foster sent Roy down to get a Coke while he tried to get the band straight. "For three hours, they experimented with different arrangements," said Bill Porter. "When the arrangement was worked out, we were about two hours and forty-five minutes into a three-hour session. Ray Edenton was one of the [guitarists] and he came into the control room and said, 'I wish they'd get this thing finished, I want to go home.' But when we got together, two takes and we had it." Guitarist Jerry Kennedy suggested the layered guitar intro in place of having all the guitars come in together. The lead guitarists on the date were Kennedy, Billy Sanford (who later worked with Don Williams), and Jerry Moss. Although Porter remembered rhythm guitarist Ray Edenton being present, surviving session logs don't bear him out. Edenton was on the equally grueling follow-up session, so perhaps Porter confused the two dates. Bill Dees sang the harmony vocal on "Pretty Woman" and dueted with Roy on the flip side, "Yo Te Amo, Maria." Released in 1964, "Oh, Pretty Woman" became Roy's biggest hit, selling—by most estimates—seven million copies, and reaching Number 1 worldwide.

Through all the success, Wesley Rose and Fred Foster disagreed bitterly. The trouble started when Foster brought Roy to D.C. in 1960, just as "Only the Lonely" was breaking, and signed him to a five-year contract without Rose's say-so. Every non–Acuff-Rose song stoked Rose's determination to get Roy Orbison off Monument when that contract expired on June 30, 1965. "Oh, Pretty Woman" was followed by the spectacularly unsuccessful "Goodnight," which sold less than 200,000 copies. Its complexity, according to Bill Dees, stemmed from the fact that it was three or four songs cobbled into one. Probably no more than a handful of people worldwide can hum it. Foster says that Rose chose the songs for the last sessions and had a hand in the production, thus engineering a downturn in Roy's fortunes in order to facilitate his removal from Monument. This is possible, although it's likelier that Rose told Roy that he was negotiating his exit from Monument and that Roy should save the best new songs for the new deal. "Wesley wanted complete control over those last four sides," said Foster, "and the low sales were astonishing to me. Believe me, I worked that record because I wanted to sell as many as possible." Just as the termination of Roy's contract with Monument became effective, Foster released another single from the last session, "(Say) You're My Girl," which sold less than 100,000 copies.

Virtually every record label expressed an interest in Roy's contract but he signed with MGM for a guarantee of one million dollars and the promise of a career that would be broadened to include movies. If all the options were exercised, it would be a twenty-year deal. The London Records division of British Decca (which distributed Monument in the United States and overseas) fronted half of the advance in exchange for rights outside North America. "The money was so big it was scary," Roy told John Pugh. "I could never have dreamed that anyone would have given me that much money in one day."

The deal still rankles Fred Foster. "I would have, and did, offer the one million dollars," he has asserted, "but Wesley was also insisting on prime time television appearances and a motion picture deal. I thought that was management's job." Rose never told his side of the story. He was the parish priest who knew all the secrets but spoke not a word. In his defense, MGM looked like a good bet in 1965. The record division had Herman's Hermits, Sam the Sham and the Pharoahs, Eric Burdon, and a full roster in all fields. Even so, it was a sweetheart deal. The ties between MGM and Acuff-Rose were strong, dating back to 1947 when Wesley's father, Fred, placed Hank Williams with the newly formed label. For many years, the Roses virtually ran MGM's country division, and MGM later distributed their Hickory label.

If Roy had remained on Monument the results might not have been markedly different, but there's simply no escaping the fact that Fred Foster was the first and only producer to coax the specialness out of Roy Orbison. Sam Phillips missed the point, as did Chet Atkins. Once on MGM, Roy's sessions were handled by Wesley Rose and MGM's Jim Vienneau. Vienneau's major qualification was that he was related to MGM Records founder Frank Walker. After being dismissed from MGM, he took a job with Acuff-Rose. Incestuous business.

Wesley Rose's dream came true and went sour at the same time. For six years, Roy's singles and albums would contain only Acuff-Rose copyrights, but they didn't sell. Even faced with plummeting sales figures, Rose couldn't let go, persuading Roy to draw from Acuff-Rose's vast back catalog. The result was tribute albums to Hank Williams and Don Gibson, forlorn ideas that Orbison should have stopped in their tracks. Unlike Foster, Wesley Rose kept a tight rein on session costs. The sessions came in on budget, but none of the recordings sold. Rose was not a producer; he was a former accountant who came to see himself as a music man. Even so, he sold his company as a hugely profitable concern to Gaylord Media in 1985, the same year that Foster, who had already lost the Monument presidency, lost his controlling interest in Monument real estate and Combine Music after accumulating debts of over $7.3 million. In 1987, Monument was acquired by CBS Special Products for a pittance—just $810,000.

The deal with MGM Records was the longest of Roy's recording affiliations: eight barren years. The first single, "Ride Away," was a modest success, peaking at Number 25, but it would be Roy's biggest hit on the label. The MGM contract called for three albums a year, an impossible goal. Roy simply couldn't write that much; *no one* could write that much. The emphasis shifted from quality to quantity. "I remember Roy would come in off the road on Friday and say that we needed six songs by the following Thursday," recalled Bill Dees. Foster was scathing: "You couldn't work like that with Roy," he said. "You had to work him up to the point where he gave you one good performance, and *that* was the session." Rose also failed to appreciate the changing nature of the business. Traditionally, albums had contained one or two hits and nine or ten filler tracks, but the mid-to-late 1960s marked the dawn of the concept album. Roy mingled among the stars of the day, so he must have known this, but there seemed to be timidity at his core. His disenchantment with Wesley Rose eventually surfaced, though: a $50 million lawsuit filed in 1982 alleged mismanagement and the underaccounting of royalties.

Lack of success was compounded by two tragedies. On June 6, 1966, Roy and Claudette were riding their motorcycles back from a drag race near Bristol, Tennessee, when a truck pulled out from a side road near Gallatin and collided with Claudette. She died two hours later. (Roy and Claudette had divorced earlier, just as the song she'd inspired, "Oh, Pretty Woman," was cresting, but, ironically, a motorcycle accident had prompted their reconciliation in 1966. Roy had been touring England when he'd broken his foot falling from his cycle in Hawkestone Park near Birmingham. Claudette flew over and they reconciled, later to remarry.

Despite falling sales, Roy continued recording in Nashville, and still made his home there. He built a ranch-styled house in Hendersonville with a pool just inside the door. When home, he indulged his passion for museum scale-model airplanes with his three sons, Tony, Roy Jr., and Wesley. It was there beside the lake that tragedy struck again in September 1968. On tour in England, Roy received the news that his house had burned and that Tony and Roy, Jr. had died. His parents were taking care of the kids, and, after the fire started, Orbie Lee tried to get the children out of the basement, but an explosion drove him back. In the patois of the

The house that burned; the motorcycle (behind the car) that crashed. Courtesy Colin Escott.

day, it was dubbed "tragic karma." Coming less than two years after Claudette's death, the grief would have sent most people into a tailspin, but Roy did what he had always done: he went back to work.

At the time of the fire, Roy had been dating a young German woman, Barbara Anne Wellhonen Jakobs, and he brought her to Nashville for their marriage on March 25, 1969. The accompanying reports in the local papers showed how marginally Roy had integrated himself into the community: "Since coming to Nashville several years ago," said the *Banner*, "he has remained something of a mystery, largely at his own instance [*sic*]." Immediately after the wedding, Roy and Barbara went to Germany to visit her parents and then on to England for a three-month tour. The road went on forever.

After the MGM deal ended, Roy signed a one-year contract with Mercury Records, then re-signed with Monument in an attempt to get back to where he once had been. The second Monument term proved that you really cannot go home again. Some of Roy's contemporaries, notably Jerry Lee Lewis and Conway Twitty, had reverted to country music, and although Roy scored a one-off country hit with Emmylou Harris, he still felt that there was a place for him in rock music. He was right; it would just take another decade to prove it. In 1978, he signed with Elektra-Asylum Records, but the album, *Laminar Flow,* was a tepid affair. Then came Linda Ronstadt's ten-million-selling "Blue Bayou," ironically on the same label as the dismal-selling *Laminar Flow.*

Roy always dated his comeback to Ronstadt's revival of "Blue Bayou," but it was David Lynch's cult movie *Blue Velvet* that made him, in his words, "contemporary again." Lynch apparently played "In Dreams" to the cast at four-hour intervals during the filming, and gave it a surreal context in the movie. Initially, Roy was shocked. "I sneaked into a little cinema in Malibu to see it," he said. "I was mortified because they were talking about 'the candy colored clown' in relation to a dope deal. Then Dean Stockwell did that weird miming thing, then they were beating up that young kid. I thought, 'What in the world . . . ' But later, when I was touring, I got the video out and I really got to appreciate what David gave to the song, and what the song gave to the movie." He also came to appreciate what the movie did for his career.

Barbara played a greater role in Orbison's career than Claudette ever had, eventually taking over his management. She provided much of the steeliness he lacked. As Roy's stature grew, there was a *Rolling Stone* cover story, and induction into the Rock 'n' Roll Hall of Fame. George Harrison brought him into an informal supergroup, the Traveling Wilburys, and the success of the first Wilburys album set the stage for an album of new songs, and a video with famous friends for Cinemax. Roy looked good; age sat better upon his features than youth.

The new album was finished in November 1988, and Roy headed to Europe for some television appearances and advance promotion. Barbara remained in Germany visiting her family while Roy returned to the United States for a few more shows. He went on to his mother's house in Hendersonville, and flew his model airplanes during the afternoon of December 6. Early in the evening, he complained of chest pains, and, at 11:00 P.M., he collapsed in the bathroom. He was rushed to

Hendersonville Hospital, where he was declared dead of a massive heart attack just before midnight.

Even before his death, musicians rarely had a bad word to say about Roy Orbison, perhaps because he wasn't competition. He was his own category. No one could do Roy Orbison better than Roy Orbison. He didn't seem to be influenced by anybody, and, in turn, hardly influenced anybody. True, there are traces of him in Raul Malo of the Mavericks, Chris Isaak, Bruce Springsteen, and others, but, in general, Roy Orbison was in a category of one.

So many of Roy's contemporaries died looking back, unable to cope with fame and then unable to cope with its loss. "All artists go through a period when they turn on success, or success turns on them," he said shortly before his death. "Most can't ride that out, but I was fortunate because I had been singing and playing for thirteen years when success came. It touched me deeply, but it didn't drive me crazy." And although he never actually said as much, you always got the feeling that every day out of west Texas was a good day for Roy Orbison.

Check It Out

There are hundreds of permutations of Roy Orbison's Monument recordings. The first CD compilation to go back to the original masters and remix them with the original mix as the template was Rhino's anthology *For The Lonely* (R2-71493). It sounded good on release and sounds good still. The Sun recordings are infinitely available, but as always it's up to Bear Family to do the definitive job. *Orbison 1955-1965* includes every song and every alternate take from Je-Wel, Sun, RCA, and Monument, together with a few live recordings. It's all on seven CDs (BCD 16423). The MGM recordings have been subject to legal action, and so are generally unavailable. The comeback album, *Mystery Girl*, and the remade greatest hits are still available on Virgin in the United States.

CHAPTER 2

Perry Como

R.I.P.

So he left, seventeen months into the century in which he didn't belong. His timing was always pretty good. Perry Como saw it all, from singing through megaphones to sampling. A lot of history died with him. He was an unlikely cultural icon, and he'd dismiss the notion with a shrug. But a cultural icon is what he was. He reflected a culture back at itself. He was what they wanted to be, the millions who saw him every week: not just rich and successful, but decent, family-centered, even-handed, and quietly confident—an ideal neighbor.

Perry Como figured out understatement. How much effort does it take before it appears effortless? Perry didn't carry it off with quite the panache of Dean Martin, but neither did he take it to the point where "no sweat" became "no interest." Perry figured out television, too. If you came of age between 1948 and 1963, he was in your living room at least once a week. Intuitively and instinctively, he knew what it took to work the new medium. Had he tried to be something he wasn't over those fifteen seasons, he'd have been unmasked as an impostor. In person, he was a little saltier, a little funnier, a little sharper, but still very Perry. People felt they knew him because they invited him into their homes, and, for all intents and purposes, they really did know him.

Pietro and Lucia Como arrived in the United States from Italy around 1903. They settled in Canonsburg, Pennsylvania, just southwest of Pittsburgh, and just across the river from Steubenville where Dean

Perry Como and Mitch Ayres, c. 1957.

Martin, another son of first generation Italian immigrants, grew up. For the Comos, the New World was an almost exact replica of the Old. Pietro worked at Standard Tin Plate Corporation, but he and Lucia continued to speak Italian, never learning more than a few words of English until the day they died. They ate the food and drank the wine of the old country, attended church, and sang the songs they'd always sung. Women with less than five children were thought barren; the Comos had thirteen. Some were born in the Old World, some in the New. Pierino, or Perry as he became known, arrived on May 18, 1912, the seventh son of a seventh son.

Third Avenue in Canonsburg is now Perry Como Avenue. The mere idea elicited a wince from Perry; he didn't like that sort of thing. His mother, who was sturdily built by the time Third Avenue was renamed, had to climb uncertainly up a stepladder to affix the sign, and that certainly wouldn't have happened if Perry had been there. For the first five years that Perry ran up and down Third Avenue he didn't speak English. He only began picking it up when he went to school. The mines and the mills where many of the immigrants worked were not for him: he would be a *barbiere*. Nick Tosches reckoned that between one-half and two-thirds of Italian immigrants declared that they were *barbieri*. Even the great Caruso had been a barbiere. Perry started apprenticing when he was twelve, and took over an established business when he was fourteen, with two grown men working for him. "A haircut was fifty cents; now I pay twenty bucks. Maybe I got out too soon," he said. Another shrug. Maybe he'd told that joke too often. Perry had a guitar, and led his own barber shop quartet in his own barbershop, and played valve trombone in a brass marching band. On July 4 and Italian saints' days, they would parade around Canonsburg. "My father walked right alongside me in the crowd," said Perry. "That's-a-my boy, you know. He loved music."

When it came to singing, Perry freely admitted to two influences, Russ Columbo and Bing Crosby. Columbo might have been as big as Crosby if a gun barrel hadn't fragmented and killed him under still mysterious circumstances. Shortly before he died, he cowrote one of the loveliest songs in American popular music, "Prisoner of Love." It must be a great song because it's the only one that both Perry Como and James Brown have taken to the charts. Perry always went out of his way to acknowledge Crosby's influence. Crosby has been portrayed as an unlovable man, sour-tempered and miserly, but that's not the way Perry remembered him. "He was supposed to be surly, tough, but he was never that way with me," he said. "He was gentle. We got along. Played golf, did each other's shows, but he couldn't take a compliment. One time we did a duet on television, and I said, 'If it hadn't been for him, folks, I'd still be cutting hair.' He was embarrassed, almost insulted. Afterward, he said, 'Perry, don't say that.'"

Around the time that Crosby was starting to become really popular, 1931 and 1932, Perry was getting up on stage around Canonsburg to sing the hits of the hour. Then, during a spring vacation in Cleveland in 1933, he went to see a local band leader, Freddie Carlone, and auditioned. Carlone offered him a job, but Perry's barber shop was a thriving business, netting him around $40 a week, and he needed some prodding from his father to go with Carlone, who was only offering $28. He met the band at a park in Meadville, Pennsylvania. His girlfriend, Roselle Belline, went there with him. Neither could face their parents if they weren't married so they went to see a justice of the peace in Meadville on July 31, 1933, just a few days after Perry officially changed profession. For years, he kept up his membership in the barbers guild—just in case, you know.

Carlone led what was known as a territory band. It had thirteen pieces and they toured up and down the Ohio Valley, and did a little radio but never recorded. When they weren't working, Carlone's brother would take Perry to a club in Cleveland where he would sing for tips. "Some guy would ask to hear 'Melancholy Baby,' I'd sing it, he'd put a buck into a jar," said Perry. "I did better with that than I did with the band." It was around this time that amplification became commonplace. Prior to that, singers would use megaphones. Perry had a megaphone with stardust painted on it. Now he was confronted with the new technology, but was slow to embrace it. "Freddie would say, 'Sing in the goddamn thing!'" he remembered, "and I'd say, 'No, I want to sing with the megaphone,' so in the end I sang through the megaphone into the microphone and it sounded awful. I don't think I ever knew how bad."

Carlone's band was run by three brothers, and Perry was treated as the fourth Carlone. After a show, they'd pay off the band, then do a four-way split. Perry felt so much a part of the outfit that he didn't even respond to a wire from the self-styled "King of Jazz," Paul Whiteman, offering him a job. Carlone tried to persuade him to leave, but Perry was adamant that he wanted to stay, and, when an offer came from Ted Weems in 1935, Carlone had to push him out the door. Weems had heard Perry at a casino in Warren, Ohio, and he wired an offer. "Ted was the same kind of man as Freddie," said Perry. "Gentle. A gentleman. I was doing well, sending money home to my dad, $10, $12. Roselle came with me on the road. We had an old Packard, we'd load it up, put a mattress in there for my son Ronnie who was just a few months old, and we'd hit the road. California. Wherever."

Perry was just one of several featured vocalists in the Weems outfit. Elmo Tanner was a star whistler and singer, Red Ingle did comedy vocal numbers, and Parker Gibbs sang too. Perry often felt that he drew the short straw when it came to deciding who sang what. "They'd get the hits; I'd get the song some guy had written on the back of a menu," he said. He was at a double disadvantage when it came to recording because Weems recorded for Decca, and Perry sounded so close to Bing Crosby, who also recorded for Decca, that the label balked at using him. On one of his first sessions, Dave Kapp, the brother of Decca president Jack Kapp, said to Weems, "Why are you letting him sing? Hell, we got one Crosby." Perry didn't hear this, but he saw the confusion, and an engineer told him later. "It was like someone was stabbing me," he said. "Here I was trying to get on record."

Perry was happy with Weems, but the constant touring irked him to the point that when the band broke up after Weems's enlistment, in December 1942, Perry decided he'd had enough. Over Roselle's objections, he went back to Canonsburg to pick up where he'd left off. He said he came to his decision during a show date in New Orleans. "We were playing the Roosevelt Grill," he said, "and I noticed a little boy about eight. He was the son of one of the musicians in the band. I looked at this kid, sitting there among the strangers, lonely and restless, and I said to Roselle, 'Is this what's going to happen to Ronnie?' There and then I decided to quit."

It was 1942, one of those moments when all the cards are in the air. War had started and the big bands were dissolving because of the draft and gas rationing. Former star vocalists, like Frank Sinatra, Peggy Lee, and Dick Haymes, were testing the waters on their own. Then the American Federation of Musicians threw a curve into everyone's plans with a recording ban. Booking agent Tommy Rockwell called Perry as soon as he heard he'd gone back to Canonsburg. The story goes that Perry was on the verge of signing a lease on a barber shop when he got Rockwell's wire. "He was the top agent," said Perry. "I'd have been a fool not to go with him."

Recognizing that Perry hated the road, Rockwell mapped out an alternative strategy. He put him in some New York nightclubs, and landed a sustaining (i.e., nonsponsored) show on CBS radio at 4:30 in the afternoon. It looked like a downwardly mobile move, from $700 a week in the clubs to around $75, but Rockwell gave Perry a little stash of money to draw on, and told him to keep the faith. When Perry returned to the clubs, Rockwell got him into the Copacabana, where his two-week stint was extended to thirteen. By the time Perry began at the Paramount, he was getting the screams and squeals reserved for Sinatra, and drawing lines around the block. Perry Como—Teen Idol. Perry shrugged and winced at the memory. Even at the time, he was dismissive. "It's just a trend," he said in 1945. "Press agents have planted [the screaming] in the kids' heads."

Ad for Perry's first record, 1943. "And we do mean silver . . ." Courtesy Colin Escott.

Rockwell talked to RCA Victor Records, a company that needed a crooner to go head-to-head with Crosby and Dick Haymes on Decca and Sinatra on Columbia. RCA vice president Manie Sacks signed Perry on June 17, 1943. The first sessions were held during the recording ban. Musicians couldn't work, but vocalists could, so Perry recorded a cappella. "That was murder," he said. "I had two boys with me who had perfect pitch, so I put them next to me, but it was hard because if the singing got loud, you'd get a little sharp. We messed up take after take." The music business was more-or-less controlled by a dozen music publishers who hired song pluggers to get their hottest new songs to the biggest names. Payola began right there, and later spread throughout the industry. Several stars would record the same song at the same time, with the release date controlled by the publisher so that all versions would appear simultaneously. This left entry-level artists with the choice of picking through the leavin's or reviving oldies. For his first record, Perry was handed "Goodbye Sue," a minor-league song by Nashville songwriter Jimmy Rule, who is best known for ghostwriting Hank Williams's booklet *How to Write Folk and Western Music to Sell*. The song got onto the charts for one week.

Starting in April 1944, Rockwell got Perry on NBC radio's *Chesterfield Supper Club*. Perry did three nights a week and Jo Stafford did two. Then came *The Perry Como Show* on CBS radio. And then came movies. "Oh, please, *please*," said Perry. "I get sick to my stomach when I see them." *Something for the Boys* was the first, followed by *Doll Face* and *If I'm Lucky*. "I was out there twelve weeks at a stretch, played a lot of golf," he said. "If I'd known anything about acting, I'd have done okay, but what the hell did I know about acting? My name was starting to mean something, and they just wanted it up there." Perry asked to be released from his movie contract in 1947 after filming his spot in the star-studded *Words and Music*. In 1953, he was asked to take the lead in a biopic of Russ Columbo. It was the one role that might have tempted him, but his other commitments were too heavy by then.

The recording ban ended, but the big hit remained elusive. During the closing months of the war, Perry recorded a xenophobic jive number, "(Hubba Hubba) Dig You Later," rivaling Carson Robison's "We're Gonna Have to Slap the Dirty Little Jap." In the song, B-29s were heading for the Japanese mainland: "A friend of mine in a B-29 dropped another one for luck/As he flew away, I heard him say, 'Hubba, hubba, hubba, yuk yuk.'" A few verses on, we meet a buddy "in the know" who assures Perry it's getting "mighty smoky over Toke-ee-oh." Perry shrugged at the mention of the song: wartime, you know. Then, in July 1945, he cut "Till the End of Time." Based on Frédéric Chopin's "Polonaise in A-flat Major," it was the tune everyone came away humming after seeing the Chopin biopic *A Song to Remember*. The following year, Perry revived Russ Columbo's "Prisoner of Love," and it, like "Till The End of Time," reached Number 1. Now he was getting the music publishers' top picks. Even Perry admitted that everything was looking swell, but then the musicians union called a second ban that lasted throughout most of 1948. RCA had exhausted its little stockpile of Perry Como recordings by the time the studios reopened on December 14. Photographers and reporters were on hand when Perry returned to the studio, and an interview given that day showed how tight his schedule had become. "We worked [on the record] from 5:02 until 6:00 P.M.," he said. "Then I had to knock off to do the supper club show. I was back at 7:30 and we worked right through 'til 10:30. Then the record was on sale just 12 hours later."

Ten days after that session, on December 24, 1948, *The Chesterfield Supper Club* moved to television. Perry did three fifteen-minute spots a week. Most of his contemporaries were still ignoring television in favor of movies, radio, and concerts. He reduced a complex equation to a blindingly simple one. "I don't want to sound like Methuselah," he said, "but people had just started buying television sets. They'd tune in, and if they liked you, they kept tuning in." Perry didn't shout at people while they were having supper. He quietly charmed them, and by the time the 1950s dawned, he no longer needed to do personal appearances.

Record sales went up and down, but for three decades Perry seemed able to recover from inevitable sales slumps. He was the last to take the credit for this, acknowledging that most of his biggest hits were songs that he did not want to do. "Every piece of crap I hated became a really big hit," he said. "I'd tell the A&R (artists and repertoire) man, 'I can't sing that garbage,' and he'd say, 'Just do one take—one take for me.' I'd say, 'I'm gonna get ill if I do two.'" The first song that Perry remembered hating in that way was an ersatz polka, "Hoop Dee-Doo." There was no reason not to hate it, but who could argue with the fact that in June 1950 it became Perry's first Number 1 hit in a year. Television seemed to like a special kind of song: a dumb one.

"Don't Let the Stars Get in Your Eyes" was Perry's biggest record from the early 1950s. First made as a hillbilly record by a deejay named

Slim Willet, the original version was so wretchedly sloppy and off-key that no one could see its potential. Willet was forced to issue it on his own label, and, after plugging it himself, it became a regional breakout in Texas. Very quickly, there were half a dozen country cover versions, and then Steve Sholes, the head of RCA's country division, suggested that it might be good for Perry. Pop covers of country songs were doing well (Tony Bennett's "Cold, Cold Heart" and Patti Page's "Tennessee Waltz," to name two), but Perry hated "Don't Let the Stars." It was out of meter, and it wasn't his type of song. But just a few weeks before the session, RCA had lured him out of the television studio long enough to do a tour of distributors. He'd been told how the jukebox operators came in, listened to the first few bars of a record, and decided whether or not to stock it. The distributors were looking for songs with short, loud introductions and snappy tempos. Traditionally, Perry had always favored the exact opposite, but now it was time to rethink this strategy. Arranger Mitch Ayres set "Don't Let the Stars" to a brisk Latin rhythm, and kicked it off with a loud, brassy intro.

The session got off to a bad start when Perry came in, looked up into the control room and saw Dave Kapp, the man who had refused to record him when he was with Ted Weems. "I walked in, and I said to the engineer, 'What's he doing here?' The engineer said, 'He's with RCA now. He's the A&R man.' I got on the microphone so everyone could hear. I said, 'Hi Dave, get the hell out of there. Get that son of a bitch out of there.' I had him put out. I told him why and he said he was just kidding back then." Perry's version of "Don't Let the Stars Get in Your Eyes" was a great record. The engineers took the vocal and the forty-piece orchestra, mixing them down on the fly to single-track tape, which was an incredible achievement in itself. The sound leaped out of the grooves, and the record streaked to Number 1. By June 1953 it had sold one-and-a-half million copies, just in time for Perry's tenth anniversary with RCA. As a token of gratitude for total sales then estimated at thirty-five million, RCA built a pressing plant in Canonsburg.

Then the rules began to change. Perry was studiedly diplomatic when it came to rock 'n' roll. Someone else's negative comment might elicit a knowing nod from him. Maybe he'd grimace, shrug, or make a vaguely disparaging sound, but he knew that every generation had to have its own music. "Play 'Stardust' or 'Till the End of Time' to the kids," he told *Saturday Evening Post* in 1960, "and it doesn't mean a thing. It's strictly for

Spanish-American War veterans. I can imagine that twenty years from now when somebody sings 'Hound Dog,' it'll make some guy in his late thirties recall some beautiful nostalgic moment. When I hear 'Hound Dog' I have to vomit a little . . . but in 1970 or 1975 it will probably be an ancient classic." Perry Como: prophet of the reissue record business.

Perry also knew that too much was happening too quickly to rock 'n' roll's first stars. They didn't have the grounding in the business, much less in music. When he worked Vegas in the 1970s, he saw the toll it had taken on Elvis Presley. Elvis would come to Perry's dressing room. "He'd sit there by the hour and never say a word," said Perry. "Just sit there. I'd say, 'How's it going Elvis?' He'd mumble something, 'Fine, Perry, fine, fine.' I wondered why he came down." Perry knew something strange was going on, but never really wanted to know what it was.

For Perry, rock 'n' roll compounded his problems. In September 1955, he'd moved from CBS back to NBC, and his new hourlong Saturday night variety show was pitted against Jackie Gleason's *Honeymooner's*. At the time, Perry downplayed the contest, saying that those who wanted comedy would watch Jackie, and those who wanted musical variety would watch Perry Como, but it was a rivalry both intense and awkward because Gleason was a neighbor and friend. "Sunday morning the phone would ring," said Perry, "and I'd say, 'That's Jackie.' I'd pick it up, and he'd say, 'Old silver throat, I knocked your ass off last night.' Another night, we'd get a point ahead of him in the ratings and I'd phone him and say, 'Hey big ass, last night we knocked your ass off,' and he'd hang up on me." Perry's mother-in-law, who didn't understand English, loved Gleason. She called him "Jackie Glissi." Knowing how much it would mean to her, Perry phoned Gleason and asked him to put in an appearance at the Como house while his mother-in-law was there. "I was worried he was gonna turn up stark naked with a lampshade on his head," he said, "but she was sitting in the kitchen at nine o'clock one morning, and Jackie knocked and walked in. 'Well hello there Mrs. Belline. . . . ' I swear, she thought she was dreaming. Here was Jackie Glissi. He prattled on, danced around the table with her. Finally, he said, 'Well, Mrs. Belline, I have to get the hell out of here. I have to work a show opposite this old fart here.' She didn't know what the hell he was saying. I called him later, I said, 'Anything you want, you got it. In fact, I'll even do one of your shows so the ratings will be better.'"

One difference between Como and Gleason was that Gleason pre-taped while Perry still went out live. Perry thought that going live gave his show the spontaneous edge that variety needed, but it had its pitfalls, too. He remembered one show with Esther Williams that, over the course of an hour, went from damage control to disaster. As soon as she appeared, she tore off the piece of lace designed to camouflage her cleavage. Then the lighting crew messed up, and the audience laughed hysterically through the romantic number. At the end, Esther was in a pool on the set, so Perry just said "Goodnight folks," and jumped in fully clothed. Another time, Julie London insisted on wearing a very low-cut dress. Perry's producer tried to talk her out of wearing it, and Perry walked into rehearsal to hear her screaming, "Goddamn, if he wants boys why doesn't he get boys?" Perry tried to calm things down, but, as he said, "It's tough telling people to change their act. They knew what they were selling. People would call me Father Como, but we weren't playing holier than thou, we just knew our audience. We didn't try to offend, we just tried to entertain."

Perry finally bested Gleason in the ratings, as he would later best Sinatra on ABC. His success led rival production companies to assume that any personable singer could fly in the ratings, but the *Perry Como Show* was the only musical variety show to consistently place in the top five. Like him or not, Perry Como was woven into the fabric of life. The only shows to outdraw him were *I Love Lucy* and *Gunsmoke*. It all seemed so informal that journalists were astonished to learn that the show actually took the best part of a week to assemble and rehearse. It aired on Saturday night, and at eight o'clock on Monday morning the production team met to begin planning the next one. Perry never minded the pace, because he loved what he was doing. Recording sessions were sandwiched between television commitments. The choice of material was left to RCA's A&R staff, and, much as he detested their picks, the fact remained that while his peers from the 1940s and early '50s were swept aside, he hung on to his core audience and still got Top 40 airplay. Songs like "Tina Marie," "Juke Box Baby," "Hot Diggity," and "Round and Round" hinted broadly enough at rock 'n' roll to get played, but never so broadly as to alienate the longtime fans. It was a skilled tightrope act.

"I owe television everything," said Perry. "It sold records, sold everything." He used television to test-market songs. "Round and Round" was previewed on the show and the response persuaded him to cut it, despite the fact that he (of course) hated it. In April 1957, it hit Number 1, and stayed twenty-nine weeks on the charts. "Hot Diggity" made Perry wince, too, but he sang it on the show and the crowd seemed to like it. If he checked *Billboard* on May 5, 1956, he would have found that it had dislodged Elvis Presley's "Heartbreak Hotel" from the top slot. Perry also has the distinction of having the first record certified gold by the Recording Industry Association of America. Until 1958, published sales figures had been highly unreliable, but, starting that year, the RIAA tried to verify and audit record company claims, and the prestigious gold record was awarded for actual sales of one million copies. The first of four records certified gold in 1958 was "Catch a Falling Star," backed with "Magic Moments." The latter, incidentally, was an early entry from Hal David and Burt Bacharach.

Magazine writers were assigned to penetrate the Como enigma. Was he really that mellow? Was he really that nice? Was he really the God- and family-loving man he seemed? It didn't make very good copy, but the writers usually came away believing that Perry Como was more or less as he appeared. No one could keep up a front that long. The only criticism that seemed to hurt was that of laziness. Perry had never known a lazy person work so hard. "I'd like one of these writers to follow me around for six months," he said. "They'd start panting quick." But, try as he might, he couldn't lick the illusion that he spent an hour a week on his television show, cut a record in five minutes, then headed for the golf course. No interviewers were invited back to the house on Long Island to meet Roselle and the family, and he remained one of the few show business personalities to refuse an interview on Edward R. Morrow's *Person-to-Person*.

In the fall of 1959, Kraft Foods took over the sponsorship of Perry's show. In an unprecedented deal, Perry's production company, Roncom (for Ronnie Como, his son), produced the show for Kraft, which in turn sponsored it on NBC. Roncom was paid the unprecedented sum of $25 million for two years. Out of that, Perry had to meet all expenses. Even the casual asides scripted by ex–Milton Berle gagwriter Goodman Ace cost him $11,500 a week. The Kraft Music Hall went out every week, at its peak attracting around forty-five million viewers in North America. Then in 1963, as the ratings sagged a little, Perry gave up weekly television in favor of specials—first eight a year, then six. By the time he quit the weekly schedules he had become part of the family. "Television will do that," he said. "You can't consciously go out and try to build that kind of thing. We tried to bring on guests that people wanted to see, and we could tell from the letters what we meant to people. I've still got some of the letters." Perry truly loved his audience. He didn't talk down to them. He was a good neighbor who dropped in once a week and didn't overstay his welcome. Quitting in 1963 was a good move. Perry was inextricably bound to the fifties, and if you reckon that the fifties really ended around 1964, then 1963 was the time to go. Six months after he did his last weekly show, the Beatles arrived. The turbulence of the mid-to-late sixties was on the horizon, and the fifties' quiet, buoyant optimism, which seemed to find its embodiment in Perry Como, forever disappeared.

The six years with Ted Weems had cured Perry of any desire to tour, and he'd steadfastly refused all offers for concert appearances, even in Las Vegas, since 1950. Now he began to think about it once again. He had never been overseas, with the exception of a twenty-fifth wedding anniversary trip to Italy with his wife, which included an audience with Pope Pius XII. So he would tour again. The changes ran deeper: now Perry could give up the novelty songs that had gone over so well for so many years. After a year and a half out of the studio, he took up an offer from Steve Sholes, now RCA's vice president of pop A&R, to record in Nashville.

Perry liked Nashville. In New York, there would usually be twenty, thirty, or forty musicians and singers at a session, together with a small army of arrangers and copyists. In Nashville, Perry walked in to find six or eight players, four singers, and no arrangements. "I'm a musician," he said, "and I looked over to see the arrangements and all I see is I–IV–V–II, and I say, 'What the hell's that?' They said, 'That's the arrangement.' It was just a chord sequence, and they'd change key and make up the arrangement as they went along. Same thing with the vocal group." Once he got over the culture shock, Perry liked it. He would run through the songs, record the bed tracks with the musicians, and leave Chet Atkins to overdub the strings while he headed for the golf course. The relationship with Nashville was cemented when the first single pulled from the initial Nashville sessions, "Dream on Little Dreamer," became his biggest hit in several years.

There was a late-sixties lull. Then, in 1970, Perry got into the Top 10 for the first time since "Kewpie Doll" in 1958. The song that did it was "It's Impossible." What sold "It's Impossible," he said, "was its simplicity. You learn to stop showing off and creating a bag of nothing." The last big North American hit was another Nashville recording, Don McLean's "And I Love You So." When it exited the charts in August 1973, it had been almost thirty years since Como's first chart entry, "Goodbye Sue."

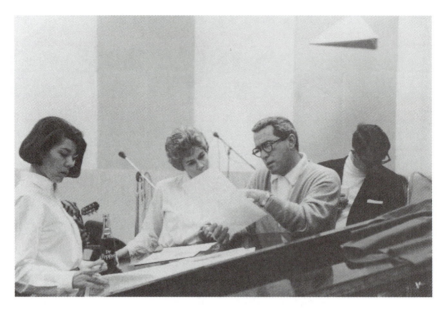

Recording in Nashville. Courtesy Colin Escott.

Perry had charted records in the 1940s, '50s, '60s, and '70s. As music, those records haven't endured too well, but as time capsules, they can't be bettered. You'll find none of Sinatra's dark soliloquies buried on Perry's albums—nothing the equal of, say, "It Gets Lonely Early." And while Perry could swing, his arrangers couldn't. His records were strictly of the moment: impeccably crafted, but rooted in their place and time. Sinatra's bipolar mix of melancholy and exuberance finds new listeners every year, while Perry's audience slowly dies off.

Perhaps the key to Perry Como's success was his "small-town-ness." Even his face was that of a man who had long ago come to terms with himself. "Some people like dogs," Perry said. "I like people." His audience instinctively knew that, and reciprocated. "I never wanted to give the people the impression that I was above them," he said. "People would come up to me like I was a friend, and then they'd realize at the last minute they'd never met me." He applied the same philosophy to his music. On the early records, he hit the neo-operatic notes, but they soon disappeared, not because he couldn't hit them, but because he stopped singing *at* people and started singing *to* them. The goofy singles underscored the fact that he didn't take himself too seriously. He didn't become greedy and demand a share of the music publishing or insist that songs be drawn from his publishing companies. While Elvis was nodding out in the corner of Perry's dressing room, he might have asked Perry about that. There are still plenty of lessons to be learned from Perry Como.

Postscript

I interviewed Perry in 1993, and his memory wasn't too good. If you could supply names, he'd keep the story going; if not, he'd shrug and fall quiet. It was, he kept saying, a long time ago. And it was. Asked about life with Roselle at home in Jupiter, Florida, he said, "We stare. We stare a lot. At one another, at the ocean. At space. At night when we sit on the sofa, she stares at me. I stare at her." Roselle died in August 1998, just weeks after their sixty-fifth anniversary. Perry sat alone on the sofa until May 2001.

Check It Out

There are literally hundreds of Perry Como CDs. RCA issued a big ol' box o' Perry, *Yesterday and Today* (RCA 66098-2), encompassing his entire career. There are other CDs of rarities, early hits, later hits, and two-on-one CD compilations of his LPs.

CHAPTER 3

OKLAHOMA BLUES

Consciously or not, most artists reach a point of no return: can't go home again; can't go back to the local clubs; can't marry the boy or girl down the street. The only way is forward. For Patti Page, that realization came early. It came before her first hit, even before her first record. She was a nightclub singer in Chicago when her manager persuaded the local press to take some notice of her. In one of those first interviews, Patti said, perhaps as much to herself as to the interviewer, "I can't ever settle for Tulsa again."

Patti Page left Tulsa in 1946. Four years later, she was a star. The price of success was that she has been shortchanged as a singer. Frank Sinatra recorded some egregiously dumb songs that have almost been expunged from the history books ("High Hopes," to name just one); Tony Bennett is so hip you'd never know that one of his biggest hits was "In the Middle of an Island." But poor old Patti Page will forever be yoked to "How Much Is That Doggie in the Window?" (cue barks). Sinatra managed to draw a line between his singles and his albums, somehow letting everyone know that his heart was in the latter. Patti Page's great albums were ignored at the time, so they stopped coming. But the good stuff is very, very good, even if you can't find it. And the bad stuff is very, very bad, and you can find it just about anywhere.

Patti Page, like Will Rogers, was from Claremore, Oklahoma, twenty miles northeast of Tulsa. She was born Clara Ann Fowler on November 8, 1927, the next-to-youngest of Benjamin and Margaret Fowler's eight **57**

"Tra-la-la, twiddly-dee-dee . . . " Courtesy Colin Escott.

daughters and three sons. Later, Patti wrote a song called "Oklahoma Blues" that includes the line, "Got eleven in my family, don't need you to get my kicks!" You might read something into that, but Patti says you'd be wrong. Benjamin was a section hand on the MKT Railroad (featured in many Texas blues songs: "She caught the Katie"). The job entailed many moves. After Claremore, the Fowlers lived in Hardy and Fouracre, Oklahoma, and in Wichita, Kansas. "Behind us, in a house adjacent to our alley was the Dinning Sisters," says Patti. "I used to go over and baby-sit their little brother while they went up to the barn dance." There were six years in Avant, Oklahoma, then on to Muskogee. Patti and her sisters Rema and Ruby were on the radio in Muskogee. "My older sister was very aggressive," said Patti. "She went to the station and said, 'We can sing good.'"

In 1938, the Fowlers settled in Tulsa. Benjamin was a foreman by this point, and the family was able to put down roots for the first time. "I went into junior high in Tulsa," said Patti. "People put me in different contests. Then, when we went over to the high school, the freshmen had the balcony as their place in the assembly hall. Whatever entertainment they had scheduled didn't show up. The principal was talking, and he said, 'Is there anyone here who would like to entertain us?' Nobody volunteered. My homeroom teacher had come over from junior high, and he said, 'We have a little girl over here who'd be glad to sing for you.' They had a piano player, and he came up and played for me. I sang 'Frankie and Johnny.'"

It was the summer of 1943 when the dean of girls at Webster High took Patti's class out to look for summer jobs. Patti hired on with Western Union and delivered a few singing telegrams. She worked at the five and dime, then went to KTUL radio looking for a job as an illustrator. Waiting for her interview in the sales department, she met the program director, who had been responsible for the entertainment that didn't show up at Webster. "You know how fate brings you to a certain place at a certain time," says Patti. "That day another singer didn't show up, and he recognized me, and he said, 'Clara Ann, would you like to sing for us until the entertainment gets here?' Later he asked me if I'd ever thought of doing anything on the radio with my voice. I said I hadn't, and he said he had a full-time organist–piano player on staff, and after we were through I could put something down on acetate with him. I said, 'Oh, okay.' So I got the job in the art department and went down to look for this staff pianist. His name was Glen Hardman, and he was married to Helen O'Connell's sister. That really flipped me out, because I'd heard Helen O'Connell on some of my sister's records." Hardman had also recorded what is even now a cult jazz item, "Upright Organ Blues," still anthologized because Lester Young was on the session. He and Patti went on to work several shows together on KTUL.

By the summer of 1944, Patti was all over KTUL's schedule. As Ann Foster she was on KTUL's *Melody and Stars,* and, as Patti Page, she hosted *Meet Patti Page* for the Page Milk Company of Coffeyville, Kansas. She sang pop songs for Page Milk, then became a western singer with Al Clauser on KTUL's *Oklahoma Rhythm Rodeo.* Clauser had stumped the Midwest with Huey Long, and worked on WHO radio in Des Moines with Ronald Reagan as his announcer. He'd starred in fifteen or more shoot-'em-ups, and somehow ended up in Tulsa. Patti made her first recordings with Al Clauser for Okla Records in 1945 or early 1946.

Some years later, when Patti was a star, pop singers rushed to cover every fast-breaking country hit. Almost alone among her contemporaries, Patti understood country music from the ground up. Her father listened to nothing else. No one would maintain that "How Much Is That Doggie in the Window?" is a country record, but something "country" stayed with Patti Page. The simple, unaffected delivery, perhaps.

By 1946, Patti Page was too big for Tulsa. Her ticket out was provided by Jack Rael. Jack was Patti's manager for fifty years, but, as their partnership dissolved in the mid-1990s neither wanted to give the other credit for anything. For most of their years together, though, they worked not just as artist and manager, but as fifty-fifty partners, a deal that became a template for the arrangement between Elvis and Colonel Parker. Rael, whose name was a truncation of "Israel," came from Milwaukee. His father was a cousin of Benny Goodman's mother, and, like cousin Benny, he played the clarinet. After World War II, he joined the Jimmy Joy Orchestra as a clarinetist and saxophonist. Joy led a very popular territory band, switching from hot jazz to sweet music during the Depression. In the summer of 1946, he came to Tulsa, and the band checked into the Bliss Hotel. Jack Rael got to his room and found that there was still some time left on the coin-operated radio. He turned it on and heard *Meet Patti Page.* Patti sounded so assured that he thought he ought to know who she was, but he didn't. He called down to the station, asked who was singing. They told him, "That's our own Patti Page."

He said, "Yeah, but where's the show originating from?" They said, "Right here in our studios." He asked to talk to her, and was told to call back after the show.

"I had a mind filled with fantasy," said Patti.

All I could think of was the Mann Act, the white slavery act which was about taking young girls across state lines for immoral purposes. Jack did pay me a compliment. He said he'd really liked what he'd heard, and asked if I would be able to come out to the ballroom where he was going to be performing. I said, "Well, I have another job that I go to, a little supper club. Why don't you come there?" He said he would. I called my sister, and another sister and her husband. Jack was sitting out at a little table, and he was eating away, and I was thinking, "Is this a big time agent? Is this what they look like?" I went over to talk to him, and he said he was looking for a girl singer because the one they had wasn't cutting it. He asked me if I'd be interested, and I said I didn't know if my mother would let me do it. He said I should do some airchecks and send them down to him at Pappy's Showland in Dallas. He was going to be there six weeks. I said, "Okay," thinking I wouldn't do it. I was planning on getting married and staying in Tulsa.

Jack called me about two or three weeks later from Dallas, and in the meantime my boyfriend, who was one of the announcers at the station, had given me his pin and given another girl an engagement ring. Jack called at just the right time. I said, "Sure I'll send those airchecks." I recorded "To Each His Own" and a few other songs, and then he called me back. When he'd seen me in person, he didn't like me at all. I wasn't what he had in mind for a band singer. I was five feet tall, and I still had my baby fat. I wasn't everyone's conception of the band singer with the legs crossed, and that look they had. But when he heard the aircheck, he heard what he heard originally. He wanted me to come to Dallas and try out with the band. I flew down. Borrowed the money from my sister, and owed it for a long time. I stayed overnight with the girl singer who was leaving. I was too naive to see that I was being auditioned to take her job. I tried out with the band, and sang some of their group things. I think Jack knew by this point that he would not be with the band long and he would become my manager.

Patti left Tulsa on December 9, 1946. She opened with Jimmy Joy at the Club Martinique on the South Side of Chicago several days later.

It didn't take long for a power play to unfold within the band. Jimmy Joy saw Patti's potential and wanted to manage her. Jack saw that he would be shuffled out of the deal if he didn't act quickly, so he signed Patti to a management contract and they left the band. The rift came in Omaha. Jack took Patti back to Chicago, and found her a few small-time jobs. One of the first was at Helsing's Vodvil Lounge on the north side of Chicago. "You were over the bar and I hated every minute of it," said Patti. "I was on WBBM and WMAQ. There was one point I thought one of the shows was networked, but no one really heard it." Jack's army savings tided them over for a few months.

"Patti stayed at a little hotel," said Jack. "She didn't even have any luggage. She came with cardboard boxes and one piece of luggage." For one week starting April 14, 1947, she was on Don McNeill's networked *Breakfast Club*. "People liked Patti," said Rael. "They'd write in." The little momentum gave Rael something to talk up when he went to see Mercury Records a few weeks later. There were very few record companies in Chicago, and Mercury, small as it was, looked like the best bet. Launched in September 1945, it had just gained a toehold in the pop market with Frankie Laine's "That's My Desire." Patti was signed by A&R man Jimmy Hilliard, and the first session was slated for July 23, 1947.

Just a few months into her contract, the American Federation of Musicians called a recording ban, to take effect on January 1, 1948. Mercury, like all record companies, scheduled sessions day and night as the deadline approached. One of the songs Patti recorded was "Confess," on which she overdubbed a duet with herself. Deejays, intrigued by the overdub, spun the record, and made it into a hit. Overdubbing is a fact of life these days (even "live" albums are often overdubbed), but it was fiendishly difficult before tape came into use. You recorded onto an acetate, then played it back into one microphone while overdubbing into another microphone. The engineer would mix the overdub with the original (itself no mean feat), then cut the results onto another acetate. If the singer flubbed just one note, or the engineer messed up the balance, they'd have to start over. Les Paul was experimenting with overdubs around this time, but neither he nor Patti was first. Jazzman Sidney Bechet had cut a session back in 1941 when he overdubbed five parts on top of his original

Patti Page hawks the latest in jukebox technology, c. 1947–48. Courtesy Colin Escott.

track, but the musicians union frowned on it, and the quality of the final master was compromised by layer upon layer of hiss. Jack Rael certainly wasn't aware of Bechet's record. "It was just logical that it could be done," he said. "We were desperate, and we had no budget."

Patti spent 1948 in Chicago. She married that April, but the state of the union was never good. In June, she worked a short stint with Benny Goodman at the Click in Philadelphia, and then, on December 28, 1948, she opened at Café Society in New York. "I think Jack expected people to know me," said Patti. "He took me up to audition for a couple of television shows that were starting. We didn't get on those. My sister came with me, and Jack got her and me a room at the Shelton Hotel. He knew the manager. He'd gone to college with him. We had a room where you shared the bathroom down the hall."

It was in New York that Patti and Jack became business partners. "My first contract with Jack was that he would make 20 percent over $150 a week," said Patti, "and I certainly wasn't making that. I said, 'This is unfair. This is all you have except your army savings,' so I gave him 20 percent of whatever I made, and then I gave him half of everything I made." For his part, Jack Rael lived and breathed Patti Page. "I have no office," he said in a 1953 interview. "My office is my car. I have never missed a date. Where you see Patti Page, you'll see Jack Rael. Patti's sole job is to sing. I handle everything else." After "Confess," Rael persuaded Mercury to give him the responsibility for picking songs and commissioning the arrangements.

The recording ban ended in December 1948, but, with just a couple of small hits behind her, it was still hard for Patti to get the pick of the best new songs. Jack Rael went all out for novelty value, overdubbing three vocal parts onto Patti's version of "With My Eyes Wide Open I'm Dreaming." Just in case anyone missed the point, it was issued as the Patti Page Quartet. Early in 1950, it reached Number 11. In October that year, she went into the studio to cut a Christmas record.

"Boogie Woogie Santa Claus" needed a flip side. "Tennessee Waltz" had been a hit in 1948 for its writer, a dwarfish Polish country singer named Pee Wee King. R&B bandleader Erskine Hawkins had recorded it, and his record was just hitting the streets as Patti and Jack were looking for a flip side for the Christmas record. Jerry Wexler, then a columnist for *Billboard*, said "Tennessee Waltz" might work. "Patti knew the song," said Jack. "I didn't. She said, 'That's my daddy's favorite song.' We did it with five pieces. The baritone player from Ellington's band was on the date. We copied the arrangement from Erskine Hawkins. Joe Reisman wrote it out for us." The first intimation that it might be a hit came when Patti opened for Joe E. Lewis at the Copacabana. "I was hired to do five songs," she said. "Three shows a night, no encores, and I hated it. Nobody listened. Nobody looked. Everyone was waiting for Joe E. Lewis or the dancing girls. Then one night I finished my five songs with 'With My Eyes Wide Open I'm Dreaming.' I was walking off the stage, and someone in the crowd said, 'Sing the waltz,' and then other people said, 'Yeah, sing the waltz.' I went upstairs, and Jack came in later, and I said, 'People were asking for the waltz. What does that mean?' Jack called Harry Rosen, the Mercury distributor in Philadelphia, and Harry told Jack that everyone was on 'Tennessee Waltz,' not 'Boogie Woogie Santa Claus.'"

By the end of January 1951, "Tennessee Waltz" had sold 1.75 million copies, and Mercury had four pressing plants working night and day on it. It spent twenty-six weeks on the charts, half of them at Number 1. It was one of those inexplicable, uncontainable phenomena. Patti now headlined her own show, and her asking price jumped from $2,000 to $5,000 a week.

Her sister, Rema, sang harmony to re-create the recorded sound. It would be another two years before Patti and Jack found a song to halfway eclipse "Tennessee Waltz," but almost every record she released until the end of the 1950s found its way onto the charts. And if she ever tired of "Tennessee Waltz" she needed only to remind herself that her career might have been very different without it.

In the wake of "Tennessee Waltz," Patti recorded a ten-inch album of country songs, *Folk Song Favorites*. One session was held in Cincinnati with the group that had backed Hank Williams on "Lovesick Blues." Steel guitarist Jerry Byrd was quite simply the best in the business back then. Patti's versions of "Detour" and the ancient folk ballad "Who's Gonna Shoe Your Pretty Little Feet?" are exquisite. Had Jack Rael not come to Tulsa it would have been no stretch for Patti Page to become a Western Swing band vocalist. *Folk Song Favorites* was her first album, and it's still worth searching for.

The next big hit was "Mockin' Bird Hill." It offers another little lesson in how the record business operated in simpler times. "I had just closed in Chicago," said Patti. "It was a Saturday morning, and I was leaving, and I was at the airport on my way back to New York, and I was opening at the Fontainebleu in Miami on Sunday. I was being paged at Midway Airport. I went to the American Airlines counter and took the phone call. It was Art Talmadge at Mercury Records. He said, 'Don't take the flight to New York.' He said he was coming out to the airport with a little record player and a record he wanted me to hear. I said, 'What?' He said, 'If you like it, I want you to cut it in New York.' I said, 'Art, I don't record without Jack, and he's in Miami.' Art came out with a little 45-rpm player. He played me Les Paul and Mary Ford's record. He said everyone was going into Lyon's Music in Chicago asking for me singing 'Mockin' Bird Hill.' He said, 'This could be big.' He said he'd talk to Jack, and he'd booked studio time in New York and the musicians. They had a limo at the airport, took me to Bob Fine's studio. I cut just that one song. I was very happy with it, and I couldn't wait to let Jack hear it. He said, 'This is really very good.' He called Art, and Art said, 'I'm so glad you like it, Jack, because we've already shipped 200,000 records.'"

And then, of course, came "How Much Is That Doggie in the Window?". It had already been turned down by Mindy Carson, the wife of Eddie Joy, who ran the publishing company that owned it. "I knew it was a hit before we even recorded it," says Jack Rael. "I added the barks, and rewrote it." Patti remembers that the song came up for consideration just at the time another dumb Bob Merrill song, "If I'd Known You Were Coming, I'd Have Baked a Cake," was a hit. Novelty songs seemed to be selling, and this seemed as good as any. The barks were by the arranger, Joe Reisman, and the contractor, Mac Ceppos. "Joe and I became friends in the Jimmy Joy Band," said Patti. "Mac was a violinist. His speaking voice was really gruff, so he could do that bark. They did the barks at the same time I added the second voice. I couldn't finish a lot of times, it was too funny. They had to put me where I couldn't see them." Patti's record is so quintessentially early 1950s: pure, innocent, and irredeemably dumb, but strangely beguiling.

By 1952, Patti Page was on television. Perry Como had already shown how to do it, becoming the first to prove that television was not a poor relation, but just needed a set of skills very unlike those necessary for the stage or movies. Perry realized that people were inviting you into their home, and you had to act accordingly. Television, like radio back then, was mostly packaged in fifteen-minute sponsored time slots, and the shows went out live. Patti's first show, *Music Hall,* was a summer replacement for Como, and went on the air in July 1952. It was picked up by Scott Paper when Como returned, and became the *Scott Music Hall* on NBC between October 1952 and August 1953. Patti returned to television in July 1955, with seventy-eight pretaped fifteen-minute shows filmed in conjunction with Screen Gems and GAC. The shows went out twice weekly, and were later syndicated worldwide. The soundtracks were recorded in stereo, as unheard of in 1955 as overdubbing had been in 1947.

Patti was off the air in 1956, the year rock 'n' roll erupted. She tried covering R&B tunes, including Brook Benton's "The Wall," but never sounded entirely comfortable with the sledgehammer backbeat. She also recorded Burt Bacharach's first song, "Keep Me in Mind," which proved that not everything from Bacharach's pen was unalloyed genius. Soon enough, Patti reverted to Plan A. The next big hits, "Allegheny Moon" and "Old Cape Cod," could as easily have been hits in 1950. Let the kiddies rock and roll: the world hadn't changed *that* much.

As 1956 drew to a close, Patti married choreographer Charles O'Curran in Las Vegas. She had seen the show that he'd staged for Betty Hutton. "I saw her at the Palace Theater when she made her comeback," she said, "and it was the most brilliant show I had ever seen. I had to find out who did it. Charlie was married to her at the time. He would never

Patti with Jack Rael on sax and the Treniers. Courtesy Colin Escott.

worry about money, and no expense was spared." After O'Curran separated from Betty Hutton, he and Patti dated. His work kept him in Los Angeles, and Patti's kept her in New York. It was July 1957 before they managed to get away to Europe for a honeymoon. Patti returned in late August to start work on her new television show, *The Big Record,* for CBS-TV, while O'Curran went off to work on *Jailhouse Rock.*

Television variety shows tried to cover all the bases, and Patti's guest list included Fats Domino, Will Glahe ("Beer Barrel Polka"), Webb Pierce, Eddie Cantor, and Count Basie. Her show was cut from one hour to thirty minutes in March 1958, and zapped from the schedules in June of that same year. In September, Patti returned as host of *Patti Page's Olds Show* on ABC-TV. There had been eight female singers hosting their own shows in 1957, but only Patti and Dinah Shore survived into the 1958–59 season. The *Olds Show* lasted until March 1959, leaving Patti free to relocate to the West Coast when it ended. In September 1959, she took her first dramatic role, in the film *Elmer Gantry.* Director Richard Brooks wanted her for the role of Sister Rachel, a dessicated choir director nursing an unrequited passion for the charismatic preacher Elmer Gantry, played by Burt Lancaster.

By the late 1950s Patti's chart placings were trailing off. She wanted to do concept albums, as Sinatra was doing. Her version of Gordon Jenkins's *Manhattan Tower* suite was brilliantly realized, as was her collaboration with jazz arranger Pete Rugolo on an album called *In the Land of Hi-Fi.* Two more albums, *East Side* and *West Side* (which had initially been released as the double LP *East Side/West Side*), appeared on Mercury's jazz imprint, Emarcy. Patti's crowd stayed away because there were no hits, and the sophisticates couldn't think of her as a jazz singer. Taken together, those four albums stand near the apogee of 1950s pop. "I've Stayed Too Long at the Fair" from *East Side/West Side,* is as good as it gets. Singing, acting, and personal experience seem to crossfade and coalesce.

Mercury missed its chance to transform Patti Page into an album artist. They shunted her from the jazz department to Shelby Singleton, who had just taken over Mercury's New York A&R office in addition to heading the country division in Nashville. Singleton's response to Patti's waning fortunes was to bridge pop and country. If Jim Reeves was coming from country toward pop, then maybe Patti could go in the opposite direction. In November 1961, Singleton brought her to Nashville to cover a fast-breaking record by Marion Worth, "Go On Home." It became her biggest country hit since "Tennessee Waltz" and her biggest pop hit in a couple of years. It also gave her some leverage when the Mercury deal was up in June 1962, and she departed for Columbia. "We left because they weren't selling albums," said Patti. "I did a lot of good albums for Mercury that never did anything. Columbia just did a much better job promoting albums back then." In 1965, still on Columbia, Patti made her last Top 10 chart appearance with "Hush, Hush Sweet Charlotte."

In 1970, Patti returned to Mercury. By then, Shelby Singleton had left to start his own Plantation Records, and his one-time assistant, Jerry Kennedy, headed the Nashville division. Kennedy signed Patti as a country artist. There were several chart entries, one of them a jokey duet with Tom T. Hall, "Hello, We're Lonely." It reached Number 14 on the country charts, but set no new highwater mark for either artist. After Mercury, Patti signed with Epic Records in Nashville, and then Avco before joining Shelby Singleton's Plantation Records. When her last country hit left the charts in June 1982, it had been thirty-four years since "Confess" had charted.

The 1970s and '80s were largely barren. Patti and Charlie O'Curran adopted children from troubled backgrounds, and O'Curran himself was

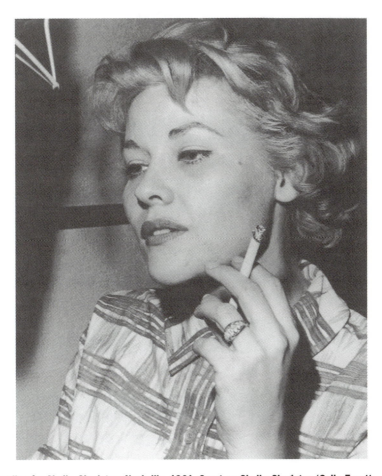

Recording for Shelby Singleton, Nashville, 1961. Courtesy Shelby Singleton/Colin Escott.

not without problems. They divorced, and Patti subsequently married retired aerospace executive Jerry Filiciotto. With Filiciotto, Patti Page found some peace and financial stability. They live comfortably, dividing their time between Solana Beach, California, and a maple syrup farm in New Hampshire. On many levels, life is good, but without actually saying as much, Patti seems jealous of Rosemary Clooney's self-reinvention as a jazz singer and Tony Bennett's recently acquired hipness. There's the nagging feeling that she has been shortchanged. And perhaps she has. The singles are the 1950s incarnate, but the albums tell a different story. Who else could tackle Patsy Montana's "I Want to Be a Cowboy's Sweetheart" as convincingly as Noel Coward's "Mad About the Boy"? She could still make another great album, but if the idea ever comes up around the A&R table, someone probably shoots it down by singing a snatch of "Doggie in the Window." Cue barks.

Check It Out

A four-CD retrospective issued by Mercury Records, *A Golden Celebration* (Mercury 314534720), covers Patti's entire Mercury career, but the great albums, *Manhattan Tower, East Side/West Side,* and *In the Land of Hi-Fi,* are unobtainable in their entirety, as is her first country album, *Folk Song Favorites.* The hits are on an almost infinite number of compilations.

PART II

Fabor

Fabor Robison (standing) with Carolyn Bradshaw (seated left) and Jim Reeves. Courtesy Bear Family Archive.

The next few stories relate in some way to Fabor Robison. Fabor was one of the hyperbolic characters who populated the music business before it was overrun by accountants and MBAs. He was never interviewed, but those who knew him remember his stories, and a few of those stories might even have been true. He claimed, for instance, to have looted a bank in Germany after the Second World War and buried the money, but then forgotten where he had stashed it by the time he got back. If so, it was a metaphor for his life: he discovered, managed, and recorded a rich roster of talent, and lost every one of them. All Fabor's acts began by seeing him as their salvation, then quickly came to hate him. When the record business soured, he turned to scams like the cold weather tanning tube, and when everything went wrong, he would disappear. Brazil was home for a few years.

Robison was born in Beebe, Arkansas, on November 3, 1911. He was a cook in the army during the war, then apparently came home to find his wife with someone else. He went to Hollywood with thoughts of making it as an actor, but became a cook and prop setter instead. He bore a passing resemblance to Robert Young, and claimed to have been a stand-in for him in movies. His first venture into the music business came when he signed rube comedian Les "Carrot Top" Anderson as a managerial client. He placed Anderson with a small California label, Cormac Records, then discovered Johnny Horton, placing him with Cormac, too.

Cormac folded, and Fabor started Abbott Records in 1951 as a partnership with a drugstore owner, Sid Abbott, who is a story in himself. Originally from Boston, Abbott had a degree in pharmacy and opened his first store at a time when druggists manufactured their own pills and suppositories. He had a sideline in whiskey, which he peddled under the counter. Somewhere along the way, Abbott heard about Johnny Horton. "I went to Harmony Park, a country dance hall. Someone had told me there was a good singer there, and it was Johnny Horton," said Abbott. "Listened to him. Liked him. Went back and talked to him, and that's when Fabor came into the picture. He was a handsome man, and it all looked promising. Fabor had Johnny Horton's contract, and we decided to go into partnership."

At the same time, Abbott had business interests in Mexico, including a candy factory that took him to Mexico City twice a month. He was also a wholesale jewelry manufacturer, and went to New York every month for supplies. Add to that three drugstores, an appliance store, and a record store, and it is no small wonder that Abbott was unaware that, in October 1953, Fabor had started another label, Fabor Records, without him. At some point in 1953, Sid Abbott and Fabor Robison fell out. Abbott Records was a going concern at the time, thanks in part to Jim Reeves, and in part to a pop act, the DeCastro Sisters. According to Abbott, he discovered the DeCastros, although the surviving sisters remember Fabor finding them.

Abbott dabbled some more in the music business, but without much success. Both Fabor and Sid Abbott appeared to have issued records on Abbott for a while. Abbott kept diversifying, going into the restaurant business in addition to his other ventures. In 1958, Fabor started a rock 'n' roll label, Radio Records, but sold all his labels the following year to Jamie and Guyden Records. He restarted Fabor Records in 1962, reissuing his 1957 recording of Ned Miller's "From a Jack to a King," which had originally appeared on Dot Records. After the song became a hit, Fabor

Records became a going concern again for a couple of years. Then Miller's contract and masters were peddled to Capitol, and Fabor disappeared to Brazil. He started a studio in Rio de Janeiro, buying a sixteen-track recorder from Bill Justis with the intention of becoming a major player in the Brazilian music business. But that didn't work out, either.

There's no doubting Fabor's ear for talent. He signed or recorded Jim Reeves, Johnny Horton, Dorsey Burnette, Bobby Hart, the Browns, Ned Miller, and the DeCastro Sisters. This was more than enough talent for an independent record label, if he'd been able to keep half of them. Instead, they all came to despise him, and left as soon as they could. Most wanted out at any cost. Fabor's only apologist these days is his one-time partner (and cousin) Russell Sims, who went on to launch Sims Records. Sims's explanation is that Fabor was a good man and a Christian man who lost God and became angry and twisted.

The Abbott, Fabor, and Radio labels were peddled several times to several different companies through the years. At some point, Fabor offloaded everything he owned, and much he didn't, to Shelby Singleton. During the 1970s and '80s he could have rehabilitated himself by talking to journalists, and telling his side of the story (the artist's side isn't invariably right, after all). Instead, he laid low, avoiding creditors, and died in his home state, Arkansas, in September 1986.

Sid Abbott was interviewed by Todd Everett and Richard Weize in January 2001.

CHAPTER 4

Jim Reeves

SAY "YES" TO RUGS

Jim Reeves was a paradox. Not an especially intriguing one to most people perhaps, but one that tells us how country music came out the other side of rock 'n' roll. You'll usually find Reeves bracketed with Slim Whitman (without even Whitman's kooky appeal), but Reeves had a vision and the cussedness to stick with it when everyone was telling him to do something different. He grew up in Texas in the 1920s and '30s, but he didn't sing Western Swing or Texas beer-joint music; instead, he sang country music for people who didn't like country music—or didn't even know what it was. When nearly all his contemporaries were trying to rock and roll, Jim Reeves went low and slow. "Four Walls" was not only a great record, but a groundbreaking one. Most of what happened in country music in the late 1950s and '60s took its cue from that one record.

For many years, Jim Reeves was the only country artist selling overseas. He was certainly the only country artist selling to Jamaicans, the bog Irish, and black South Africans. Jamaican record shops in London had huge Jim Reeves sections because, believe it or not, his records were considered "make out" music. In South Africa, he was almost a demigod. News of his death was greeted with disbelief, and his records were pressed on 78s for sale in the black townships well into the 1960s.

Somewhere along the way, Reeves acquired the nickname Gentleman Jim, which made those who'd worked with him shriek with laughter. In what was then the small, easygoing town of Nashville, Gentleman Jim was

Courtesy Colin Escott.

legendarily difficult. Although photographed in front of blazing fires wearing Perry Como cardigans, he was sour tempered, deeply suspicious of people he didn't know, and blunt to the point of rudeness. A typical story: sitting in a barber shop in Madison, Tennessee, he saw a tall church spire, and, out of the blue, told the barber he'd like to see how far he could get that spire up the ass of a promoter who'd shortchanged him. Gentleman Jim.

James Travis Reeves was born on August 20, 1923 (not 1924 as most sources state). This means that the man who showed the way forward after Hank Williams's death was actually older, by a month, than Hank himself. He was born between Deadwood and Galloway, in Panola County, Texas. Shreveport, Louisiana, was thirty-five miles to the northeast, and Carthage, Texas, eight miles to the west. Jim was the ninth and last child of Tom Reeves and Mary Beulah Adams Reeves, and the eighth to live. Tom died on May 1, 1924 when Jim was less than one year old, leaving Beulah to raise the family alone.

If times were tough because of the Depression, they must have been tougher still for the Reeves family, but you'd never know it from the few times Jim talked about his earliest years. The one clear fact to emerge from the studied triteness of Reeves's interviews is that he was fiercely determined to get off the farm one way or another. Baseball seemed the best ticket. He was a star pitcher for Carthage High School, and always insisted that he won a baseball scholarship to the University of Texas in Austin in 1942. He said he majored in "speech, phonetics, articulation, pronunciation, enunciation," but the university has no record of James Travis Reeves attending. He rid himself of his backcountry accent somewhere along the way, though. By the time he recorded his first transcriptions a few years later, it was impossible to tell where he came from.

Reeves volunteered for active service in World War II, but was turned down because of enlarged muscles around the heart, the result of rheumatic fever. He worked in some wartime munitions plants, and was picked up for the St. Louis Cardinals farm system in 1944, a system depleted by the war. On March 25 of that year he was offered a minor league contract and sent to the Piedmont League farm club in Lynchburg, Virginia. In 1945, he broke a collarbone and a finger in a road accident and was released. By that point, his record was 0-0 in ten appearances. The following year, he played for Natchez, Mississippi, and Alexandria, Louisiana, in the Evangeline League and had a 10-8 record in twenty appearances.

Early in 1946, Jim Reeves met Mary White at a dance in Marshall, Texas. Mary graduated from high school in May of that year, while Jim was playing baseball. The following year, Jim was still pitching for Alexandria, and after going 5–2 in nine games, was traded to Marshall, Texas, then Henderson in the Lone Star League. And then, in August, he was injured. Mary says that in trying to pick a runner off first base, he twisted around on the pitching mound, slipped, and tore his sciatic nerve. Jim said he was batting and tore a ligament trying to reach first base. In any event, he reached home plate with Mary. They were married on September 3, 1947 at the Methodist church in Carthage. By then, his baseball career was over.

Shortly before leaving for Houston to work on an oil pipeline, Jim interviewed for an on-air job at KGRI, a 250-watt station in Henderson,

Texas. "We had moved to Henderson," said Mary, "and some of Jim's buddies asked him if he had ever thought of doing disc-jockey work. He said he hadn't, but as there was a vacancy at the radio station he decided to go ahead and try for it. The same people that owned the radio station also owned the baseball franchise, so he was under contract to them anyway. The program director gave him some news to practice on, and told him to come back the next day and audition. He brought it home, and practiced reading while I listened. The next day he auditioned and got the job."

In 1950, Jim made his first records for Macy's Records, an offshoot of United Record Wholesalers in Houston. The owner's wife, Lela Macy Henry, ran the label. The launch date was July 1, 1949, and Jim probably recorded early the following year. "I rented a car and drove to Houston," he remembered, "and I blew a couple of pistons out of it trying to get home, and had to buy a new engine for the car. And I had to pay for the session, and pay the musicians. That took my life's savings." The Henrys sent him a watch for Christmas 1950, and that was all the remuneration he ever saw. The Henrys probably figured that they could sell enough copies of Jim's records around Henderson to break even, and could then rely on him to spin their product. It was a common enough bargain in those days. The two Macy's records show that Jim had discovered his natural range, but had yet to learn to be intimate with the microphone. He was a little edgier than Eddy Arnold, but not much.

"In that part of the country," said Mary, "Dallas was *the* place to record. We were unlucky with the recording companies there, so then we made the move to Longview, Texas, and Jim took another radio job at KSIJ and another in a big nightclub where he sang with a band." Trying to pay the bills, he sold insurance for the local affiliate of National Life and Accident, the company that owned the Grand Ole Opry. Talking about his stint as an insurance salesman, he said, "My boss could tell I wasn't happy and he asked me why. I told him I wanted to make my living as a singer. He asked me what kind of singer, and I told him folk songs and country music. He told me that if I'd stay with his company, he'd arrange a business trip to Nashville so I could see the Grand Ole Opry. I told him the first time I saw the Opry, I was going to be up on the stage." Jim loved those Horatio Alger moments: rejection and redemption. He later bought KGRI in Henderson, the station that once employed him.

The "big nightclub" Mary was talking about was the Reo Palm Isle club in Longview. Often, Jim would close the club at 2:00 A.M. and sleep

Working the Texas country circuit, c. 1950. Courtesy Bear Family Archive.

on the couch at KSIJ, leaving word with the telephone operator to call him in time to get up and sign the station on air at 5:00 A.M. Jim and Mary sent copies of the Macy's records to all the country record labels, but found no takers until Fabor Robison came on the scene. Fabor had started Abbott Records in 1951 to record Johnny Horton, then peddled Horton's contract to Mercury in June of the following year. When Horton got a gig on KWKH's *Louisiana Hayride* in Shreveport, Fabor came east with him. KGRI deejay, Tom Perryman, told Fabor to check out Jim Reeves at the Reo Palm Isle club, and Fabor signed him to the newly relaunched Abbott Records in November or December 1952. At around the same time, Jim joined the *Louisiana Hayride* (the radio barn dance that made stars of Hank Williams, Elvis Presley, Webb Pierce, Johnny Horton, and many others) as an announcer, not a singer. Every night, he was on the *Hayride's* home station, KWKH, as a deejay. As radio jobs went, this was as good as it got because KWKH blanketed much of the eastern United States and Canada with its 50,000-watt clear channel.

When KWKH was off air, between 1:00 A.M. and 5:00 A.M., the studio was used for recording. The *Hayride's* biggest star, Slim Whitman, recorded there, as did Dale Hawkins ("Susie Q"), and many others. One of the songs on Reeves's second Abbott session was Mitchell Torok's "Mexican Joe." Torok, the son of Hungarian immigrants, was a student in nearby Nacogdoches. Caricaturing Mexicans as lazy, feckless, and simple, "Mexican Joe" was the sort of record you couldn't make today, even if you wanted to, but it was a smash in 1953. Just as it was breaking, another *Hayride* performer, Billy Walker, rushed out a cover version on Columbia Records using the same arrangement, in fact the same band. Jim stared daggers at Walker the next time they met. Walker hoped that Columbia's stronger distribution would blow Abbott out of the water, but this was Fabor's moment, and he seized it. Jim Reeves's record was Number 1 for nine weeks.

Ironically, it was Billy Walker, not Jim Reeves, who sang "Mexican Joe" on the *Hayride* because program director Horace Logan didn't see Jim as a singer. Fabor was on the ball, though. He had Colonel Parker's ability to focus singlemindedly on a task and had the same carny instinct for a good sideshow. Those skills were now used in the service of Jim Reeves. At Fabor's instigation, Jim covered another cretinous novelty song, "Bimbo" ("Bimbo, bimbo, where you gonna go-wee-oh"), and, dumb as it was, it too reached the top of the country charts. "Beatin' on a Ding-Dong" was, if anything, even dumber, but at least it failed to chart. Fabor Robison put Jim Reeves on the map, but at a price. At Fabor's instigation, Jim not only sang truly dreadful songs, but sang high, trying for the nut-clenching Webb Pierce notes that weren't his natural terrain.

Unlike most record company execs, Fabor wasn't prepared to assume a background role. He assembled a touring package called Fabor Robison's String Music Show, featuring Jim and other newly signed acts like the Rowley Trio, the Browns, and Mitchell Torok. "We toured all over the West Coast with Jim," said Dido Rowley. "All over Colorado too. Fabor went with us. He had a little ukelele. We were all onstage the whole show. The whole cast was onstage, and we'd take turns performing. Fabor would come waltzing around with his ukelele, but he couldn't keep a beat. He was having a ball, thinking he was keeping time, but he wasn't."

Disillusionment set in. "He was a great discoverer of talent as well as songs," said Mary Reeves, begrudgingly, "but he was wired up a little bit different from most people. He was very hard to get along with. He was a bit of a dictator, and that doesn't work too well with intelligent artists." Jim's buddy from KGRI, Tom Perryman, elaborates: "He always thought someone was after him. He carried a little pistol. He said, 'They're trying to get me. The distributors won't pay me, and the major record labels are trying to put me out of business, cut my throat.' He was paranoid. Weird. I never had any trouble with him, but he never paid me either." Jim Ed Brown says that Fabor tried to rape his sister, Maxine. Money and control seem to have been the issues that irked Jim. He saw his records atop the charts, saw sold-out halls wherever he played, and saw Fabor driving a new Cadillac and building a beachhouse studio in Malibu, yet he was told that the records weren't selling and the tours weren't making money.

Jim made his first overseas trip between Christmas and New Year 1954–1955, touring frigid Army bases in France, Germany, the Azores, and Newfoundland, Canada. After he returned, the arguments with Fabor became increasingly heated. Fabor had Jim Reeves tied up in every conceivable way: recording, music publishing, and management. Details of the final blowup are sketchy. Earlier, Jim had grabbed a gun and driven to Fabor's house with the intention of killing him, but cooled down and decided that Fabor wasn't worth shooting. In the final scene, it was Fabor waving the gun, cursing Jim for his disloyalty. Jim apparently grabbed the gun and held it to Fabor's head, telling him he would record whatever he needed to get out of his contract. Fabor wasn't getting much sympathy from the other artists on his roster. "Jim should have killed the bastard. Somebody should have," said Maxine Brown.

Fabor had Jim Reeves under contract until June 1956, and as part of the severance package, Jim had to sign over royalties on all unreleased sides. His chances of getting royalties on the released sides probably weren't great, either. Interviewed shortly after the blowup, Jim seemed disillusioned and talked of getting out of the recording end of the business and into music publishing. "After being with Fabor, you just want to give up," said Maxine Brown. "You don't want to fool with it, if that's the way the music business treats you." The Browns wanted off Fabor's new Fabor label, but had to sign an even less favorable agreement in which they handed over all songwriter royalties and $10,000.

Jim had been approached by Paul Cohen at Decca Records and then by Steve Sholes at RCA. On March 23, 1955, he cast his lot with RCA. Even before the first RCA single hit the streets, Fabor had rolled out a new Jim

"String Music Show" poster. Courtesy Colin Escott.

Reeves record, and then a Jim Reeves album (country albums were almost unheard of in those days). Sholes saw that his new releases would be undermined by old recordings, and so concluded a deal with Fabor to buy the back catalog. This was a lesson worth learning. When Sholes signed Elvis Presley from Sun later that year, he made sure he got the back catalog as part of the deal. Around the same time, Jim was approached by WSM's Jack Stapp, who wanted him on the Grand Ole Opry. The country music business was nowhere near as Nashville-centric then as it is now, and Jim had worked almost a decade in country music without any involvement with Nashville, but in May 1955 he packed up and moved there.

The first RCA session was on May 31, 1955. Jim drove up from Shreveport, fooling with a new song, "Yonder Comes a Sucker," based on an old nursery rhyme. Sholes scheduled it as the first RCA single, and it reached Number 4 on the country charts, reportedly selling around 250,000 copies. One of the reasons that Jim wanted to be free of Fabor was that he wanted to sing ballads in his natural register instead of up-tempo novelties in high keys, but "Yonder Comes a Sucker" could easily have been an Abbott record, albeit a *good* Abbott record. While in Nashville, Jim signed with Tree Music, a newly formed partnership between the Opry's Jack Stapp and bass player Buddy Killen. In fact, signing with Tree might very well have been part of the deal that brought Reeves to the Opry. Killen remembers, "I waited for Jim to complete the session, then I told him who I was and explained about the contracts which he signed. I said, 'Jim, thanks for placing your songs with Tree.' He said, 'I might as well place them with you as anybody else, you're not going to pay me anyway.'" Anyone dealing with Gentleman Jim had to get past comments like that, and Jim eventually warmed to Killen to the point of bringing him into his band.

These days, artists signing major label deals can expect some serious front money, but when Jim and Mary Reeves moved to Nashville in October 1955, they could barely afford a trailer on low-rent Dickerson Road. Around the same time, Jim ditched the Western outfits he'd worn in Shreveport in favor of evening attire. He knew where he was heading. The cowboy hat had to go, too, but it was hiding a receding hairline. Jim went shopping for a toupee. "He was a fair looking guy," says Tom Perryman, "but he was always self-conscious about his hair. When he changed his style, he quit wearing the hat, but he hated the hairpieces. You had to use spirit gum, and he worked and worked at it. I remember one time, one of my kids was up at Jim's house, and he had washed his hairpiece and had it laying on the edge of the bathtub. My little girl accidentally dropped it in the toilet."

Jim Reeves signed with RCA just a few months before rock 'n' roll erupted. He'd watched Elvis on the *Hayride*, and so had a much better idea of what was in store than anyone around Nashville, and he'd already made up his mind that he was having no part of it. From the beginning of 1956, Chet Atkins took over RCA's country sessions. Even when Sholes headed country A&R, he was based in New York, but, from 1956 onward he was consumed with Presley-related issues. "Steve had moved on to what the company considered more important things," Atkins recalled in 1973, "so he turned Jim and Hank Snow over to me. That didn't go over too well, and they kinda resented the fact that Mr. Sholes was not making their records, and they didn't know if I had any talent in the studio. Jim wasn't too warm at first, but he saw I had some talent and wasn't trying to push any bad tunes at him. Jim liked to go out and have a drink after recording. Maybe the third time I recorded him, I went with him. He was a great conversationalist. He was so graphic in his descriptions of things that had happened to him. We came from about the same background. He'd talk about how he'd often sleep in the courthouse when he was going to school, get up in the morning, bum some breakfast somewhere, and go on to school. I think Jim had been kicked around pretty bad, because he was suspicious of people until he got to know them."

Together, Chet Atkins and Jim Reeves forged Nashville's response to rock 'n' roll. Hard-country instruments, like the fiddle and steel guitar, dropped out of the mix, to be replaced by the piano, electric guitar, strings, and vocal chorus. This was the "Nashville Sound," and the first great Nashville Sound record was "Four Walls." Its quiet, claustrophobic desperation made it the perfect song to usher in the new era: "Four walls to hear me, four walls to see / Four walls too near me, closing in on me." The demo and lead sheet were sent to Atkins, and were sitting in a pile on his desk that toppled over into the trash. Jim was sitting in Chet's office, and retrieved "Four Walls." He read through the lyrics, and told Chet he'd like to cut it. Chet was both guitarist and producer.

"It was a lot of stress," Atkins told Dave Bussey, "because I had to run back and forth to the control room, but Jim liked my guitar sound and wanted me to play the introduction and the bridge. He also wanted the Jordanaires, and I called and couldn't get them. Jim said he wanted that sound, so we moved the session back to when we could get them. He also wanted to rehearse the song, and we were both working on WSM, and we arranged to rehearse 'Four Walls' one evening after the radio program. The Jordanaires were there, too."

Atkins was always painfully self-effacing. "All great things are an accident," he said. "You don't just sit down and say, 'I'm going to develop this or that.' I wasn't trying to change the business, just sell records. I realized at that time you had to surprise the public and give them something a little different. At that time, we had an engineer from New York who was from the old school and he didn't believe in artists getting too close to the

Recording at RCA, with Chet Atkins watching from behind the glass. Courtesy Colin Escott.

microphone in case they popped a *P* into it. Jim wanted an intimate sound and wanted to get real close and whisper the lyrics, and he had many arguments with this engineer. Then it so happened he left, and we recorded 'Four Walls' with [engineer] Selby Coffeen, who was from Springfield, Missouri. Steve Sholes was amazed. He said, 'How did you get that beautiful vocal sound?'"

Studio musician and songwriter Tommy Hill remembered the session because he hoped Jim would cut one of his songs. "Jim recorded roughly two inches from the microphone," said Hill. "He had been one hell of a disc jockey, and he knew how to control the air hitting the mic. He would turn his head when he was hitting a *P* or something that had the air pressure. He would work that mic when he was recording. He had always sung up-tempo and real high. That was what was selling then. He was just cornball country when he hit high notes, but he was pretty on the low notes." "Four Walls" was almost embarrassingly intimate. "We loved that song so much," said Jordanaire Gordon Stoker. Listening to the playbacks in the studio, Stoker remembered Jim saying, "This is great, if they release it just like we're hearing it now." He didn't want more instruments added, and he wanted the chorus up in the mix. And that was how it appeared.

Jim had neared the mark a few months earlier with "Am I Losing You?" but there was a steel guitar in the background and no chorus: almost, but not quite. In the year or so since rock 'n' roll erupted, the number of stations programming country music had dropped precipitously. Country music's biggest stars, Hank Snow, Webb Pierce, and Red Foley among them, were cutting lame rock 'n' roll records, trying to get back on air. Some of these records catch your attention, much like a car wreck on the other side of the highway, but they weren't the way forward. Few saw it, but rock 'n' roll had presented country music with a huge opportunity; yet it wasn't the opportunity to rock. The rules that governed pop airplay were changing. Forty-piece bands and big arrangements were no longer the norm. Simple little love songs could make it. If the hillbilly edges were sanded down and the sound sweetened, pop airplay for country artists was suddenly very attainable. It's hard to know if Jim Reeves sensed this or stumbled upon it, but much of what happened in Nashville over the next decade or more was predicated by his recording of "Four Walls."

"Four Walls" also set Jim on his quixotic quest for the perfect record. In an era of imperfect studios, imperfect musicianship, and imperfect pressings, he wanted everything just right. He really belonged in the Digital Age. He didn't exclude himself from criticism, although he usually had his vocals worked out by the time he entered the studio. The pickers came in cold, and when they goofed, Jim tore into them. "He was an old maid," said Stoker. "He always complained he wasn't getting the best of this or that. I remember one late session, and the musicians had already done one, two, maybe even three sessions that day. Buddy Harman, the drummer, had gone into RCA Studio B to lie down and rest before Jim's session, and Jim came in and said, 'Well, that's what I always get, a bunch of broken-down musicians that are worn out before I get here.'" Atkins simply learned to live with this. "Sometimes," he remembered, "Jim would say something to one of the musicians and you'd feel a chill in the place. Most artists want to excel, but Jim was something else."

Just as "Four Walls" was being readied for release, Jim prepared for another overseas junket. Routine today, these overseas trips were very unusual and fraught with peril in 1957. The emcee of the 1954 tour, Dick O'Shaughnessy, was conscripted again, together with Hank Locklin, Del Wood, Janis Martin, and the Browns. With the exception of O'Shaughnessy, all were RCA acts. The revue assembled in Nashville and partied at the Andrew Jackson Hotel following the Opry on March 23. Jim was on a special edition of the *Tonight Show,* networked out of Nashville on March 26. He sang "Four Walls" with the Browns backing him. There was a warm-up show in Toledo on March 29, the Opry on March 30, another warm-up show in Akron on March 31, then on to New York. RCA grandees came to the airport to buy lunch and wave goodbye. They told Jim that they intended to put a big push behind "Four Walls" in both pop and country.

According to Tommy Hill, trouble set in long before landfall in Europe. "About an hour out of Iceland, I was the only one awake, and I felt something like an air pocket. I looked outside and an engine was on fire. They had something on the engine to smother the blaze, and they shut the engine down, and landed in Iceland. There were five or six couches. I grabbed a sandwich and laid down to sleep. They all said, 'We'll leave you behind, Tommy.' I said, 'I don't think so.'" The troupe arrived in Frankfurt on April 2, and began a grueling tour of bases. "It was unorganized," said Maxine Brown. "We had to ride in transport planes, wearing parachutes between our legs." Hank Locklin, who'd spent most of his career in the inexorable flatness of the Gulf Coast and Texas, was amused by farms clinging to hillsides. "I guess there wasn't enough land to go around for everybody, so they had to hang it up and farm it on both sides," he said. Janis Martin hadn't told anyone that she was married, much less that her husband was in Germany. He appeared, and she disappeared.

They flew to England in a parachute drop plane. "It was a C-40," said Tommy Hill. "They just had benches down each side and strapped the luggage in the middle. We got over London and just circled and circled, waiting for the weather to break. Then they said, 'We're gonna have to find another airfield.' All of a sudden we just went nose down. Maxine and Bonnie Brown were hysterical. I never heard Jim cuss so much. The plane ran out of fuel just as we were taxiing to the terminal."

Jim couldn't wait to get back to the United States. All indications from home were that "Four Walls" was breaking. "That's the happiest I ever saw Jim," said his steel guitarist Bobby Garrett. "It thrilled him to death to know he finally had a big ballad hit." Jim's manager, Herb Shucher, moved fast. By June 9, Jim was on the *Steve Allen Show;* then the *Patti Page Show* and *NBC Bandstand.* He was on the *Jimmy Dean Show* during the week of July 20-27, then the *Georgia Gibbs Show* on July 29. He had worked all his life for this.

"Four Walls" reached the top of the country charts and Number 11 on the pop charts, but the follow-ups did nowhere near as well on the pop charts. The best songwriters in Nashville were willingly holding their songs for a Reeves session, but nothing clicked. Jim tried going up-tempo. Roger Miller's "Billy Bayou" could almost have been an Abbott record, and although it reached the top of the country charts (displacing another Miller song, "Invitation to the Blues"), it failed to make much of a dent in the pop charts. Jim returned to Shreveport in December 1959 for a bene-fit show for Tommy Tomlinson, the guitarist who had been injured in the car wreck that killed Johnny Horton. He sang "Mexican Joe," and ran into Mitchell Torok backstage. Torok asked him how things were going, and Jim, who tended to be overly pessimistic, said he was just piddling along, selling 50,000 copies of his records, playing his show dates. He told Torok he had just recorded a song called "He'll Have to Go," and he hoped it would break the logjam and rack up some decent sales for a change.

The first to record "He'll Have to Go" was Billy Brown, an Atlanta-based artist who'd cut it for Columbia. Chet Atkins heard it when Jim was out on the road. "When he came in I played it for him," said Atkins, "and the boy who recorded it didn't have much of a voice because he couldn't hit those low notes." Jim waited to see if Brown's record would be a hit, and when it wasn't, he covered it. Jim and Chet framed the vocal with vibraphone, piano, electric bass, and acoustic guitar, calling for take after take. Jim decided to underscore the word *low* by dropping an octave. After two-and-a-half years, he knew he'd finally found a follow-up to "Four Walls."

The song was by Joe Allison, a California disc jockey who later became the head of Capitol Records in Nashville, producing Wanda Jackson, among others. The idea came from his British wife Audrey's soft telephone voice. "Put your sweet lips a little closer to the phone," he'd often tell her. "He'll Have to Go" showed up in the country charts early in December 1959, and, during the first week of February 1960 it knocked Marty Robbins's "El Paso" from the top. It stayed at Number 1 on the country charts for fourteen weeks, and reached Number 2 on the pop charts: a career record for Reeves.

International stardom began to kick in. British Decca Records, RCA's licensee in Europe, began second guessing RCA Nashville's choice of sin-gles, pulling songs from Jim's albums that seemed better suited to the European market. In South Africa, RCA was represented by Teal Records, and Jim was so popular there that Teal bankrolled a tour that brought Jim, Chet Atkins, and Floyd Cramer in for three weeks in August 1962. Only Elvis sold more records in South Africa than Jim Reeves, but, unlike Elvis, Jim fanned the flames, recording four songs in the Dutch patois, Afrikaans. The troupe flew from Nashville to New York, New York to Rome, and Rome to Johannesburg. There was a Jim Reeves Moment in Rome when the airline levied a $600 surcharge for excess baggage. Jim threatened to go back to Nashville, and the plane sat and waited. The bags were offloaded and reloaded while Jim argued his case. Eventually, Floyd Cramer and Chet Atkins paid the surcharge.

"We didn't know if any of us had even been heard of," said Cramer. "It was so far away, but it was some reception. The airport, everywhere we played, it was like Elvis. It was a very interesting tour." Atkins confirms that there were literally thousands of people waiting to see them at the airport. It was, he says, the only time a crowd really scared him with its size. The troupe was ferried around South Africa in an ancient, unpressurized Viking airplane with a fuselage made of canvas and wood. Jim was just starting to learn how to fly, and took the controls from time to time, heightening the anxiety level among the passengers.

As the tour neared its end, Jim and his entourage tried to get from Johannesburg to Cape Town for a concert when the weather became turbulent. Cramer was petrified. "I got suspicious," he said, "when all air traffic out of Johannesburg was grounded, and then Trek Airlines, who had chartered the plane to RCA, got permission to take off. We shouldn't have left because the weather was so bad." Despite the fact that the airplane wasn't pressurized, the pilot took it up to 17,000 feet to avoid the turbulence and told everyone not to exert themselves. The wings iced up, and it was bitterly cold in the cabin, but the airplane landed safely. There were separate concerts for black South Africans, and a detour into what was then the British colony of Rhodesia (now Zimbabwe). "You don't realize how far you are from home till you land in a field in a strange country and there ain't even a building around," said Cramer. "Then some car comes out, and it's some inspector. We just sat there in the field." Alone among his contemporaries, Jim Reeves was willing to do this. Cramer never again left the United States. For Jim, it was an excuse to take his natural pugnaciousness up a notch.

In March 1963, Jim was back in South Africa to star in a movie. Almost no one in North America has seen *Kimberly Jim,* and that's probably not a bad thing. Musical arranger, Bill Walker, was assigned to the project, and Jim admired his work. He told Walker that he was planning to work with bigger orchestras and invited him to come to the United States to write the arrangements. Walker agreed, arriving the weekend that Jim died. But he stayed, becoming an in-demand arranger as other artists followed Jim's lead in opting for the bigger sound.

Early in 1964, Jim was off overseas again, this time to England and Ireland. There were several frustrations involved in working England; the most annoying was the stipulation by the local musicians union that one British musician must go to the United States for every American who came to England. Until Beatlemania, there weren't many English musicians that Americans would pay to see, so visiting American artists had to work with local bands. Jim was in the charts over there with "Welcome to My World," a song he had yet to release back home. It sold an incredible 450,000 copies in England. The writer, Ray Winkler, co-owned KZIP radio in Amarillo, Texas, and wrote songs as a sideline. Every time Jim came to Amarillo, Winkler would pitch another song. Jim would always refuse them, but he'd say, "Keep trying, Ray, you're getting better." Finally, Winkler came up with "Welcome to My World," and Jim bit. Winkler sweetened the pot by offering Jim half of the music publishing royalties. The song had another payday when Eddy Arnold cut it, and an even bigger payday when Dean Martin used it to introduce a segment of his top-rated television show.

Later that year, Jim was back in Europe. RCA's licensee, Decca, released an album track, "I Love You Because." Jim was infuriated until he saw the sales. It had sold over 300,000 copies by the time he arrived in England, and, at the height of Beatlemania, spent the remainder of the year on the charts, eventually selling over one million copies. It became the first record by an American artist to top one million since Elvis's "It's Now or Never." At times, Jim and Roy Orbison were the only American artists on the British charts.

Reeves's itinerary was grueling: Germany, Austria, Denmark, Sweden, and Norway on successive days, then back to Germany, on to Holland and Belgium, then across to England. When Jim accepted a silver record in Oslo, he complained bitterly of sleep deprivation. "Of course, I know a promotional tour like this is necessary," he said in Holland, "but I don't think it's fair to the audiences. We have been getting an average of three or four hours sleep a night." Then he lost the little grip bag that contained his toupee. "He was fit to be tied," said Chet Atkins, "'cause he couldn't go onstage without that toupee. We rushed around and got another one from somewhere." As usual, Jim wasn't shy in expressing his opinions. "He'd cuss these people out," said Atkins. "He'd say, 'You build a $300,000 building and you put a $50 PA system in it.'"

The last album that Jim released during his lifetime, *Moonlight and Roses*, hit the top of the country album charts in July 1964. That month, Jim cut his last session. His old drinking buddy, Hank Cochran, had gotten a divorce on the day of the session. Jim recorded one of his songs, "Make The World Go Away," and after the session ended at 1:00 A.M., they went out and drank until dawn. Some say that Jim Reeves had decided to take it easy now that he was forty years old and an international star, but that seems unlikely. He was too driven and too insecure. "Jim had premonitions that he would die early," said Maxine Brown. "He used to talk about that all the time." Chet Atkins remembers Jim talking about dying young on the European tour. He said he'd never live to be fifty because everyone in his family died young.

If Jim was interested in living past fifty, he wasn't improving his odds by flying small planes without much in the way of navigational skills. He got his pilot's license in March 1963, the month that Patsy Cline, Hawkshaw Hawkins, and Cowboy Copas were killed in a small plane piloted by Cline's manager, Randy Hughes. Talking to *Country Music People*, his guitarist, Leo Jackson, remembered Jim commenting on the Patsy Cline crash. "We'd be on the bus and Jim would be preaching. He'd say, 'Randy Hughes should not have been flying that plane. He made a mistake. You can't make a mistake in an airplane. Randy was a daylight pilot. He wasn't trained to read the instruments. He should not have been flying at night and it's a mistake on his part; that's the reason they're dead. I'll never make that mistake.'"

Jim told Chet Atkins that he found tranquility when flying. Chet reminded him that insurance questionaires asked if you flew on anything other than scheduled airlines, and, if the answer was Yes, you couldn't get life insurance. That, said Chet, should have told Jim something. On the morning of Thursday, July 30, 1964, Jim rented a single-engine, four-seater Beechcraft Debonair from Southeastern Beechcraft in Nashville and flew to Arkansas to look at some land he was thinking of buying in Bull Shoals. Fabor Robison's cousin and business partner, Russell Sims, had been to Arkansas and met a local developer named Bill Tucker—the "land man." Sims took his card and gave it to Jim. "I said, 'This guy's got some land. If you've got some pesos, go take a look. You might do real well.'" His idea was to develop it into a fishing and recreational area.

Reeves stayed over at a motel in Batesville on Friday night. The trip was one of several he'd taken in the Beechcraft Debonair. No one was particularly comfortable flying with him because of his lack of experience. Maxine Brown wanted to see her parents back in Arkansas, but turned down Jim's offer of a ride. Mary wouldn't go with him, and Tom Perryman refused Jim's offer to pick him up in Texarkana and fly to Batesville and then back to Nashville. On August 1, Tom and Jim had planned to celebrate the fact that they had paid off the $50,000 loan they had taken out to buy the Texas station, KGRI, where Jim had once worked. On July 31, RCA was breaking ground on a new building, and Chet Atkins had asked Jim to attend the dedication, but Jim told him that he would be away on business. "Groundbreaking is kinda like a funeral," said Chet, "everyone dressed up and sticking a pick in the ground. I remember thinking that we would all be at a funeral in a few days."

Jim's pianist, Dean Manuel, was from Batesville, and flew with Jim to see his family. The outbound trip was uneventful, and they left Batesville for Nashville at around 2:00 P.M. on July 31. Jim called the Federal Aviation Administration in Walnut Ridge, Arkansas, requesting weather information, then took off. Shortly before 5:00 P.M., he was cleared to land in Nashville, but the air traffic controller wanted to vector him around a thunderstorm. With typical cussedness, Jim thought he could go around the storm in another direction and save a few minutes. Instead, he hit another storm on his approach to Nashville airport. On a clear day, he would have had good sight of the airport when he ran into trouble, but in the heavy rain he became unsighted and lost control over a hilly area just south of the city. The plane circled low over a swimming pool owned by a Mr. Puryear Mims, and several people on the ground remember hearing the plane's engine sputter out. At 4:58 P.M., seconds before the crash, Jim radioed the Nashville tower, and the traffic controller asked him if he was clear of the rainstorm. Jim replied "Negat—" and his airplane disappeared from the Nashville radar, and nosedived into the ground.

One of those who heard the crash was Marty Robbins. He was taking a shower, and he'd read that it was good for the hair to rinse it in rain water, so he was in his yard rinsing off when he heard the plane crash. Despite the fact that the plane crashed in the suburbs, it took forty-four hours to find it. The dense foliage closed in behind the wreckage making it invisible from the air. Seven hundred people, twelve airplanes, and two helicopters started searching as soon as the storm broke. Opry stars joined the search parties. There was a heatwave that weekend, with temperatures topping 100 degrees.

"I thought, 'This is ridiculous,'" Mary Reeves told Dixie Deen. "They can't just have vanished. Then I began to think about where to have the ceremonies, and what kind to have." The wreckage was found in a wooded area four hundred yards east of Franklin Road, one of the major routes heading south out of Nashville. It was on property owned by a Mr. A. L. Jerdan, who was out of town. Bob Newton, a member of the Davidson County Civil Defense Rescue Team, found the wreckage by plotting a line on a map from the last sightings. Jim had been thrown thirty feet, completely dismembered, then eaten by buzzards. It was a grisly sight. Manuel's body was still in the plane and had been burned in the fire that followed.

Jim had always said that he wanted to be buried in Texas, so his remains were sent back to Shreveport in a National Guard airplane, then brought to Carthage, Texas in a hearse. He was buried in a bleak little two-acre plot three miles east of Carthage on the Shreveport highway. The Civil Aeronautics Board later concluded that he was flying by vision in conditions in which flying by instruments was essential, and the crash was laid to poor conditions and inexperienced piloting. Jim Reeves had paid the ultimate price for his obstinacy.

Very few artists sustain a posthumous career. There's usually a buying frenzy around the time of death, then sales slowly sink beneath the radar. Hank Williams's album sales remained buoyant, but his singles sales quickly slipped to nothing. Mary Reeves took over Jim's career and managed the thus far unreplicated feat of five posthumous Number 1 country hits, and a steady stream of increasingly smaller hits—the last one an amazing twenty years after the crash. In England, his records were on the charts for a total of 322 weeks, the sixteenth best ranking, in front of Diana Ross, Michael Jackson, the Beach Boys, and Madonna. Inevitably, though, the pendulum swung the other way. Mary operated their old house in Madison, Tennessee, as a museum, but fewer and fewer American visitors came, and then only foreigners, and then almost no one. Mary developed Alzheimer's disease, and died on November 11, 1999. Thirteen years earlier, Fabor Robison had died impecunious and crazy in Arkansas.

"If Jim had lived," said Chet Atkins unsentimentally, "he would either have been very big, or the most unhappy guy in this world. I often think that what made Jim so mean and so hard to get along with was that he wanted to be perfect, and he knew he wasn't. It bugged the hell out of him. He tried to be perfect in his music. He wanted the best songs, the best arrangements, and perfect records. When they weren't perfect, it tore him up."

Check It Out

There's a posthumous CD collection with one of the all-time great titles, *The Unreleased Hits of Jim Reeves* (Soundies Records). It makes no more sense when you look closer because it consists of demos that *might* have been hits had they been overdubbed. Earlier, someone discovered that Jim Reeves and Patsy Cline recorded several of the same songs, and faked up a ghoulish beyond-the-sunset duet album that ranks among the most tasteless endeavors in the history of the record business. Avoid both at all costs.

There are literally hundreds of other Jim Reeves CDs, but in general, you get what you pay for. The premium-priced collections, like *The Essential Jim Reeves* (RCA 66589-2), have been reengineered to capture the warmth and presence in Reeves's vocals; the budget collections have not. Anyone who wants it all should locate Bear Family's epic sixteen-CD collection, *Welcome to My World* (BCD 15656).

CHAPTER 5

Mitchell Torok

WHEN MEXICAN JOE GAVE UP THE RHUMBA

Some songwriters work purely from inspiration, and can no more write to order than they can find a word to rhyme with *orange*. Others are pure craftsmen: if you want a song any time about any subject, they can dash it off. Mitchell Torok falls proudly into the latter category. For fifteen years, he was in and out of the charts as a songwriter and performer. Jim Reeves's "Mexican Joe" was Torok's song and a Number 1 country hit. His own recording of "Caribbean" was not only a Number 1 country hit but a pop hit several years later. Another of his records, "When Mexico Gave Up the Rhumba," stiffed at home, but became a huge hit in England. Add to that his salute to bubbadom, Vernon Oxford's "Redneck," several songs for Glen Campbell's movie *Norwood*, and an album track or two for Dean Martin and you get some sense of Torok's prolificacy. (As a footnote, he also cut the original version of "Pledge Of Love," a charmingly innocent teenage ballad that became a Top 20 pop hit in 1957 for the otherwise forgotten Ken Copeland.)

Torok has chased his dreams back and forth across the United States, and once to Europe. He has lived in Texas, Missouri, Nashville, and Los Angeles. These days, Nashville is home, and artwork is his business. If you want a sign or painting, he will produce one to order, much as he wrote songs thirty years ago. He's still vigorous and prolific, and he can handle anything from a miniature to a mural. Like many of those who broke into the music business several decades ago, he's a little contemptuous of

today's stars and today's music, and probably jealous of the huge rewards that country music now delivers. More than anything, he'd dearly love to have back some of the opportunities that once were his.

The Toroks were Hungarian immigrants. Mitchell's father, Nick, emigrated to Gary, Indiana, to build boxcars, then sent for his wife, Irene. "All she had," said Mitchell, "was a few bags tied with rope. When I was four, I was playing under the table, and she went out to get the mail. When she came back she was crying, and I asked what was wrong, and she said in Hungarian that her mother had died. She and my father never went back.

She lived to be ninety-five; he lived to be eighty-six. They only spoke Hungarian around the house."

From Indiana, the Toroks went to Wisconsin. Nick wanted to be a postmaster, but Irene caught pneumonia, and her doctor told her that she needed to be somewhere warmer. The family moved to Florida. "We had seven acres in Orlando, and this monstrous hurricane came and blew everything away," said Mitchell. "They packed up again and moved away. They were broke, so they just left everything. I wonder to this day if that seven acres isn't sitting under Disney World. It's still ours, I guess." In its absolute implausibility, that's a very Torokian moment, not said light-heartedly, but with deadly seriousness.

From Orlando, the Toroks went to Houston, where Mitchell was born on October 28, 1929. He was named for the Dr. Mitchell who delivered him. He got a guitar when he was twelve, but seemed likelier to excel in sports than music. Unlike most country singers from that era, he didn't grow up with country music around the house. There were no family get-togethers with grandmaw and grandpaw breaking out the fiddle and banjo. That's probably why his music didn't quite fit.

Mitchell Torok's recording career started on FBC Records, a lilliputian label named for Fort Bend County, just southwest of Houston. The Schulze brothers owned a hardware store that sold records, and a radio station. Mitchell and two friends had a show on the Schulzes's station, KFRD, every Saturday. "Mr Schulze called and said, 'Hey, you sound pretty good. Do you want to cut a record?'" remembered Mitchell, "and I said, 'Yes sir.'" "Nacogdoches County Line" was a creditable debut, and when Mitchell went to Stephen F. Austin State College in Nacogdoches, Texas, in the fall of 1949 he found that it had sold well around there.

Mitchell won a football scholarship to Wharton County Junior College, sixty miles south of Houston. A promoter in Houston, Jimmy Franklin, signed him to a five-year contract, and landed a deal with Royalty Records. Royalty is a deeply ironic name for *any* record company—especially this one. Based in Paris, Texas, it was owned by Jimmy Mercer, who claimed (implausibly) to be Johnny Mercer's brother. Apparently, Mercer was busted for bringing "party" records across the border from Mexico soon after Mitchell's second Royalty single was issued. Mitchell might have thought he'd heard the last of the deal, but, the music business being what it is, Jimmy Franklin reappeared three years later. Mitchell had just started scoring hits, and Franklin showed up, brandishing his contract. "I went home to see my parents after 'Mexican Joe' hit," said Mitchell, "and he found me and served me with some papers. He sued me for $50,000, and settled out of court for five hundred." In 1954, just as "Caribbean" was coming on strong, Franklin leased two Royalty titles to Imperial Records.

The next player to enter Mitchell Torok's life was Fabor Robison. Mitchell had just written his two-chord novelty song "Mexican Joe." "I wrote it in January 1953," he said.

> It took me thirty minutes. I think I was basing it on "Polly Wolly Doodle." I was in Nacogdoches in my last semester of college. For two weeks I went up and down the highway to radio stations trying to give an engineer half of the song if they would cut me a demo tape. They never had time. Two weeks later, Fabor came by. He was in Nacogdoches, and he went into Mr. Johnson's music store. He asked if there were any local songwriters he should know about, and the Johnsons told him about me. Fabor called me, and said I should meet him at the local drugstore. I recognized him by his sharp perforated shoes and silk shirt. We went back to my house, and I played him "Mexican Joe." He said he had a singer by the name of Jim Reeves. He asked if I'd heard him. I said we'd heard Reeves's first Abbott record on the radio sometimes. He said, "Well, I'm recording him tonight, and I'd like to take your song." He took "Mexican Joe" and "Butterfly Love." We signed a little deal and he left. A few weeks later I got a wire, then a box of 78-rpm records. I didn't have a record player so I ran back down to Johnson's, and they were so proud because they'd help set it up. The record wasn't what I'd had in mind. I'd thought of doing it Hank Snow style, with shakers. I wanted a tight little Nashville record. I said, "I think they ruined the song." He signed me to a five-year deal. I was young. Didn't know any better. I just thought "Goll-eee."

Inevitably, Fabor came back to the well. Mitchell played him "Caribbean." A big smile crossed Fabor's face, but Mitchell wasn't about to surrender this one. He wanted to sing it himself on Abbott Records. "Jim's hot, and you're not," Fabor told him, but Mitchell stuck to his guns, and got an Abbott contract. "We cut at KWKH between one o'clock and five o'clock in the morning when the station was off the air," said Mitchell. "I loved those Latin records that Johnnie and Jack, and Hank Snow, made.

"Best Beer in Town"; Torok works the honky-tonks.

The drummer, Ron Lewis, who was related to Stan Lewis [owner of Jewel/Paula Records] played the hell out of that samba or rhumba or whatever it was."

Mitchell truly didn't know what it was. He was receiving Latin music third- or fourthhand. Some guys in New York heard the real stuff, and came to Nashville with RCA's A&R man, Steve Sholes, to flog the local pickers a lick or two. The local pickers played on the Hank Snow and Johnnie and Jack records that got on the radio, and that was Mitchell Torok's exposure to Latin music. So it really shouldn't be a surprise that "Caribbean" had a tenuous connection with the islands.

Mitchell didn't know what the hell he was singing about, but neither did his audience. On December 12, 1953, "Caribbean" dislodged Webb Pierce's "There Stands the Glass" from the top of the country charts. But then Mitchell and Fabor came with one dumb song too many. "Hootchy

Kootchy Henry from Hawaii" was as ghastly as it sounds, but not as bad as its follow-up, "Edgar the Eager Easter Bunny." "These days," said Torok, "I give it to people with children and tell them, 'This ended my recording career.'" And then, in one of his many moments of need, Fabor offered Mitchell's contract around Nashville, and found a taker at Decca Records. There were several Decca singles, but none amounted to much.

Decca's Paul Cohen had the responsibility of finding the next Elvis, and thought that Mitchell could be it. Mitchell had never really been country, and so had no problems deserting it. His second rock single, "When Mexico Gave Up the Rhumba," was written under the name Gale Jones to sidestep Fabor's publishing deal. "When I got through with that session," remembered Mitchell, "I said, 'I finally got the answer now.'" "When Mexico Gave Up the Rhumba" sank without a trace at home, but then Mitchell took a call from Paul Cohen. "Hey man, you got a smash overseas." A booker in England advanced a plane ticket and some money, and Mitchell was whisked off on a four-month tour. He was a star in a land he hadn't thought about, headlining a show that ran across a bomb-pocked country in the depth of winter. "When Mexico Gave Up the Rhumba" was about Mexicans forsaking their traditional music for "Blue Suede Shoes."

Cohen's avarice might have cost Mitchell a big hit with "Pledge of Love." "I moved to Dallas just before I went to England," said Mitchell,

> and my wife Gail hooked up with a music publisher in Gainesville, Texas, who was a columnist for the *Dallas Morning News*. He introduced her to Joe Leonard, who owned Lin Records in Gainesville. He signed up four songs, and we demoed them. One of them was "Pledge of Love." It was a rainy Sunday night. I remember we listened to the demo at the hotel. I said, "This is a hit." We called Paul Cohen at home in New York, and played it for him over the phone. He said, "Well, guy, it sounds good, but we need that Nashville sound." In December '56 I came back to Nashville and cut it. Then I went overseas. Joe Leonard had the demo, and I'm told that Paul Cohen called Joe Leonard for part of the publishing. Leonard said, "No way." In the meantime, this kid, Ken Copeland, who's now a big-time TV preacher, came to Joe Leonard. He was about to be drafted. He said, "Mr. Leonard, I want to put out a record. My daddy's got the money. Have you got anything you can put my voice

on, then I can get in Special Services in the Army." That damn Joe Leonard took my backing track for "Pledge of Love" and said, "Can you sing this?" He pressed some records, sent some around to a big 50,000-watt radio station in Fort Worth, and the phone rang off the wall. Imperial Records bought the master, and my record was in the can. Paul rushed mine out, but I'd lost the hit.

Copeland's record was huge, peaking at Number 12 on the Hot 100. Mitchell had indeed lost the hit.

The final Decca session was held in April 1959. The major label experience had been altogether less satisfying than it was cracked up to be. "The bottom line," says Mitchell, "is that you've got to have someone out there working for you. Fabor was out there on the road, talking about me, talking about Jim. He went into radio stations. No presidents of big record companies went into radio stations. The deejays would put Fabor on the air. The Decca records were all over the place. Someone should have said, 'Mitch, get some Latin stuff together.'"

In August 1959, Mitchell was touring Oklahoma promoting his last Decca single when the unexpected happened. Not just unexpected, but unprecedented. "Caribbean," a country hit from 1953 became a Top 30 pop hit in 1959. "I went to see a distributor," said Mitchell, "and he said, 'What do you think about "Caribbean" hitting again?' I said, 'What are you talking about?' No one had told me anything." Fabor Robison was always ready to offload his assets, often selling the same master to different people. No one better epitomized the "do it and duck" mentality of the old record business. After selling Jim Reeves, the Browns, and the DeCastro Sisters to RCA in 1955, he offloaded the rest of his masters to Jamie and Guyden Records, a Philadelphia company in which Dick Clark held a surreptitious stake. For some reason no one can remember, Jamie decided to re-release "Caribbean," and it was a hit. It broke just as Mitchell was free of Decca Records. Milt Gabler, head of pop A&R at Decca, offered to extend the contract for six months, but Mitchell passed. Jamie offered a little front money, and seemed the better bet.

The owner of Jamie and Guyden Records, Harold Lipsius, was a lawyer—not a music man. Just as "Caribbean" was breaking, Fabor Robison reappeared from somewhere, offering to produce Mitchell, and Lipsius agreed. Fabor still had some lingering credibility as a producer. "Guyden wanted to see if the magic would come back seven years later," said Torok, "and of course it didn't. The fun days were over. Everybody hated Fabor. Jim Reeves wanted to kill him. I didn't have a special place in my heart for him, but I tried to work with him because you never knew when someone like him would come up with a hit."

To his credit, Fabor tried desperately hard to stay abreast of what was happening. He had figured out the limp Philly teen pop sound, but Mitchell didn't care for the results. "The boys down in Shreveport," he said, "they had soul. Maybe the piano was a little out-of-tune or whatever, but the sound had soul. Those Guyden recordings were just a little too perfect."

In 1966, Mitchell moved from Dallas to the West Coast to work with Jimmy Bowen at Frank Sinatra Enterprises. Dean Martin had already cut one of Mitchell's songs, "Face in the Crowd," and while Mitchell was in California, he cut another, "Open up the Door," which became a middling hit in 1966. Mitchell had his last country hit, "Instant Love," on Sinatra's Reprise Records in 1967. The Toroks moved back to Houston after the Bowen deal ended, and then on to Nashville. Gail died there in August 1985, one week shy of their thirty-fifth year together.

Today, Mitchell does a little art, a little songwriting, and hopes that one of his old songs will get covered. He thought his moment had arrived in 1995 when Jeff Foxworthy's "redneck" act was all over radio and television. He wasted no time getting over to Foxworthy's office with a copy of Vernon Oxford's "Redneck," but Foxworthy's people didn't bite. Up and down Music Row, the record companies and music publishers are now staffed by kids who have no idea why Mitchell Torok is leaving messages. "It would make a weak man pack it in and leave," he says. Still, he can't quite let go. Success is addictive. Fifteen minutes penning the right song can pay an awful lot of bills. And you never know.

$\mathcal{N}ed\ \mathcal{M}iller$

FROM A JACK TO A KING

One night in California, some forty-five years ago, Henry Ned Miller sat down to play a game of solitaire. An idea for a song came to him as he turned the cards slowly onto the table. "From a jack to a king, from loneliness to a wedding ring." It's a testament to the song's strength that it's so familiar. Miller himself has done little to promote it; he's a painfully shy, self-effacing man, who went as far as to send his buddies out on tour as himself. Fame involves screaming "Look at me, look at me!" but Miller couldn't do it. Uneventful as it is, his story adds a little postscript to the Fabor Robison stories.

Interviewed in the late 1980s, Miller admitted that he still sometimes got ideas for songs, but never developed them. For three decades, his only involvement in the music industry has been driving to the mailbox to pick up the royalty checks. He moved to the desert, all the better to preserve his anonymity. He says he makes a living from his old songs, which include "Dark Moon" and "Invisible Tears," and, of course, "From a Jack to a King."

Ned Miller must be the only country singer from Utah. He was born in Raines on April 12, 1925, and his family moved to Salt Lake City when he was small. It was there that he first heard Western, not country, music. He worked as a pipe fitter and air conditioning installer, then moved to California in the mid-1950s. "I had to keep groceries on the table and my wife, Sue, worked at waitressing," he said. A friend in Salt Lake City knew

Courtesy Bear Family Archive.

that Ned wrote songs and suggested that he look up Fabor Robison in Malibu. Fabor had just launched the Fabor label; in fact, and true to form, he had already launched it, folded it, and relaunched it by the time Ned appeared. Ned cut one record that went nowhere, then cut "From a Jack to a King." The date was early 1957, and, according to Miller, it first appeared on Fabor. The guitar lick that dances in your head for days was played by the great Roy Lanham.

Around this time Ned wrote "Dark Moon." Robison planned to record it with Dorsey Burnette, but Bonnie Guitar, then a staff guitarist at

Robison's studio, wanted a shot at it, and clinched her chance by offering to forgo artist royalties. Fabor couldn't turn down a deal like that. Around March 1957, Bonnie Guitar's record started getting a little action, and Fabor hastily concluded a deal with Randy Wood at Dot Records, giving Wood first refusal on all his masters. The first side covered under the deal was "Dark Moon." Bonnie Guitar's record, featuring Ned Miller on acoustic guitar, had mystery and longing. It was a beautifully spare record. Randy Wood saw it as a country record and figured that someone would cover it for the pop market, so it might as well be him. Gale Storm's pop version was overornamented by comparison, but it was a giant hit. Fabor's credibility rocketed, and he leased Ned's "From a Jack to a King" to Dot. Once again, Dot killed their own release by rushing out a pop cover version, this one by Jim Lowe. Ned was given one last chance on Dot, and he recorded another hauntingly lovely song, "The Lights in the Street," which failed to show up. No one even bothered to cover it. Shortly after this, Fabor sold his remaining assets to Jamie and Guyden Records and disappeared.

In 1958, Ned cut one record for Jackpot Records, the country subsidiary of Gene Autry's Challenge Records. It coupled two of the strangest songs in his oeuvre, "Ring the Bells for Johnny" and "The Girl from the Second World." Asked about these very atypical songs, Miller said only that they were "a new thought." New, but not especially good. Two years later, Miller reemerged on Capitol Records in a deal probably midwifed by Fabor Robison. The Spade Cooley song "Cold Gray Bars" was delivered in a style that bore an uncoincidental likeness to Marty Robbins's Western songs. The lyrics had been written by Cooley just days before the session, and their graphic realism was no accident: Cooley was awaiting trial for the murder of his wife. Despite the fact that details of the trial were carried on a daily basis in most newspapers, the song failed to get much attention.

In 1962, just as Ned Miller was contemplating premature retirement from the music business, he was contacted by a jukebox operator in Seattle who said that if someone rerecorded "From a Jack to a King" he would order several thousand. "I always thought it had the potential to be a hit," said Ned, "so I got hold of Fabor and he decided to rerelease my version." The record was a hit *despite* Ned Miller, who played a few television shows in Los Angeles, and a few concerts in the Northwest, but suffered so badly from stagefright that he avoided public appearances whenever possible.

When he did appear, his shyness made him appear standoffish, which went dead against the country singer's credo. "From a Jack to a King" nevertheless entered the country and pop charts at the tail end of 1962 and became one of the biggest hits of the following year, reaching Number 2 in country and Number 6 in the pop charts.

The immediate follow-ups flopped, but in 1964 Ned and Sue Miller wrote "Invisible Tears," and it became a country hit, peaking at Number 13, and a pop hit for Ray Coniff. The follow-up was based on a saying Ned had picked up from his father, "Do What You Do Do Well." It had none of the quiet gloom that settled over most of Miller's work; in fact, its jolliness was more in keeping with Mitch Miller than Ned Miller. Nonetheless, it reached Number 7 in country and Number 52 on the pop charts.

Once again, Fabor decided to bail out. He sold Ned's contract to Capitol, and some minor hits followed, but Capitol's country A&R chief, Ken Nelson, liked artists who worked the road. He was fond of saying that he could look at his sales reports and tell who was touring and who wasn't. Ned Miller wasn't, so he was dropped. There was a brief fling with Gene Autry's new label, Republic Records, which resulted in one small hit, "The Lover's Song," in 1970. Then Ned Miller quit the recording end of the business and retreated to the desert. He wrote his last song during the mid-1970s. "I'll get an idea," he says, "but then I think, 'Who wants to go through the hassle of getting someone to record it?' I have nothing to do with recording. My kids have nothing to do with the business. If you love shows and like to perform, it's a great business, but if you don't, you shouldn't be in it."

Apparently, you can still live off a couple of big hits, provided you live quietly in the desert. "Dark Moon" will probably show up in an ad or a movie sooner or later, and Ricky Van Shelton cut "From a Jack to a King" some years back. But don't sell Ned Miller short. Many, including Elvis Presley, have tried their hand at "From a Jack to a King." They've brought more sweat to it, without coming close to eclipsing the original.

Check It Out

Predictably, the only Ned Miller CD is on Bear Family: *From a Jack to a King* (BCD 15496).

PART III

Town Hall Party

CHAPTER 7

Skeets McDonald

YOU OUGHTA SEE GRANDMA ROCK

Why should you care about Skeets McDonald? His songs are more or less forgotten, and his life was lived in the shadows. He's not a name on anyone's lips anymore. But Skeets McDonald, like Wynn Stewart, made some hard-bitten, unornamented country music that remains the perfect accompaniment to a beer. Yes, he was a bit player, but sometimes the career minor leaguers can tell us more when we can piece together the story.

Skeets has been dead for over thirty years. If you gathered all the published interviews, they wouldn't fill a page. He fell into the void between the Tex Nobodies and the stars who seemed to hog what coverage there was. There were a few short pieces in the country fanzines in the early 1950s, and then little or nothing until brief death notices fifteen years later. Capitol-EMI's British budget label, Music for Pleasure, reissued Skeets's sole Capitol album, *Goin' Steady with the Blues*, in the mid-1960s, under the mistaken notion that it was a blues album. Several years later, Nick Tosches made him one of his *Unsung Heroes of Rock 'n' Roll*, and one of his songs became a recurring motif in a bizarre British television series. Otherwise, nothing.

Stories on West Coast country music usually revolve around Buck Owens and Merle Haggard, but no one seems to care about those who laid the groundwork. Who was perfecting the beer-hall shuffle while Buck 'n' Merle were sitting on the edge of their beds with their Mel Bay chord books? Skeets McDonald, Wynn Stewart, and Tommy Collins, that's who. It was called the Bakersfield Sound: the music that Nashville forgot,

Courtesy Bear Family Archive.

warped and hardened in the isolation of the California honky-tonks. It was steel guitars and Fender Telecasters playing off each other, with drums to keep it danceable. It was music that had migrated from Oklahoma, Texas, and Arkansas, kept alive as a statement about roots in the vast melting pot of Southern California.

Skeets McDonald, like Wynn Stewart, migrated from the Ozarks to California, and, like Wynn, became a fixture at Capitol Records. Skeets is probably even less well-known than Wynn, despite the fact that he was on television in Los Angeles every week for years, played clubs across the country, and had at least one hit that almost everyone could hum at one time. He recorded some of the very best beer-joint country music, even cut a rock 'n' roll record that earned him a posthumous, if not particularly well-deserved, reputation among European rockabilly fans.

Family history has it that the McDonalds originally settled in South Carolina, and went from there to Alabama and on to Arkansas. Skeets was born Enos William McDonald on October 1, 1915 in Rector, Arkansas, near the Missouri boot heel. Out in the cotton fields one day, when he was three or four, he ran back to the house shouting, "I go home, skeets bite"; from that day on he was Skeets. His older brothers took the Hillbilly Highway north. Skeets followed them, leaving Greenway High School in 1932, heading first to St. Louis, then working his way north in hillbilly bands. By 1936, he was on WEXL in Royal Oak, about halfway between Pontiac and Detroit. He couldn't yet make a full-time living from music, so he played radio stations in the early morning, went to his day job, then worked the beer joints on weekends.

The Treeces were from Missouri, and one Sunday afternoon Mr. Treece took his daughter, Opal, to hear some music from back home. Skeets began flirting with Opal, and bought her a chicken dinner. Opal was going to high school and Skeets was working in the press room at the Fisher auto body plant (the same place Johnny Cash worked some fifteen years later). Skeets got off work around the time that Opal got out of school, so he'd walk her home. In the morning, he'd dedicate songs to her over the radio. Who could resist? Skeets and Opal were married soon after she graduated from high school in 1936. Their son, Robert Lee, was born two years later. Then, when Robert was eleven months old, Opal left. "I kept forgiving him and forgiving him," she said. "I couldn't endure him living that life. He was a very likeable guy, and he was idolized by a lot of women, and you can only take so much. It was just his weaknesses and his way of life." Skeets was ordered to pay five dollars a week in alimony, but the payments soon dried up, and he never publicly acknowledged that he had a son or first wife. In 1942, Opal married a real estate broker. Robert went on to graduate from the U.S. Naval Academy in 1962 and was in the army until 1968. Since then he has worked as an engineer. Skeets did the only thing he knew to do: make music.

Skeets's parents, Sam and Ethel, divorced in Arkansas and moved separately to Pontiac in the late years of the Depression to join their sons. Ethel had a steady job for years at the state hospital; Sam was a caretaker in an apartment building. They both retired separately back to Arkansas after the war. This may seem strange, but entire southern communities recongregated up north. Skeets had guys from Rector working in his bands. By the time war broke out, he was a local star in and around Detroit, playing music that was like word of home for the hundreds of thousands of exiled southerners.

On April 4, 1943, Skeets joined the Medical 69th General Hospital, operating in North Africa, India, and Okinawa. He came home on January 21, 1946 with a Bronze Star. On May 10, 1948, he married Josephine Harl. The Harls were southerners. The family worked a farm in southern Illinois, where the state borders Kentucky, and nine children made their way one-by-one to Detroit and Chicago. Jo, born in October 1918, was introduced to Skeets by a mutual friend when he was working at a club in Pontiac. Although nearly thirty, she had never worked, and never would. "My dad spoiled her," said Jo's sister Bernice, "and then Skeets spoiled her."

It wasn't until 1959 that a record label went coast-to-coast from Detroit. That label, of course, was Tamla-Motown. Before Tamla, there were several local independent labels, the wackiest of which was Fortune Records. Founded by an accountant, Jack Brown, the label was run by his wife, the wonderfully eccentric Devora. Fortune was initially seen as a pop label and a vehicle for Devora's music and poems. At some point in late 1946, Jack coughed up $3000 to get it going, and it's still more-or-less in business.

Skeets McDonald went to Fortune Records as part of Johnnie White's Rhythm Riders. The band appealed to two very different exiled populations: Eastern Europeans and displaced southerners. There was a huge Eastern European population in and around Detroit, so White probably had one show for Polish community centers and another for exiled southerners. Skeets's singing was hugely confident by this point. He lay back, letting the natural warmth of his voice roll over the songs. White's sides without him were cloying and limp. Skeets's first record was a local hit, although White's name was on the label. "The Tattooed Lady" was an old song, probably older than Skeets knew. It originated in seventeenth- or eighteenth-century England:

I paid a bob to see the Tattooed Scotch Lady
Tattooed from head to knee,
She was a sight to see
For over her jaw
Was a British Man o' War
While on her back
Was a Union Jack,
All up and down her spine
Was the King's horse guard in line
And all about her hips
Was a line of battleships. . . .

Then two hundred years and 3,000 miles later:
Once I married a tattooed lady
It was a cold and winter day.
And tattooed round her body
Was the map of the good ol' USA;
And every night before I went to sleep
I'd jerk down the quilt and take a peep;
Upon her butt was West Virginny
Through them hills I love to roam
But when the moon begins to shine down her Wabash,
That's when I remember my Indiana home.

The song was recorded in the United States (possibly for the first time) on September 27, 1933. The artist was Walter O'Keefe, the vaudevillian who popularized "The Man on the Flying Trapeze." Rudy Vallee recorded it on August 6 of the following year. It's anyone's guess where Skeets heard it.

Fortune followed "Tattooed Lady" with another risqué classic, "Birthday Cake," based on the old blues song "Take Your Hands off of It." By the time it appeared, Skeets had probably left Detroit. In February 1951, he and Jo and their Maltese cat Boo-Boo headed for Los Angeles. "Jo knew he had the talent," said Skeets's first wife, Opal. "When I was with him, he never had any ambition to play the Opry or move anywhere else. He was happy playing around Detroit. I give Jo the credit for getting him out to California." Jo's sister Bernice had moved to Lawndale, in greater Los Angeles, and Skeets and Jo stayed with her for several months as Skeets set about establishing himself in the West Coast country music scene.

The first stop was to see Cliffie Stone, a radio show host and de facto A&R man at Capitol Records. Cliffie managed Tennessee Ernie Ford and hosted the *Hometown Jamboree* on KXLA, Pasadena. Skeets auditioned for Cliffie, and Cliffie had him sing over the phone for Ken Nelson at Capitol Records. "I was doing *Hometown Jamboree* on radio," Stone remembered. "Skeets came to the radio show. He was immediately a hit on the show. He was as country as cornbread. He was the personification of the good ol' boy. He was a very soft man. Very easy to work with. I signed him to Central Songs. Ken Nelson and I coproduced Skeets. I attended every session because Skeets wrote songs for me, and I wanted to make sure that he did some of his songs on the session. Skeets wanted to sing ballads. I guess he was into Hank Williams, but I liked him singing the up-tempo songs. I'd get him to do up-tempo numbers on *Hometown Jamboree*." People seem to struggle for recollections of Skeets McDonald. Cliffie Stone isn't alone in not remembering very much.

The calm, ascetic Ken Nelson was the odd man out among country A&R men. Not only was he based in Los Angeles, but, unlike Decca's Paul Cohen and Columbia's Don Law, he didn't drink and party with his artists; in fact, he made it his policy not to socialize with them at all. In 1935, Nelson had been an announcer on WAAF, Chicago, reading livestock reports and cattle futures when he was told to line up some hillbilly programming, and that was his introduction to country music. Later, on WJJD, he programmed *The Suppertime Frolics,* a show that blanketed the Midwest and the South. Capitol A&R man Lee Gillette brought Nelson to Los Angeles, but Nelson, like Gillette before him, was dependent on guys like Cliffie Stone. In return, Stone managed Nelson's little secret endeavor, Central Songs. Nelson's involvement was covert (even those who managed Central Songs believed that Cliffie Stone owned it), but cutting Central's Songs was almost a prerequisite of remaining on Capitol. Skeets was signed to Capitol and Central.

Nat "King" Cole, Capitol's biggest star at the time, recorded one of the first songs that Skeets cut for the label, "I'm Hurtin'." Pop singers were rushing to cut country songs in the wake of the pop chart success of Patti Page's cover of "Tennessee Waltz," but "I'm Hurtin'" simply wasn't in that league. Skeets's trademark was lung power: high, keening sustained notes that could cut through the smoke, stale beer funk, and poor PA system of any bar anywhere. The steel guitar and the bass strings of the electric guitar worked in tandem: a classic honky-tonk combo.

And then on August 9, 1952, Skeets went into the studio to record a cover version of Slim Willet's "Don't Let the Stars Get in Your Eyes." Willet was a deejay at KRBC in Abilene, and hosted the station's Saturday night jamboree. According to a report in *Billboard*, Willet signed with 4–Star Records in late 1951 and recorded one single that didn't do well, prompting 4–Star to refuse "Don't Let the Stars Get in Your Eyes." The label did, however, offer to press the record for Willet so that he could sell it locally. Willet agreed, and records started appearing around Abilene in April 1952. He went so far as to hire a salesman to promote the disc, and the reorders were strong enough for 4–Star to reverse their decision and release it in June. It was a testament to the song's strength and unusualness that its potential could be sensed beneath Willet's tuneless vocal and 4–Star's terrible pressings. On June 28, 1952, *Billboard* reported that Skeets was working Texas nightclubs, so it was probably then that he picked up the song that would change his life.

Nelson acted swiftly, and had Skeets's version of "Don't Let the Stars Get in Your Eyes" in the stores by September 8, 1952—four weeks after the session. Ray Price recorded it on September 16, Red Foley on October 7, and Johnnie & Jack on October 17. Then, on November 4, Perry Como cut it. Willet's record reached Number 1 on the country chart on December 6, and Skeets's record began its three-week reign at the top on December 27. Perry Como's version went to Number 1 in the pop charts on January 10, 1953 and became the best-selling pop record of the year. Willet bought a new house with the proceeds. Skeets also bought a house, pooling his royalties with some money from the G.I. Bill. He and Josephine found a little place in the La Mirada suburb of Los Angeles.

When Skeets went back into the studio in November, it was unclear just what a huge hit "Don't Let the Stars Get in Your Eyes" would be, but he seemed to have some inkling because he'd written an almost litigiously close soundalike, "I've Got to Win Your Love Again." It didn't chart, and neither did any of the other twenty-plus singles he released on Capitol. The fact that his records didn't chart doesn't mean they didn't sell, though. Capitol was out on a limb in the country music business, being based on the West Coast. The charts had an eastern bias, and an artist like Skeets

McDonald could sell well without charting. Indeed, Skeets must have sold fairly well or Ken Nelson would have cut him loose. There's nothing as unsentimental as an A&R man with a sheaf of sales statistics.

One of Nelson's first ploys on Skeets's behalf was to pair him with a pop singer. The country-pop duet format had worked well for Nelson. Tennessee Ernie Ford dueted with Kay Starr and Jimmy Wakely with Margaret Whiting, and the sales had been astonishing. Nelson tried pairing Skeets with Helen O'Connell, and it might have worked if "Hi Diddle Dee" hadn't made "Hoop Dee Doo" look like "Stardust." Skeets's next best shot came with a cover version of another fast-breaking tune, Rudy Grayzell's "Looking at the Moon and Wishing on a Star" on Fabor Robison's Abbott Records. Perhaps it was a little too similar to "Don't Let the Stars Get in Your Eyes," or perhaps it was too fast for dancing. Fans of furious pickin' got a treat during Jimmy Bryant's solo. Most of us can't even think that fast.

Skeets's itinerary is an almost complete mystery, except for a few months in 1953 and 1954 when he hired a publicist to tell the world what he was up to. His comings and goings are hardly of earth-shattering importance, but they give a sense of the journeyman country singer's life, circa 1953. Country music, so regional in the 1930s and '40s, was now opening up. In April 1953, Skeets did a month in Detroit, followed by an appearance in May on the *National Barn Dance* in Chicago. He headed home via Texas and Arizona, playing dates along the way. Almost immediately, he flew up to Portland for several days of personal appearances and television. In June, he headed back to the Northwest for a series of dates in Idaho, Washington, and Oregon, then went to Salinas and El Cerrito, California. Following the "Looking at the Moon and Wishing on a Star" session in September, he was off to Texas, then on to Missouri and Arkansas, back to Chicago for another appearance on the *National Barn Dance,* and then back to Detroit. At that point, he could no longer afford a publicist.

Skeets's 1955 sessions were wonderful, unapologetic hillbilly music. The fiddle was front and center, often working in unison with Wynn Stewart's steel guitarist, Ralph Mooney. Skeets's vocals were strong and confident. He was in an excellent groove when rock 'n' roll erupted, but probably figured that he had no option but to roll with the flow. "Rock it, but don't ruin it," he called forlornly as young Eddie Cochran went into

Skeets on the bandstand. Courtesy Bear Family Archive.

the guitar break on "You Oughta See Grandma Rock." Skeets was forty-one years old, and really had no business fooling with rock 'n' roll, but he tried hard. If you didn't know his past, you could almost be fooled into thinking that he was born to rock. Certainly, European rockabilly collectors used to think so when they shelled out big bucks for this record.

"You Oughta See Grandma Rock" was one of the great Harlan Howard's earliest efforts. Harlan had grown up in the Detroit area listening to Skeets, and went on to write classics like "Pick Me up on Your Way Down," "Above and Beyond," "Streets of Baltimore," and many, many more. "I paid fifty cents to get into Town Hall Party," he remembered.

It was a big ol' dance hall, and there was a long bar on each side. Skeets came up beside me and I introduced myself. He liked me, I guess. We swapped phone numbers, and that was the beginning of my whole go-round. I was working at Pacific Press, driving a forklift truck in the bookbindery. I told Skeets about how I wanted to get into songwriting, and he introduced me to Wynn Stewart and Wynn cut my first song.

"You Oughta See Grandma Rock" was my attempt to write rock 'n' roll. Elvis was hot, but I wasn't zeroed in on it. I was just fooling with it. I was still in the factory, and when rockabilly came in, and I thought my career as a country songwriter was over before it started. Skeets was really the guy who got me started, though. He called Johnny Bond. He said, "You'd better listen to this guy." I had a tape at Johnny Bond's publishing company, but it was just laying there. You know how that goes. But Skeets made them listen to me, and they gave me my first publishing deal. Skeets introduced me to Wynn, and Wynn drove me to Bakersfield and introduced me to Buck Owens and Bobby Bare. It all began with Skeets.

"You Oughta See Grandma Rock" inhabited the same "rest home rock 'n' roll" subgenre as Jimmy Murphy's "Grandpaw's a Cat" and Carson Robison's "Rockin' and Rollin' with Grandmaw." In other words, it has a certain goofy charm. Radio gave rockin' rollin' Skeets McDonald the double thumbs-down, and "Grandma" seemed to disappear without a trace, but then it took on a life of its own in a far-off land. "I went to England in the sixties," said Harlan Howard. "Bob Powel [editor of *Country Music People* magazine] drove me around. He took me to a nightclub where some band was doing Buck Owens songs all night. Now I'd written several of Buck's big hits by then, but the band came up and said their favorite record was Skeets McDonald's 'You Oughta See Grandma Rock.' I thought of that song as a bomb, a feeble attempt to write Memphis rock 'n' roll, but the only thing these guys wanted to talk about was Skeets McDonald. I realized then how strange the world is."

Aside from those few months when he had a publicist, it's hard to know what Skeets was up to. Most weekends from 1951 to 1953 he worked on Cliffie Stone's *Hometown Jamboree*. Stone remembered Skeets as popular but sometimes erratic:

We were on from seven o'clock to eight o'clock at night on television. The Santa Fe Railroad tracks ran right alongside the El Monte Legion stadium where we did our show, and usually we could do our show without the trains bothering us. One night, Skeets was singing and along came a train. It shook the whole building. The cameras shook. Skeets stopped. He thought it was the California earthquake. Anyone who isn't from California thinks we have earthquakes every five minutes. He stopped and just stood there, looking into the camera. I was standing backstage. It really shook Skeets up, but he laughed and went on with the song.

He could be a little forgetful sometimes. I'd make out a schedule for the program. I'd say, "You go on after Merle Travis," and he'd forget where he was supposed to go on. He just wasn't there. I finally put a guy in charge of him, someone to say, "Here's your guitar. You're on in ten minutes."

Stone's major competition came from *Town Hall Party,* which had started in 1951 as a radio barn dance on KFI in Compton. According to researcher Cary Ginell, the show was actually owned by one of the performers, Les "Carrot Top" Anderson, but Anderson had no intention of revealing that fact to the other regulars and let it be thought that the manager, Bill Wagnon, owned it. The show went on television from 1953, and, from January 1955, part of the radio show was fed to the NBC network. Some of the episodes (twenty-six or thirty-nine, depending on who you listen to) were filmed by Screen Gems and went into syndication as *Ranch Party.* Ace steel guitarist Speedy West, who worked regularly on *Hometown Jamboree* and on Skeets's sessions, recalled that Skeets was among the first to defect to *Town Hall Party.* The show ran until 1960 or 1961, and Skeets was probably there till the end.

Ken Nelson gave Skeets a little session work, mostly playing bass or rhythm guitar. "He was a good country rhythm guitar player," said Speedy West. "Open chord rhythm was about the extent of what he could play, but he was steady." Work was getting scarce, and Skeets was probably happy to get the $41.25 session fee when it was offered. He had few solo spots on the syndicated *Ranch Party* shows, but mostly stood anonymously in the background while the Collins Kids took center stage.

Skeets and Josephine had no children, but acquired seven cats, and Skeets built tall fences to keep them in. Even Ken Nelson, who had little or no involvement in his artists' lives, remembers that Skeets was fanatical about cats. "He was a clean cut guy," said Jo's sister Bernice, "and he was a real home guy for a while. He had a tape recorder set up, and he'd work on his songs. He was a real nice guy when he wasn't drinking." Skeets had begun drinking heavily in Detroit, and had become a binge drinker by the time he arrived in California. Those who worked with him on *Hometown Jamboree* in the early 1950s say that he never showed up drunk, but his drinking became a problem as the decade wore on. "It got so that he'd drink and stay drunk for days on end," said his sister-in-law, Opal McDonald. "Then he'd sometimes stay sober for months."

Skeets probably felt he was being sidelined, and his feelings of isolation were exacerbated in other ways. "Capitol Records called me and Skeets and Tex Ritter to do some promo spots," said Speedy West. "We got in the studio and Skeets said, 'Speed, you go first.' He insisted that Tex go next, and Tex had something different from me to say, and this threw Skeets 'cause he had memorized what I'd said. He just couldn't do it. He said, 'Ken, I hate to do this to you, but I just don't have the education to do this.' Those promo spots were typed out for us to read, you know."

The flirtation with rock 'n' roll didn't work, and neither did a return to hardcore country. Determined to do whatever it took, Skeets tried crossover country. Ken Nelson's recordings with Sonny James and Ferlin Husky were setting the stage for the birth of the Nashville Sound a year or so later, but Skeets just didn't belong. Then, just as you would think Nelson was getting ready to scratch Skeets from the roster, he greenlighted his first LP. It was March 1958, a time when many in the country music business saw LPs as a waste of time and money. Over two nights, Skeets laid down a blues-themed album with a small group and no chorus. The low budget worked to his advantage, and the album was a tiny masterpiece. Nelson used reverb to establish a lonesome mood, and the small group seemed perfectly attuned to Skeets's ideas. New songs from Skeets and Harlan Howard sat alongside bluesy country standards. The only anomaly was "Hawaiian Sea Breeze," a cute novelty song that Skeets had written. Thirty-five years later it found its way into a bizarre British television series, *Pleasant Town*. Two ambulance attendants, charged with hauling crazed suburbanites to the asylum, play the song on every trip.

By the close of 1958, it had been six years since Skeets McDonald had been in the country charts, and so it couldn't have been a big surprise when Ken Nelson finally cut him loose. In view of Skeets's age and his track record, Nelson probably wouldn't have bet much on the chances of any more Skeets McDonald hits, but Skeets's career had a big second act.

Under the leadership of Don Law, Columbia Records was on the point of becoming the preeminent country label of the early 1960s. Starting with Carl Smith and Lefty Frizzell, Law had slowly assembled a dominant roster. It wasn't unusual in the early sixties for his productions to hog the Number 1 spot for weeks, sometimes months, on end. Smith was still on Columbia, as were Johnny Cash, Ray Price, Johnny Horton, Stonewall Jackson, Marty Robbins, Jimmy Dean, Lefty Frizzell, George Morgan, Jimmy Dickens, Claude King, Billy Walker, and Flatt and Scruggs.

It seems likely that Ray Price and songwriter Hank Cochran helped ease Skeets onto Columbia. Cochran had bailed out of a faux country brother act with Eddie Cochran, and was working in the California office of Price's Pamper Music. He had yet to dent the charts as a writer, but he interested Skeets in one of his songs, "Where You Go, I'll Follow." Price then leaned on Law to sign Skeets. Law would have been familiar with Skeets as he was a frequent visitor to the West Coast, and usually made a point of visiting one of his acts, the Collins Kids, on the set of *Town Hall Party*. Law even issued a *Town Hall Party* LP, although Skeets wasn't on it. He often recorded on the West Coast, but Skeets probably realized that the scene had shifted to Nashville. After more than two decades in country music, he had yet to record one song there.

According to Cochran, Ray Price effectively produced the first session, and sang harmony on the chorus. The 4/4 shuffle was Price's trademark, but Skeets took to the shuffle as if he'd been born to sing it. His voice sounded a little careworn, but was still in good shape, and rough edges sounded good on bar-room shuffles. There was a hit on that first Columbia session, but unfortunately not for Skeets. Harlan Howard's "Everglades" became a pop smash for the Kingston Trio on Skeets's old label, Capitol. Skeets had the original, but that doesn't count for much if no one hears it.

Skeets finally scored his second charted hit in the fall of 1960 when "This Ole Heart" got to Number 21. (Connoisseurs of the hillbilly shuffle need to seek out Skeets's early Columbia sessions. Their power and beauty simply cannot be sold short.) The harmony vocalist on the second Columbia session was Ray Price's sideman, Donnie Lytle, aka Donnie Young, aka Johnny Paycheck. Skeets had always been something of a chameleon, adapting to one style then another, but he really seemed to find himself in Nashville cutting shuffles. He was effortlessly assertive, with enough maturity in his voice to make these songs of heartbreak and betrayal come alive.

More than a year passed before Skeets was back in Nashville. It was September 1961, and six songs were on the slate. It's possible that Law was contemplating an album, although it's likelier that he was simply stockpiling some masters because Skeets didn't swing through Nashville very often. Harlan Howard, resident in Nashville since June 1960 and by then one of the hottest writers in town, contributed two songs; Skeets and his buddy Eddie Miller (composer of "Release Me") contributed three; and Law's girlfriend, Irene Stanton, wrote another. Once again, lovers of the hillbilly shuffle need look no further. Skeets and Paycheck harmonized wonderfully on the choruses, and the Nashville session crew had been hitting this groove so often that they were like a well-oiled machine with the fewest necessary moving parts.

Another year passed before Skeets was back in Nashville, and a change had come. The shuffle's day had passed. The vocal chorus, formerly muted or sidelined, was well to the fore. The assertiveness of the earlier sessions was diluted, but the results were more commercial. "Call Me Mr. Brown," written by Eddie Miller's wife, Barbara, was pulled as a single, and peaked at Number 9, thus becoming Skeets's second biggest hit. It was very similar to "Walk On By," a connection reinforced by the heavily echoplexed guitar, and its success only underscored the capriciousness of the business. Skeets had made many better records than this.

Don Law might have been close to dropping Skeets when "Call Me Mr. Brown" became a hit. Instead, the contract was renewed and Skeets returned to Nashville in September 1963 for another session. There were two more minor hits, and then Skeets McDonald parted company with the country charts. He was still fairly busy, although times were getting rougher. A short newspaper feature on him in the wake of "Call Me Mr. Brown" mentioned that he was still touring the South and Southwest regularly. His first wife, Opal, heard that he operated a club in Santa Ana for a while. Gigs were still to be had, even if the fees were slipping. Between December 3, 1964 and January 4, 1965, he toured the Far East with a group called the Westernaires. A scribbled note on the itinerary for Guam says that he was paid $535 for five days' work. He lost the house in La Mirada, and moved to an apartment in Inglewood. His son, Robert, saw him for the last time in Alaska in 1965. Robert was serving there, and his aunts had told him about Skeets's upcoming dates. Skeets was friendly but Robert felt as though his father was a distant relation.

It was November 1966 when Skeets returned to Nashville for what would be his last Columbia session. After running Columbia's Nashville office as a virtual fiefdom for sixteen years, Don Law was just a few months away from retirement. Columbia's head office had seen good profits from his productions, and let him do as he wanted. As a result, Law hung onto guys he liked even when they weren't selling. That was about to change. In his last months, he set about cleaning house, shedding the contracts that weren't putting up the numbers.

Skeets's last recording session was courtesy of Cliffie Stone, who was producing for the UNI subsidiary of Decca. Neil Diamond was on UNI, and so was Skeets McDonald—for one single. Skeets now knew that his days were numbered. He had an enlarged heart, emphysema, and suffered from diabetes. He tried to clean up his ways and curb his drinking but it was too late. He worked an exhausting tour of the Philippines between February 17 and 24, 1968, but talk of an upcoming trip to Germany was forestalled by his death. He came home from a Saturday night job in San Diego and died the following morning of a massive heart attack with Jo beside him. It was March 31, 1968. He'd told everyone that he wanted to be buried back in Arkansas, so his friends and relatives took him home to Rector on April 5.

When Bear Family Records decided to do an anthology of Skeets McDonald's entire recorded output, we began piecing together his story. As far as we knew, his wife, Jo, was still living, but, after spending months locating her, we discovered a sadly delusional woman who still believed Skeets was not only alive, but in the next room. A nurse who happened to be in Jo's trailer suggested that we contact Bernice, who lived in the trailer next door. Bernice was helpful, telling us all she could remember. She mentioned a trunk that had been unopened since Skeets's death. It sounded intriguing so we dispatched Larry Zwisohn to check it out. Larry found Bernice and her husband raising a cousin who was fully grown, but with the mental age of a child. He would play with toys, then throw tantrums that were quite threatening in a person his size. Skeets was the biggest thing that had ever happened in that little trailer, but, from talking to Jo and Bernice, it seemed as though occasional hits were worse than no hits for him.

Expectations were raised, only to be dashed again. The trunk contained his last stage uniform, a few show posters, records, and itineraries, but truly not much. Skeets McDonald remained elusive.

Check It Out

It's feast or famine: either the complete Bear Family five-CD boxed set— *Don't Let the Stars Get in Your Eyes,* consisting of everything Skeets recorded—or nothing.

CHAPTER 8

Wynn Stewart

NOT SUCH A PRETTY WORLD

Wynn Stewart was a short, peppy little man with a huge voice. It had few subtle shadings; just lung power and soul. Those who worked with him still shake their heads and say they can't figure out why it didn't quite happen for him. Had he lived, it's tempting to think that his role as an architect of West Coast country music would have been recognized and he could have renewed and sustained his career much as Buck Owens and Merle Haggard have done. It's just as likely, though, that he would have been denied airplay, and would be playing occasional stints in Branson, Missouri—close to where he is now buried.

Wynn Stewart certainly had his chances and was in and out of the country charts for thirty years, but the hits were fewer and smaller than they should have been. It's true that he was his own worst enemy, but the same can be said of Jimmie Rodgers, Hank Williams, George Jones, and many others. Wynn drank and no-showed to the point that he alienated many of those who would have been inclined to help him. Still, industry people liked him; fans liked him. They saw his talent, and saw that he was essentially a good—if flawed—man.

Winford Lindsey Stewart was, as he was fond of saying, a bigger name than he was. He topped out at 5' 5" in socks, 5' 7" in his platform shoes. He was born near Morrisville, Missouri, on June 7, 1934. His father, Cleo Winford Stewart and his mother, Golden, were from Missouri. Cleo had thirteen siblings, and, as far back as the 1930s there was a family tradition

Courtesy Bear Family Archive.

of heading back and forth to California as economic circumstances dictated. Cleo's father was killed in an automobile accident in Arizona in 1938 on one of those trips. Cleo was a farmer when Wynn was born, and Wynn had two siblings, Patty and Beverly. Cleo took the family out to Vallejo in the San Francisco Bay Area to work at the submarine base during the Second World War, came back to Missouri, and then moved to Los Angeles in 1948. His mother had remarried and was settled in the Florence area of greater Los Angeles, and Cleo settled there too, working as an upholsterer.

Even before the Stewarts left Missouri for good, Wynn had appeared on KWTO (an acronym for Keep Watching the Ozarks) in Springfield. "Music was part of Wynn from the very beginning," said his sister,

Beverly. "He used to sing with our aunts in church [a 1969 press release says his first public performance was at age five or six when he sang in church with Aunt Leota], but his first love was baseball. We had an uncle, Ken Gables, who was a lefthanded pitcher [he played parts of three seasons with Pittsburgh], and I seem to recall that he got into the record books for something. Uncle Ken told Wynn he had to be a little taller to stand on that mound. Then [Wynn] got something like athlete's foot in his glove hand, and had to have it exposed to the air." So Wynn started playing the clubs, exposing his hand to cigarette smoke and stale beer funk instead.

Wynn had picked up the guitar at age eight, and, according to family history, a salesman for Folger's Coffee saw him at a talent show and liked him so much that he bought him a top-of-the-line Gibson. Wynn had very few jobs outside music, and was playing the honky-tonks at a prodigiously young age. Cleo had to chaperone him, but didn't mind in the least. Under California law, Wynn couldn't leave the bandstand until he was twenty-one.

Carl Moore, a deejay in Huntington Park who went under the name Squeakin' Deacon, hosted regular talent shows, and Wynn entered as often as he could. At one of them, he met Ralph Mooney, who would become his, and later Waylon Jennings's, steel guitarist. Mooney developed his melodic rolling style while with Wynn. He was six years older, but they discovered that they'd been to the same junior high school, Thomas A. Edison, in the Florence school district. Later in life, Mooney would say that no matter how many sessions he made with other artists, he thought of himself for fifteen years as Wynn Stewart's steel guitarist. "Wynn and his dad would come in every Sunday to this talent contest that Squeakin' Deacon held at the Compton Ballroom," says Mooney. "He was called Winford then. He won that talent contest every time. People hated to see him come in. You'd win a wristwatch, and he would come in and show off this arm full of wristwatches."

Wynn's first records appeared on Intro, the short-lived country division of R&B giant Aladdin Records. There was just one session in February 1954, which resulted in two singles. The uncharacteristic note bends and melisma on the first songs came straight out of the Lefty Frizzell style manual, but the Intro records went nowhere. Wynn's big break came a couple of years later when he met Skeets McDonald on the set of a local Sunday afternoon television show. Skeets was recording for

Capitol and set up an audition for Wynn. Legend has it that Wynn sung over the phone to Capitol's A&R man, Ken Nelson (just as Skeets had done), and was offered a contract on the spot. Skeets also introduced Wynn to Harlan Howard. "I told Skeets about how I wanted to get into songwriting, and he introduced me to Wynn Stewart," remembered Harlan, "and Wynn cut my first song, 'You Took Her off My Hands.' I wrote it in Tucson. I wrote it and I lived it. Wynn recorded it for Capitol and offered me a Central Songs contract on it. Skeets had helped Wynn get on Capitol, and both their names were on it. I thought, 'Shit, I'm getting one-third of my own song,' but they'd done me so many favors. Wynn would get me into nightclubs for free, and he'd driven me to Bakersfield. Skeets had introduced me around. They'd done me a lot of favors, but I'd be lying if I said I was happy about it." The disappointment rankled again in 1962 when Ray Price recorded the song. Although relegated to the B-side, it did almost as well as the top side, peaking at Number 11.

"You Took Her off My Hands" was probably intended as Wynn's first Capitol single, but was held back as Nelson rushed Wynn back into the studio to record a hot new tune, "Waltz of the Angels." It cracked the charts, peaking at Number 14 during a one-week stay. Sales might have been better had Lefty Frizzell not covered it, or had anyone outside a twenty-mile radius of Baldwin Park heard of Wynn Stewart. The follow-up was Beverly Stewart's exquisite "Keeper of the Keys." Carl Perkins can be heard singing it and enthusing about it during the Million Dollar Quartet session in December 1956, and he had every reason to do both. It began, "You have gone, and yet I'm still a prisoner," an opening line as good as any in country music. Only the changing face of country airplay prevented "Keeper of the Keys" from becoming a major hit. Ironically, Perkins, who loved it so much, was one of those responsible for keeping it off of the charts. Eddie Cochran played guitar on Wynn's record.

At the time of the Capitol contract, Wynn was living in Lakewood with his mother and one of his sisters, but he often drove to Bakersfield to check out the Sunday afternoon jam sessions at the Blackboard Café. Among those present was a very young and as yet unrecorded Buck Owens. "I was at the Blackboard from '51 to '58," said Buck. "We'd have a jam session from three o'clock to seven o'clock on Sundays. The last of '54 or early '55, Wynn came in. He came back a time or two and we struck up a friendship." Around 1956, Wynn drove out to Bakersfield with Harlan Howard, introduced him to Owens, and thus unwittingly

launched one of the greatest singer/songwriter partnerships in contemporary country music.

Wynn was never especially fond of traveling. His first steady gig was
at Sherry's Red Barn in Paramont, California, bordering on Long Beach.
It was a hundred-seat honky-tonk, and he soon had the place packed. He
moved on to George's Roundup on the Pacific Coast Highway in North
Long Beach at some point in 1958. Ralph Mooney dropped back into the
lineup around this time. Wynn played six nights a week, with occasional
stints in Las Vegas and very occasional trips into northern California.
There are several stories connected with those trips across the desert to
Vegas. Ralph Mooney remembers that on one occasion they were drinking beer and needed to urinate. Parked out in the desert, they found an
abandoned building, urinated against it, then took out a spray paint can-
ister and daubed "Coming Soon—Wynn and Moon." "I think we had a
little too much fun," says Mooney, who reluctantly gave up drinking and
smoking after a 1988 heart attack.

Wynn's unwillingness to leave town probably accounted in part for
Capitol's termination notice. The other factor was his reluctance to record
rock 'n' roll. Most country singers saw no other option, but this hurt and
infuriated Wynn. In a section of a questionnaire filled out in later years for
Thurston Moore, he listed this as his darkest moment. As he explained
later to Jack Gunter, "Transplanted country folk in California took their
feel and their love for traditional country music, and there they preserved
it and nurtured it." Switching to rock 'n' roll was a betrayal of that heritage,
Wynn thought.

After being dropped by Capitol, Wynn had an approach from an
unlikely source. Joe Johnson had been a law student at Vanderbilt
University in Nashville, and had worked as an assistant to Columbia
Records' country A&R man, Don Law, between 1952 and 1956. In 1956,
he heard Wynn's "Waltz of the Angels" and it was apparently at his suggestion that one of Law's acts, Lefty Frizzell, covered it. Later in 1956,
Johnson went to California to work for Gene Autry's music publishing
company, Golden West Melodies. He acquired "Just Walkin' in the Rain"
for Golden West, and it became a huge hit for Johnnie Ray. Autry raked
in about $60,000, and Johnson persuaded him to sink it into a record com-
pany. Autry wanted to call it Champion Records in honor of his wonder
horse, but found that although Decca Records had retired the name, they
still owned it. Instead, they hit on Challenge. "Challenge meant we were

going to challenge Decca and all the others," said Johnson, "and it was an answer to the challenge of not being able to use 'Champion.'" Challenge was launched in March 1957, and, within a year, was in the charts with the Champs' "Tequila!" and the Kuf-Linx's "So Tough." Then, in October 1958, Autry sold his controlling 56 percent share to Johnson and his sales manager. Despite the fact that he had been recording since the 1920s, Autry never really understood the capriciousness of the record business. "Once I brought him a deal I thought was fantastic," said Johnson. "I said, 'Gene, this is a good deal.' He said, 'Son, we don't take the good deals, we take the sure things.' The record business wasn't enough of a sure thing for him."

After a year or so in pop music, Johnson decided that he would expand into country, and started a new company with different distributors. "I figured we'd have to be lucky to make it work, so we called the label Jackpot," said Johnson. After a few months of toughing it out with two sets of distributors, Johnson folded Jackpot into Challenge. Wynn Stewart was one of the first artists on Jackpot. The contract was dated June 9, 1958, and the first record, "Come On," was a three-chord rockabilly bash, and a pretty convincing one at that. Wynn had clearly decided he would rather switch than fight. Johnson says he nudged Wynn toward rock 'n' roll, telling him he had potential in both markets. There were two aborted sessions around this time, which included Vern Stovall's soon-to-be-classic "Long Black Limousine." It's the story of a small town girl who returns home in the long black limousine she always wanted: a hearse, of course. Pianist Jim Pierce, who later joined Wynn's band, not only played piano on Stovall's original, but on Wynn's version as well as on versions by Rose Maddox and Gordon Terry. Wynn's version wasn't released, and the song went into abeyance for almost a decade before Jody Miller scored a minor country hit with it, prompting Elvis Presley (who bought the music publishing company that owned it) to cut it in 1969.

By the time Wynn went back into the studio in December 1958, he had decided to stand or fall with unadorned country music. His second Jackpot single was Harlan Howard's "Above and Beyond," which created enough of a stir for Buck Owens, then not much better known than Wynn, to cover it. Owens got the hit. "I heard Wynn's record on a pop station in Seattle," Owens recalled. "This time I was on a big label [Capitol] and he was on a little label. I inquired about it, and the guy said it wasn't doing much, so I thought I'd do it. I had 'Under Your Spell Again' out at that time, and 'Above and Beyond' put me in mind of 'Under Your Spell Again,' but I made a totally different record out of it than Wynn." In 1989, Rodney Crowell made a Number 1 country hit out of it.

Wynn's first single of 1960 was "Wishful Thinking" "We wrote that in Lakewood in 1956," said Beverly Stewart. "It was our sister Patty who inspired it. She was out of town somewhere, and she wrote, 'I wish I was with you folks, but I guess that's just wishful thinking.'" Beverly sang the soprano harmony. It was everything you need to know about West Coast country music circa 1960: a slightly harder take on the Ray Price beer-hall shuffle. The sweetening, then very much a feature of Nashville recordings, was minimal. All told, "Wishful Thinking" spent twenty-two weeks on the charts, peaking at Number 5, but Johnson says that country sales were so poor at this point that the Number 5 spot only equated to 35,000 or 40,000 copies.

During this period, Wynn's buddy and sometime bass player, Hap Arnold, reckons that Wynn wrote "Lonely Street," which became a big hit for Andy Williams. "There was a street in Los Angeles called Lonely Street," said Arnold. "Wynn wrote the song, and sold it to Carl Belew for $50." Wynn, says Arnold, needed the money to pay off some debts. (Belew, ironically, had also been known to sell-off songs.) Some dismiss Arnold's claim, but when Wynn listed his own compositions for his first RCA press release, he too mentioned "Lonely Street." Jackie Burns, who later opened for Wynn, confirms that Wynn indeed wrote it, and had given it to Belew, saying it was a no-count pop song. Arnold also insists that Harlan Howard gave Wynn the first crack at "Heartaches by the Number," but Wynn turned it down only to see Ray Price make it into a Number 1 country smash. Wynn also performed Ralph Mooney's hit song, "Crazy Arms," for some time before Ray Price cut it. There was almost a career to be had from Wynn Stewart's reject pile.

Wynn didn't help his cause by disappearing right after "Wishful Thinking." "Distributors would say, 'When's the next record coming out?'" said Johnson, "and I didn't know where he was. He went off to upstate Washington or Oregon and just hibernated for six months. Then he just called one day. He was in Sacramento, and he'd be in Los Angeles the next day, and he wanted to record. I said, 'Wynn, come on . . .' I don't think he knew how much it meant to back up that record and be exposed out there to the people buying it when it's hot."

The follow-ups included some classic West Coast beer-hall shuffles, like "Playboy" that was coupled with another top-drawer Harlan Howard song, "Heartaches for a Dime."—amazing value for 89¢. "Playboy" wasn't a charted hit, but became an underground classic. Dwight Yoakam loved it. "It always appealed to me," he said. "I'd bring it up from time to time as an illustration of that Bakersfield sound. I love Wynn Stewart's vocal style and his recording of it." Some years later, when Yoakam cut an album of other people's songs, *Under the Covers,* he recorded it.

By the fall of 1961, Wynn had a new band. His pianist, Pete Ash, had been killed in a car wreck. He'd had an argument with his girlfriend and was driving home for the rings he'd bought her so that he could throw them at her, but crashed into a phone pole. Ash was replaced by Jim Pierce from the house band at the Foothill Club. At Pierce's suggestion, Wynn hired the great Roy Nichols, another member of the club's house band, who later played guitar with Merle Haggard. Bobby Austin played bass, and Helen "Peaches" Price was on drums. This lineup followed Wynn to Las Vegas.

Wynn opened his own club in Las Vegas, the Nashville Nevada, in partnership with the manager of George's Roundup, Don Spafford. It was located on East Boulder Highway, and opening day was set for November 14, 1961. Wynn owned 33 percent in exchange for being the regular attraction. Band members were supposed to get points as well, but no one ever collected. "Every night after we were through at George's Roundup, we'd go back in the office," remembered Ralph Mooney, "and we'd plan the club. The size of the stage, the curtains, everything." It was more a honky-tonk than a Vegas showroom. The prevailing motif was Western, and when the curtain was lowered around the bandstand it simulated a covered wagon. There was a button behind Peaches Price's riser triggering the curtains, although Mooney insists that the device never worked, and the curtains usually had to be raised and lowered by hand. In theory, the curtains scalloped back, revealing the band. There would be a jukebox playing, and Wynn would open each set by picking up whatever was playing on the jukebox in midsong.

At first, there were no slot machines, but Wynn and Spafford eventually brought in a syndicate that installed eight or ten slots and a blackjack table. The club never closed, and so as part of the opening celebrations, the door key was dropped into the desert from an airplane. Wynn played from 9:00 P.M. to 3:00 A.M. on weekdays, and until 6:30 A.M. on Saturday nights. They worked from Tuesday to Sunday. Wynn settled in quickly, buying a house and relocating his mother, his sister Beverly, and her

At the Nashville Nevada with Jackie Burns and Ralph Mooney. Courtesy Bear Family Archive.

daughter Kathy. Wynn's father, Cleo, had died of a heart attack, brought on by alcoholism, in August 1959. He was just forty-nine. "There was always a big crowd at the club," insists Ralph Mooney. "Everybody from the country bands would stop by after their set was over. Patsy Cline came by just before she died and told me she was going to record [my song] 'Crazy Arms.'" And she did.

In 1962, Bobby Austin gave notice that he was intending to pursue a solo career. He had just recorded a song he'd written, "Apartment #9," for Tally Records. It looked likely to become a hit, and might have done better if Tammy Wynette hadn't covered it for her first record. Later, Austin wrote Glen Campbell's megahit, "Try a Little Kindness," and, after quitting the music business, became a reclusive mural artist in the Northwest until his death in January 2002.

Just as Austin was giving his notice, Merle Haggard and his buddy, Dean Holloway, arrived in town, and made the Nashville Nevada one of their first stops. Haggard wasn't long out of San Quentin. "There was a half-moon bandstand right down the center of the room," he wrote later. "The sound just moved right through your danged body. It was the best sound system I'd ever heard. Of course, I hadn't heard too damn many." Wynn was nowhere in sight when Haggard arrived, but Roy Nichols recognized him from somewhere and hauled him onto the bandstand because he wanted to take a break. "He just went to wavin', almost throwing his guitar at me," Haggard told Bill DeYoung, "a double-neck Mos-Rite. He had a big ol' bird painted on the back. Where Ernest Tubb had 'Thanks,' he had a big ol' fuckin' bird. He said, 'Take this son of a bitch, and play it for a minute, and let me get to the bathroom.' It was like a guy being thrown into the New York Yankees, and they say, 'Hey, pitch one.' Ralph Mooney said, 'Can you sing?' I said, 'Yes, I believe I can sing something. Let's do "Cigarette and Coffee Blues."' Before I had it out of my mouth, he had kicked it off. We did three songs. The third was 'Devil Woman,' a Marty Robbins song you won't hear too many guys singing because it's got a high note in there that will embarrass you if you don't hit it. I was doing that song and in the middle of the dance floor I looked and there was Wynn Stewart, standing looking at me with his arms crossed and his head kind of cocked over to one side."

Far from being upset, Wynn liked what he'd heard, perhaps because Haggard's style was partly his. "The first thing he said to me," remembered Haggard, "was 'I've been all over America looking for someone to replace my bass player. I walk in my own joint, and the guy's standing onstage singing. Where in hell are you from, and what's your name?' I told him I'd been working over in Bakersfield, and he asked me what I was making over there. I said, 'Well, around $125 a week.' He said, 'I'll double that if you come play bass.' I said, 'Shit, I don't know how to play bass. I can't do that. Not with this band.' He said, 'Yeah you can. This band will teach you.'"

"Merle learned to play bass on stage," recalled Ralph Mooney. "But he sang so good Wynn had to have him in the show. He'd do Marty Robbins songs. Roy Nichols would play all the runs on 'El Paso,' and Merle would sing it." At first, Haggard roomed with Jim Pierce in a trailer near the club, then brought his wife out to Vegas.

One night Haggard heard Wynn do a number he'd never heard, "Sing

Hangin' with his country buddies. Left to right: Merle Haggard, Wynn, Biff Collie, unknown, Bob Kingsley. Courtesy Colin Escott.

a Sad Song." Wynn had written it at the small bar near the door of the Nashville Nevada. There was an octave jump on the bridge that very few singers could handle, but Haggard was confident he could do it. "It took me two or three days to get up the courage to talk to him about it," he wrote. "Finally, I walked over to the table where he was sitting, and pulled up a chair. 'Wynn,' I said, 'if it was in your power to make me a star, would you do it?' 'Sure I would,' he said. 'It is within your power. Give me that song you wrote, "Sing a Sad Song." Let me record it.' 'You got it,' Wynn said.'" Haggard told Bill DeYoung that he went to the phone, called his producer, Fuzzy Owen, and said, "Fozzo, we got the song."

"Sing a Sad Song" became Haggard's first hit, and as it began to break, he left Wynn's band. "Wynn told me that Merle was the worst bass player he'd ever heard," said Hap Arnold, "but Merle really wanted to be a lead guitar player. He'd work with Roy Nichols. He'd do great impersonations, too. Lefty and Marty. Merle learned so much from Wynn Stewart. He learned how to phrase from Wynn. Even little things, like

Wynn would carry his keys in his back pocket, and Merle still does the same thing." It wasn't just the lure of success that drove Haggard from Vegas, though; the gaming tables and the licentious climate had been his undoing. "I must have been trying to make up for those three years I was in prison," he wrote. "I played music until it was comin' out of my ears, and when I wasn't playin' music, I was gamblin' with the rent and grocery money. Whatever time I had left over from music and gamblin' was spent either fishin' or foolin' around." Merle and his wife, Leona, fought constantly. He lost his car, his money, and everything else he owned, and returned to Bakersfield.

It wasn't just Haggard. "Wynn was heavy into gambling," says Hap Arnold. "Hell, we all was. I was three paychecks in the hole." Wynn gambled heavily on pinball machines. He'd finish his shows then gamble until 11:00 A.M. before going to bed. "Wynn couldn't live there," says Ralph Mooney. "He was losing too much money. The rest of the band had families. Wynn didn't. We took a vote, and we stayed, and Wynn left. I stayed in Vegas until 1969." Soon after Wynn left, his partner, Don Spafford, lost everything at chemin de fer, literally gambling away the club. The band arrived one day to find that the Internal Revenue Service had padlocked the door—the door that was never to close. Spafford eventually went to Alaska and made a fortune as a truck operator serving the pipeline industry. When asked why he had quit Vegas, Wynn replied that it had turned into a weekend town. The truth was that it had turned into one long weekend for Wynn.

Contrary to what Mooney believed, Wynn married twice while he was in Vegas. He and his first wife, Claire Anne Douthit, had one child, Gregory. My mom met Wynn at his club," Gregory said later.

> She was the executive secretary to the VP of finance at Reynolds Electrical and Engineering. They were a prime contractor to the Atomic Energy Commission at the Nevada test site. My mom grew up in Pilot Rock, Oregon, so she was a country girl but she didn't care for country music. She preferred rock 'n' roll. When she first invited Wynn over to her house, she played Johnny Mathis.
>
> My mom is 5'7" and Wynn was 5'5" in his boots, so she would wear flat-soled shoes to go dancing at the club. She thought he was cute, and they got married on June 24, 1962. They bought a house in Las Vegas and he put in a recording studio in the garage.

Musicians like Roger Miller came over, sitting around the kitchen table, writing songs. But it didn't take long for Wynn's mother, Golden, and Beverly, and Beverly's little girl, Kathy, to move in with them. That didn't sit well with Claire, and she told Wynn that if she had known they were part of the package, she never would have married him. Friction between Golden and Claire led to the divorce. She thought he was a mama's boy. Pregnant with me, my mom moved to Klamath Falls, Oregon, to live with her divorced mother. That's where I was born on April 23, 1963.

On June 9, 1963, less than two months after Gregory was born, Wynn married Dolores Morris. "My best friend at the time was Simone Cerrone," said Dolores.

Simone was a high school girlfriend from Cheektowaga, New York, who worked in Las Vegas as a beautician. She did Wayne Newton's mom's hair as well as Ann-Margret's hair. Jerry Newton, Wayne's brother, had a lounge act at the Freemont Hotel in 1963. I dated him occasionally. The four of us all ran around together. Simone and I loved to dance and the Nashville Nevada had the largest dance floor in town, not to mention great music. We went there to dance a lot. As I was dancing, I noticed this cute little guy singing onstage and I caught him watching me . . . several times. During the break, he came over and invited himself to sit at our table and offered to buy us a drink. After several more meetings at the club he finally asked me out and gave me a ride home. I had an apartment in Vegas, and two little boys from a previous marriage.

While we were dating, Wynn was a deejay at a local radio station. He would often play songs just for me and dedicate them in a special code that only I would understand. We often double-dated with Bobby Bare and his wife, Jeannie. We decided to get married, but Wynn's schedule was so busy we ended up marrying at a chapel on the Vegas strip . . . between sets at the club. Wynn was a bit of a mama's boy, and since he had already experienced a quickie marriage he was afraid to tell his mom about me. He was living with his mom and Beverly and Kathy, so even though we were married I had to go back to my apartment alone. After a few months, he finally got up the nerve to tell his mom that he had married again, and he told her, "By the way, there's a baby coming soon."

Wren Dee Stewart was born on March 8, 1964. Delores realized that she and Wynn needed to get away from Goldie, which probably accounts for the second marriage lasting longer than the first. Wynn and Dolores left Vegas in late 1964 or early 1965 and rented a house in La Puente, close to Baldwin Park. Their second daughter, Tatia Wynett, was born there on August 14, 1967. Wynn had told his first wife, Claire, that if he couldn't have custody of Gregory, he wouldn't see him, and he petulantly listed Wren as his sole child on a 1965 questionnaire. "Mom didn't like to talk about him," says Gregory, "so the Phonolog [an alphabetical listing of records by artists carried by most record stores] was the only way I knew he existed."

Back in California, Wynn assembled another band. Bassist Dennis Hromek, guitarist Robert Wayne Edrington, and drummer Dave Allen worked at the Sandalwood Inn in Modesto, California, and booked artists into the club. Wynn played there a few times as a solo act, then offered to hire the trio, together with steel guitarist Jimmie Collins. Ken Nelson had caught Wynn at the Nashville Nevada, and re-signed him, probably with the proviso that he work the road. Wynn signaled his intent to leave town by naming his band the Tourists. Jim Pierce reckons that Wynn had worked just one date outside Vegas in the three or four years they were there, and that was a private function.

The early Capitol sessions picked up where the late Challenge sessions left off, with tough, uncompromising, West Coast country music. The first Capitol single, "Half of This, Half of That," cracked the charts, reaching Number 30 during a fifteen-week stint. Subsequent singles failed to make much of an impression, though. Buck Owens, in comparison, was hitting Number 1 with nearly every record, and Merle Haggard had just signed with Capitol. Artistically, Wynn was in their company; he simply lacked their grim determination. "Buck was a businessman," said Wynn's former supporting act, Jackie Burns. "Wynn partied. He'd roar all the time."

In 1967, Wynn finally found his song, Dale Noe's "It's Such a Pretty World Today." Noe had kicked around the scene as a singer, songwriter, and guitarist, and had been recording since 1951 (beginning with a lame "Tennessee Waltz" answer-disc, "I'm Sorry I Got in the Way"). He'd worked in California and Shreveport with Jim Reeves and Johnny Horton, and his first hit as a songwriter was Webb Pierce's "Missing You" in 1957 (a posthumous hit for Jim Reeves in 1972). The first Dale Noe song that Wynn recorded was "Angels Don't Lie" (another posthumous hit for Reeves). "It's Such a Pretty World Today" came to Noe one afternoon in Phoenix. "I was sitting at home," he said, "The clouds were so pretty. Big white fluffy clouds, and we rarely saw clouds out there. I was talking to my ex-father-in-law and some relatives from Oklahoma. They didn't like the look of the clouds because they thought it looked like rain, but rain was beautiful to us. The song just came to me, and I took off into the bedroom to write it down as fast as I could."

Dennis Hromek remembers that Wynn rehearsed "Pretty World" to death: "We did it six months straight. We did it in every little demo studio along the road. We did so many different arrangements before we arrived at the one we used. Then we cut it in Nashville with the road band and the Anita Kerr singers." It reached Number 1 in June 1967. "We were playing a little club in Denver," said Hromek. "Someone from Capitol called and told Wynn that 'Pretty World' would be Number 1 next week. We were making three hundred bucks for that job. After the show, Wynn took the three hundred bucks, turned out the lights, threw it up in the air, and let the guys scramble for it."

Wynn's steady gig for most of 1966, 1967, and 1968 was as Buck Owens's opening act. He usually worked ten days a month with Owens and the remainder on club dates. Owens was so hot at the time that the troupe often worked the usual "off nights," Monday and Tuesday. In some clubs and bars, you could see Buck Owens, Wynn Stewart, and Rose Maddox for a $1.20 cover. "He had that big record, 'Such a Pretty World Today,'" said Owens, "and he wanted to get out and do something. He joined my booking office and management firm, but not my publishing company. I had Wynn, Freddie Hart, Rose Maddox, Tommy Collins, Merle Haggard, and so on out on the road. Wynn was with me maybe three years. The strange thing was he was very often not in his hotel room when you went looking for him. He'd get spooked and rent himself another room. It was just some kind of phobia, I guess."

Wynn's asking price increased in the wake of "Pretty World." "The fan base really started to grow," said Dennis Hromek. "Up till then he was a singer's singer, but he really became much better known. Our nightly fee more than doubled from $300 to $600 or $1,000 a night. We were still playing the same places, but we got more money." The financial fallout from "Pretty World" enabled Wynn to buy a twenty-acre ranch in Mansfield, Texas. He figured that Texas was centrally positioned for touring, and he and Dolores decided that it was a good place to raise their kids.

The original Tourists broke up. Dennis Hromek joined Merle

Haggard, working with him on the road and in the studio for twenty-one years. Buddy Holly's former bassist, Larry Welborn, came in for a short stint. Ralph Mooney and Hap Arnold rejoined around 1969, and for a year or two it was like old times. Wynn had two hobbies: fishing and drinking, preferably in tandem; he drank straight gin. "He liked to go off by himself," said Hap Arnold.

> We were in New Jersey. He'd bought a $100 worth of fishing tackle and he had this big jug of gin. He walked out on a dock, and it had rusted, and it gave way on him. He just disappeared. Then he came up, and he swam to shore. He'd lost all his fishing equipment, but he'd grabbed his jug of gin. He just sat on the shore saying, "Shit! Shit! Shit!" Me and Mooney were drunked up. We stayed out on the lake till it got foggy and we couldn't find our way back to shore. We had a bunch of fish, but by the time we got back there was no time to cook them so we left them in this cabin we'd been loaned. The owners didn't come by for another two weeks, and oh God it stank so bad they told us never to come back.
>
> Another time, we were in Iowa. Wynn had to do an interview at a radio station. Me and Ralph and Wynn went to the radio station. We'd been roaring all night. We got to the studio. Fifty-thousand-watt station. The control room had these big old tubes and there was knobs in the control panel, and Wynn was listening to the station in the car. He'd say, "That station's weak for a 50,000-watt station." We got in there and Wynn was waiting to go on. He saw those knobs and turned those things wide open. 'Bout the time Wynn was due to go on the air, the whole station blew, and went off the air. Ralph said, "I don't know about you, Hap, but I'm outta here." I said, "I'm with you." We lit out through the back door. They made Wynn pay for those tubes.

Wynn's follow-up singles did all right, but no one remembers them now, and there's no reason to seek them out. "In Love" was probably the worst ("Life is a trip if you've got the fare"). It's a shame in a way that Wynn found success with a dippy number like "It's Such a Pretty World Today," because he immediately figured that he needed more songs in that vein. Meanwhile, Merle Haggard was playing the hardscrabble country that Wynn had more or less originated, and the tough stuff survived.

Things slowly fell apart. Pianist Jim Pierce quit in 1969. By then, Wynn was many house payments in arrears, and Pierce had arranged for Buck

Owens's manager, Jack McFadden, to book twenty straight dates to make enough money to save the house. "There were some long hops," said Pierce. "It was a real hard twenty days. Wynn got his money, but he found out I'd talked to Jack McFadden, and he was mad at me. It just got harder and harder to work for Wynn. He was drinking heavily. We'd need to leave to go to the gig, and he'd be holed up in his room. I'd say, 'It's time to go, Wynn,' and he'd say, 'You worry too much.' Often, he'd sit in the station wagon and drink maybe two pints of gin a night. When I first knew him, he'd say that he wasn't going to end up an alcoholic like his father, but he did. Del Reeves offered me a job, and I left." Hap Arnold and Ralph Mooney quit around 1970, and shortly thereafter Wynn was off Capitol. He was sneaking gin into his sessions, and the ascetic Ken Nelson did not approve. Dolores left in 1970, too. She found it hard to cope with Wynn's absences, and with musicians hanging around the place when he was home.

Bobby Bare persuaded Chet Atkins to sign Wynn to RCA Nashville, but after one year and three middling hits, Wynn was out the door. His movements are hard to trace from this point on. Several of the RCA songs were written by Bozo Darnell, a comedian, musician, and songwriter from Burkburnett, Texas. Bozo knew an Arizona-based songwriter, Jack Gunter, and they began writing songs. Gunter and Darnell then went to Texas to meet Wynn, persuading him to pack up and move to Phoenix. Wynn had now married again, this time to Doris Massey, the daughter of a songwriter he'd known during the Capitol years. Gunter produced Wynn for his own Copre Records, licensing the sides to Atlantic Records' Nashville label. After a couple of years and few hits (none of them by Wynn), Atlantic vice president Jerry Wexler pulled the plug on the country division, perhaps a little prematurely. Willie Nelson had recorded two albums for Atlantic Nashville, and was cut loose along with Wynn Stewart. Willie signed with Columbia, and his next album, *Red Headed Stranger*, became one of the biggest country albums of all time. Wynn went on to Playboy Records.

Playboy had entered the record business in 1972. In addition to its magazine, Playboy owned four resort hotels, seventeen nightclubs, a movie production company, and a book publishing house. The record business seemed the next logical step. Apparently, Playboy Records's boss, Tom Takioshi, was ordered to get into the country business after Playboy emperor Hugh Hefner developed a crush on Barbi Benton. Barbi had told Hugh that she could be a country star, and Takioshi had to deliver on it. Benton scored several hits on Playboy Records, and Wynn Stewart had the second biggest hit of his career on the label. It was another Dale Noe song, "After the Storm." "We had our ups and downs," says Noe. "I was mad at him when 'After the Storm' was recorded. I'd swear I wasn't going to have no more to do with him. Then he'd pick up one of my songs and record it."

Things seemed to be looking up again. There was an album on Playboy that, predictably enough, contained a remake of "Playboy." Jack Gunter started a club, Wynn Stewart's Country World, in Phoenix. "If it had been successful, he would have owned 50 percent," said Gunter, "but he was fighting with his wife. He brought her out to Phoenix, and they parted a couple of times, then got back together. Then we had a sold-out show for New Year's Eve 1976. He flew into Dallas to pick her up, and never came back. I never had anything to do with him after that. He could have been a millionaire if he'd stood still a while and listened. He'd be booked somewhere or have a session scheduled somewhere, but he'd rather play a joint on the Fort Worth Highway for twenty-five bucks and free drinks. One time, after we'd parted company, he called me at three o'clock one morning and wanted me to send him the liquor license we had in the club. He was in Nashville then, and I told him you couldn't transfer a liquor license from state to state. I said he should call me when he'd sobered up, but he never did."

Playboy folded its record division in 1978. By then Wynn had bowed to the inevitable and moved to Nashville. Beverly had married a songwriter and moved there in 1971. Wynn lived in an apartment off Nolensville Road for a while, and, after Doris left, he and his mother and Beverly moved to the Bluegrass apartment complex in Hendersonville. He seemed to have done very little for several years. He'd hang out backstage at the Opry, but didn't appear on the show. His life revolved to a great extent around gin and pills. He was in rough shape, bloated to the point that old friends sometimes failed to recognize him. Dale Noe saw him sporadically. "He was getting up and drinking gin or vodka for breakfast," says Noe. "He had gained so much weight, and was taking all those pills. I did everything I could to straighten him out and get him to give his heart to the Lord. He appreciated the effort, but he wouldn't do it."

Wynn's son Gregory visited him during the summer of 1984:

> I was traveling to New Orleans with my ex-wife, Christina, and
> asked Mom if she knew Wynn's address, which she did. We drove to
> Hendersonville, to the condo where he lived with Beverly and

Golden. I remember how little he looked when he answered the door because I'm 6'2" and he was 5'5". Golden and Beverly hugged me, and I think I shook his hand. He didn't know what to do with himself and neither did I. Christina and I sat on the couch, and he sat in his chair. There were stacks of demo cassettes and lyric sheets, and a foam beer-can cooler, which I could tell was always full of beer. His conversation opener was, 'Do ya have a dawg?' He went on to explain how he picked songs. He would read the lyrics first since it was faster than listening to the tape, and would weed out most songs quickly. He would look for lyrics that somehow said the usual things in a new way. He showed me a closet full of cassettes, stacked to the ceiling, rubber-banded together with lyrics. He said it was a never-ending job to review them all.

He was permanently a night person. Even if he wasn't playing, he would sleep in late and stay up at night watching television. He'd lost his driving license because of a DUI conviction, so I drove him to the store to get some beer. He was mildly embarrassed about that. Next door to his condo complex was a big field, and there was a circus tent. He said this was Twitty City. He'd walk over there sometimes because he couldn't drive. I walked over to see someone he thought would go somewhere. It was Reba McEntire. He stayed home. And that was the last time I saw him.

Wynn's daughter, Wren, also visited during the summer of 1984. She intended to stay for the entire summer, but, without a car, was unable to find a job. Wynn took her to Twitty City and to the Opry to meet Jan and Harlan Howard. Harlan offered to let her sing some demos, but money was very tight in the little condo, and, under pressure from Golden, Wren left after six weeks. Wynn was working very sporadically. His former bassist, Dennis Hromek, was still with Merle Haggard and occasionally booked Wynn into Haggard's resort on Lake Shasta, California. Other gigs were few and far between. It wasn't such a pretty world any more. Buck Owens's former sideman, Doyle Holly, owned a music store in Hendersonville, and Wynn's pink Fender solid-body guitar, in which he had once taken such pride, was on sale there.

By mid-1985, Wynn had a new manager, Charlie Ammerman, and was excited about assembling a new band. He called Hap Arnold and Jim Pierce. "I was driving a bus for Larry Gatlin," said Arnold. "Wynn called me around two o'clock one morning. He hated the sound he was getting from his new band. Didn't have the Wynn Stewart sound. He said he wanted me to come back and work for him. He had a bus. Some promoter had bought boots, uniforms, the whole deal. He wanted me to come back and play bass. I said I would if he would straighten himself out. He was trying to quit drinking and quit taking pills, but he had bloated up like a little ball. He was happy because he was going back to work. I said I'd take over the band and be road manager." Jim Pierce also responded to the call. "We rehearsed at Doyle Holly's music store, and I was amazed at how it all came back. All the old licks," he said.

Wynn had not been taking care of himself. A bout of rheumatic fever when he was a child had damaged his heart, and years of drink, pills, smoking, and poor diet had compounded the damage. Charlie Ammerman had arranged a warm-up tour of Texas, Oklahoma, and Louisiana, and asked Wren to join them on some of the Texas dates. The night before they were due to leave, Golden fussed around Wynn, asking if he wanted her to pack some things. He replied that he would pack himself, but he had some heartburn and needed to rest up for a few minutes. He sat down in an armchair, then slumped over dead. It was around 6:00 P.M. on July 17, 1985. Wynn Stewart was fifty-one. His buddies phoned each other through the night. Everyone was saddened; no one really surprised. The family buried Wynn back in Missouri in the little town of Willard. Beverly, Patty, and Golden remained in Hendersonville. Golden died on September 23, 1994.

Wynn surely wondered what had happened when he saw Buck 'n' Merle sell so many records with a sound so like his own. He sang with such absolute authority. He was, in every sense, a natural singer. The Nashville-centric history of country music has tended to confine him to the footnotes, but the music, or the best of it anyway, tells a different story.

Check It Out

There's a single Wynn Stewart CD, *The Very Best Of the Challenge Masters* (Varese-Sarabande 302066231); otherwise the only available collection is Bear Family's monumental complete career ten-CD retrospective, *Wishful Thinking* (BCD 15886).

CHAPTER 9

Wanda Jackson

DID SHE OR DIDN'T SHE?

Try to find some old *Ranch Party* videos. It was the syndicated version of *Town Hall Party*, the television barn dance that ran from around 1951 to 1960. There were interesting guys like Joe Maphis and Skeets McDonald mugging it up in the background, occasional guest spots by the fabulously out-of-tune Jenks "Tex" Carman, and regular appearances from the Collins Kids. At some point in 1957, Wanda Jackson was booked to sing "Cool Love." As she went into the bridge, she began to move, and the fringe of her dress began to sway in counterpoint. It wasn't a cheap burlesque move—in fact, it was almost beguilingly innocent—but there was nothing sexier in 1950s music.

Wanda Jackson discovered early that she was meant to sing, and stayed true to her calling. Unlike many of her contemporaries, she's comfortably off, but when she can't get out and sing she has a hard time coping with the ordinariness of things. Back in the 1950s when most women her age were settling into the "Honey I'm home" world of childrearing, cooking, and housework, Wanda was driving all night to Los Angeles or Nashville or some little puke 'n' holler honky-tonk. Housework holds no allure now.

The sweat and determination that Wanda put into her career becomes clear in sometimes poignant ways. She breaks out her old Martin D-18 guitar, the one with "Wanda Jackson" stenciled on it. The back has been repaired because her belt buckle and costume jewelry nearly wore through it, and the pick guard has been extended to accommodate the beating. **145**

Courtesy Bear Family Archive.

Like a slave quilt, Wanda's old D-18 is almost a piece of folk art that reveals much about the person who once used it.

Wanda never really left Oklahoma. It would probably have been a smart move to go to Nashville or Los Angeles, or even Las Vegas, but instead she settled into suburban Oklahoma City. The neighbors have no idea that the middle-aged lady with bad knees was once a rockabilly queen. Wanda and her husband, Wendell Goodman, tend to their investments and play locally at gospel revivals, but several times a year she packs up and heads overseas to play rock 'n' roll: Germany, Scandinavia, Holland, England. They love her there.

Tom Jackson was a country fiddler, originally from Fort Worth, Texas, whose family moved to Maud, Oklahoma when he was a kid. Nellie Whitaker was from Roff, Oklahoma; her father worked in the oil patch. They met at a dance; Tom was in the band. Too poor to afford a church service, they were married in a civil ceremony in April 1936 and set up house in Maud. He worked for a bakery and pumped gas at night. Their only child, Wanda Lavonne, was born on October 20, 1937. There were two waves of migration from Oklahoma to California. The first and best known was in the mid-1930s, the Dust Bowl era, but many of those who found a way to hang on subsequently migrated during the early 1940s to work in the munitions plants and shipyards. Tom went west in 1942, leaving Nellie and Wanda with Nellie's parents. As soon as he found a job, he sent for them. It was in Los Angeles that Wanda spent the greater part of her childhood. Most of her early memories of Oklahoma came from summer trips. The Okies and Texans who moved west took their music with them. Wanda didn't grow up wanting to be on the Opry; she wanted to be a girl vocalist with a Western Swing band. After the Second World War, Tom Jackson became a barber in Bakersfield, but Nellie became homesick, and in June 1949 they moved back to Oklahoma City. Tom gave up barbering and drove a cab.

In 1951, Wanda made her first radio appearance on KLPR, broadcasting with 250 tiny watts from the Capitol Hill district of Oklahoma City. She sang Jimmie Rodgers's "Blue Yodel No. 6." Two years later, KLPR gave her a fifteen-minute show, and, from that point, Wanda sacrificed all for music. She didn't become a cheerleader because it might make her hoarse, and she diligently typed out the lyrics to the hot songs of the day, placing them in a ring binder, patiently penciling in the chord changes. At fifteen, she was singing "Back Street Affair" and "Warm Red Wine," but saw no incongruity there. "I had a real innocent mind," she says, "and if they was popular I'd sing 'em." While others were doing homework assignments, Wanda was writing out pitches for her sponsors so that she could rehearse them. Tom Jackson had given up music, but he bought Wanda a Martin D-18 guitar and taught her every chord he knew.

Hank Thompson ruled Oklahoma City. Between 1952 and '54, he was on WKY-TV and played regularly at the Trianon Ballroom. The

Trianon was above a restaurant, but was hampered by Prohibition, which lingered in Oklahoma until 1959 (when it was repealed, Missouri was the only remaining "dry" state). Liquor was sold in Oklahoma, but only by the bootleggers hovering outside, which meant that the ballroom had to exist on food, soda, weak beer (less than 3.2 percent alcohol), and admission. The other side of the coin was that anyone of any age could be admitted or could play in bars because liquor wasn't actually sold on site.

Hank Thompson was driving around listening to KLPR, and figured Wanda to be older than she was. When he asked her to play with him at the Trianon, he was surprised when she said she'd have to ask her mom. "How old are you, gal?" he asked. "Fifteen." "Ain't that somethin'." She sang occasionally with Thompson's band, then switched to Merl Lindsay's Funspot to front Lindsay's Oklahoma Nightriders. They had a Saturday afternoon radio show and a dance at night. School couldn't compete with this.

Even before she was out of school, Wanda was on Decca Records. The deal was announced over the Capitol Hill High School intercom, and everyone applauded. Hank Thompson middlemanned the deal, cutting a demo session at his home studio and sending it first to his A&R man, Ken Nelson, at Capitol Records. Nelson felt that Wanda's voice was immature, so he passed. Meanwhile, Thompson was trying to land a contract for one of his front men, Billy Gray, and wanted a good home for a song he owned, "You Can't Have My Love." He found a taker for all three in Decca's Paul Cohen. Wanda cut her first session at Decca's Los Angeles studio with the nucleus of Thompson's band behind her. Thompson was on the West Coast cutting one of his biggest hits, "Honky Tonk Girl." Tom Jackson made the trip to Decca into the family vacation that year. "I didn't want to do a duet," says Wanda, "and 'You Can't Have My Love' was a kinda dumb song, I thought it made fun of Okies. We'd been made fun of since the Depression days and I thought, 'Here, I'm gonna contribute to this.'" But more than that she wanted to get on record. "You Can't Have My Love" really was a pretty dumb song, but it peaked at Number 8.

The Grand Ole Opry offered Wanda a guest shot, but the experience left a bitter taste. Ernest Tubb politely informed her before the show that she couldn't go out wearing the shoulderless dress that Nellie had tailored especially for the occasion, so she had to borrow a white leather tassled jacket. Then Minnie Pearl and Rod Brasfield cut up behind her, drawing laughter from the crowd while she was performing. "That one time was

Wanda with her mentor, Hank Thompson. Courtesy Bear Family Archive.

enough for me," said Wanda. The passage of more than forty-five years has done little to erase the memory.

Wanda graduated from high school in May 1955, and hit the road. Tom gave up his job driving cab to become her de facto manager. "Mother," says Wanda, "stayed at home so we'd have a paycheck coming in 'cause I was working for practically nothing. In fact, I worked the first tour for just expenses." Tom Jackson had set aside his own musical ambitions, but now revived them vicariously through Wanda. "We didn't know where to start," said Wanda, "so daddy got *Billboard* and there was some write-up or advertisement or something for Bob Neal, and daddy called him. Bob Neal said that he could use a girl singer so we started working a tour he'd organized." The first stop was Cape Girardeau, Missouri, on July 20, 1955. Wanda was on a bill headlined by Elvis Presley, Bud Deckelman, and Charlie Feathers. Wanda met Elvis at a radio station before the show, and thought he looked like no hillbilly she'd ever seen. She had neither heard him nor heard of him to that point, and had no idea why he was topping the bill. Then, sitting backstage, she heard a roar from the crowd: maybe there was a fire in the auditorium. She peeked through the curtain, only to see Elvis doing his Elvis thing. The day after the show, Elvis and her father exchanged hats, snapped silly photos, and headed in opposite directions.

In October 1955, Elvis and Wanda worked together again on a short tour of West Texas. Tom Jackson wouldn't let Wanda ride between towns in Elvis's Cadillac, but they'd go to a movie before the show, ride around, and flirt. Wanda won't say if it got any heavier than that. After the tour ended, Elvis called Wanda most days around 4:30 in the afternoon. He told her that there was a new day dawning, but she didn't believe him.

Wanda had signed with Decca for two years, and when the deal was up Hank Thompson told her that Ken Nelson was ready for her. "My one aim," she says, "was to be on the same record label as Hank Thompson, and I signed an initial five-year contract with Capitol Records and Central Songs." The first Capitol single, "I Gotta Know," looked in two directions at once, shuttling between rockabilly and country. It became Wanda's only hit on Capitol for four years. Joe Maphis took the scorching solos. To Wanda's amazement, he turned up for the session in his carpet slippers. Buck Owens, still three years away from his first hit, picked up forty-one bucks for playing rhythm guitar. His guitar case, Wanda remembered, was held together with masking tape.

Wanda and Elvis, March 1956. Courtesy Colin Escott.

Wanda played a few more dates with Elvis, one of them in Memphis. He took her back to his new house on Audubon Drive, spun blues records and his own records for her, and told her once again about that new day dawning. When Wanda returned to the studio in September 1956, she believed she had no option but to sing rock 'n' roll. "My daddy loved rock 'n' roll because it was bluesy music," she said. "He loved Elvis's music. I just didn't think I could sing it." But she did, starting with a silly little three-chord rockabilly song, "Honey Bop," cowritten by Mae Axton. Raised in Roff, Oklahoma, alongside Wanda's mother, Mae had moved to Florida where she'd cowritten "Heartbreak Hotel." "Honey Bop" boiled down to nothing, but incredibly it took three people to write it. For the record, the others were Tommy Durden (who'd come up with the idea for "Heartbreak Hotel") and Glenn Reeves (who'd sung the original demo of "Heartbreak Hotel").

Country was now banished to the flip sides. One of those early flip sides was the original version of "Silver Threads and Golden Needles," which would surely have been a country smash a year earlier. Wanda sings with all the plaintiveness and hurt she could muster. It might just be her finest moment on record. Written by Jack Rhodes, cowriter of "Satisfied Mind," "Silver Threads" languished a while after Wanda's recording, but then Skeeter Davis cut it in 1963. The Springfields revived it, and then Linda Ronstadt made it into a minor standard. Wanda, though, sung a verse that no one else ever sang, a verse that really holds the key to the song:

I grew up in faded gingham where love is a sacred thing
You grew up in silk and satin where love is a passing game
I know now you never loved me, and I know I was a fool
To think your pride would let you live by the Golden Rule

By early 1957, Wanda was on one of Bob Neal's Stars Incorporated packages, trekking up through Ontario and across the prairies en route to Montana. The other performers on this tour were Carl Perkins, Jerry Lee Lewis, Johnny Cash, and Onie Wheeler. Mile after mile Tom Jackson drove his Pontiac Star Chief through snow, black ice, and sleet, all for those few minutes when Wanda could wriggle into one of the slinky dresses that Nellie had sewed for her, and sing and sway. An ex-musician himself, Tom Jackson understood the craziness, otherwise he would have surely told Wanda to find a nice guy back home.

The tour ended in May 1957, and that September Wanda went back to Capitol, still in search of the really big hit. A few years earlier, she'd found a song by R&B singer Annisteen Allen, "Fujiyama Mama," and she convinced Ken Nelson that it might work for her. Seven larynx-searing takes later, "Fujiyama Mama" was in the can. It barely showed up at home, but American Forces radio in Japan played it to death, and then the Japanese picked up on it, which could only be because they didn't understand it ("I been to Nagasaki, Hiroshima too / What I did to them baby, I can do to you"). "Fujiyama Mama" became a giant hit over there in late 1958, and a tour was hastily arranged for the following January. When the plane touched down in Tokyo, Wanda felt like a star for the first time. The red carpet was rolled out, and hundreds of fans bowed down before her. When everyone got up, Wanda, whose gospel hair and high heels elevated her to about 5' 7", found that most of the men were shorter than she was—unlike in Oklahoma.

Japan might as easily have been the moon. Wanda didn't understand anything they said and didn't understand why audiences bowed and threw streamers. Then there was that godawful uncooked food, and sleeping on mats. But they seemed to like it when she shook and swayed. Wanda finally flew home on March 16, slept in her own bed for a few days, then set out for Minneapolis. Appropriately, Chuck Berry was on the charts with "Back in the U.S.A" ("I'm so glad I'm livin' in the U.S.A. / Hamburgers sizzlin' on an open grill night and day"). Indeed.

Wanda decided to hire a band. Her agent, Jim Halsey, put her in touch with Bobby Poe and the Poe Kats, a racially mixed band featuring Big Al Downing on piano. A mixed band wasn't anything new (the Del-Vikings were mixed and successful, and Benny Goodman had hired black musicians back in the 1930s), but it *was* something new in the redneck pisspots that Poe played. Very often after the show, they'd have to smuggle Downing into the motel in a bass fiddle bag. "Bobby and I would do solo spots," Downing told Bill Millar, "warming up the audience before Wanda came on. Frankly, there wasn't as much prejudice as you'd expect even though I'd stand beside her and sing with her. She liked my playing and would introduce me to the audience, which helped."

In April 1958, Wanda and the Poe Kats went to Los Angeles to cut an album. Ken Nelson was a big believer in albums at a time when everyone else in the country music business saw them as a profitless inconvenience. It's hard to know if Nelson was a visionary, or simply saw albums as an opportunity to place ten or twelve songs from the publishing company he surreptitiously owned, Central Songs. Even session musicians like Speedy West, Ralph Mooney, and James Burton got a shot on LP. Nelson usually liked to cut an album in three sessions. That way, the musicians' tab was less than $750.

Wanda says that "Party" was the last song recorded for her first album. It had been written by Jessie Mae Robinson, who had written hits for R&B legends like Charles Brown and Amos Milburn long before she'd written for Elvis. Strangely, it wasn't Elvis's version of "Party" that Wanda remembered; it was the Collins Kids' cover version. Wanda and the band roared through it, but it remained no more than an album cut for another couple of years.

"It was a bad point in my life," said Wanda. She had endured five years of touring without much to show for it. "All my friends were married and having children and I didn't even have a steady boyfriend. I was always a

At the deejay convention, checking the charts with Gene Vincent. Courtesy Bear Family Archive.

bridesmaid, never a bride." Then the Poe Kats quit on her. And then Las Vegas beckoned. While Frank Sinatra, Sammy Davis Jr., and the really big names worked the main rooms, there was plenty of work in the lounges. Wanda bought into the Vegas lifestyle. She went to bed around 7:00 A.M., and, without the need for a driver, Tom Jackson went back to Oklahoma City leaving Wanda alone for the first time. Booze was cheap and plentiful, and a cast of men came and went. Wanda began to live the vale-of-tears existence that she sang about. "The hours were terrible," she said. "Five thirty-minute shows back-to-back with a fifteen-minute break. Only one guy in my band sang a little, so I knew I needed some help entertaining, and there's a difference between singing and entertaining. We were trying to think of someone and I remembered this guy I'd seen in Maryland. I knew I could draw the crowds, but I needed someone to help me keep 'em, and I thought he could."

Wanda had gone to Strick's Club in one of the D.C. suburbs and seen Roy Clark. She sent her father to Maryland to find Clark and bring him to Las Vegas. At first the band didn't have a name, but very soon and very unexpectedly they had a hit to hang a name on. Wanda had just about decided to revert to country music when a deejay in Des Moines, Iowa, started spinning "Party" as his theme song. The volume of requests convinced him to contact Capitol. Ken Nelson had nothing to lose, and issued it as a single. Just as conventional wisdom said that rockabilly was finished, Wanda had a Top 40 hit in August 1960 with pedal-to-the-floor rock 'n' roll. It was one of the ironies that only the record business can deliver. Her backing group became the Partytimers when they opened at the Golden Nugget in September 1960.

Wanda cut a couple of singles in Nashville after "Party" became a hit. "Right or Wrong" was the best: a lovely, seductive song that Wanda had written back in Oklahoma. She played it for Ken Nelson, "Where have you been keeping that?" he said. Nelson gave it the Nashville country-pop gloss, and it became a big country hit (Number 9), and a Top 30 pop hit. The flip side was the vaguely suggestive "Funnel of Love," which featured a strange, surf-like solo from Roy Clark.

Wanda never quite found the right song after "Right or Wrong." It probably wasn't a good idea to give one of her best self-composed numbers, "Kickin' Our Hearts Around," to Buck Owens. Good songs were in short supply, and Buck already had enough. Wanda couldn't put together enough of a hit streak to guarantee the pick of the best new songs, she fell between the cracks. She wasn't part of the West Coast scene led by Buck 'n' Merle, but neither was she part of the Nashville scene. She could have taken up where Patsy Cline left off, but Ken Nelson didn't seem to appreciate that Patsy, Roy Orbison, and Elvis had changed the way records were made in Nashville. The norm was four songs in three hours, but you couldn't make four Patsy Cline or Roy Orbison records in three hours. Nelson, though, remained wedded to value-for-money output from his artists. Wanda says that she never really thought of challenging him. "I always tried to do what I was told," she says. "If they'd said six songs in three hours, I'd have broke my neck trying to do it."

Nelson flew into Nashville several times a year, scheduling sessions night and day. To his credit, he was resisting the Nashvillization of country music, while nurturing the original alternative country scene out on the West Coast, but he shortchanged his Nashville artists. Even when he finally bowed to the inevitable and opened a Nashville office in 1961, he remained out west. RCA, Columbia, Decca, and Mercury already had their country A&R chiefs in Nashville working with the music publishers to find the best new songs. Nelson had an intermittent relationship with the Nashville publishers, and a strong predilection for Central Songs. In Nashville, hot new songs tended to create a buzz, and were very often recorded within hours of being written. Songwriters wanted to see an immediate return on their work and didn't want to hang on in case Ken Nelson ran out of Central Songs.

"I'd come to town with songs I'd written, or songs people had sent me," says Wanda. "Ken would bring what he had, and we'd let the word be known in Nashville when I was recording. I've come to believe I got the culls—the songs people had already culled through. Sometimes Central Songs was all I heard. There was always a sackful of them. The schedule was so tight that many times I would learn a song and record it the same evening." Wanda wouldn't arrive until the day before a session. "We had a misconception," says Wanda's husband-manager, Wendell, "that it was more important to be out there on the road making money that you could see. Most country artists thought that way then. We'd fly in, squeeze in three sessions for an album, and go home." Wendell sat with Ken Nelson in the control booth, sharing the candies that Nelson munched compulsively. Dig deep, and you'll find some treasures among Wanda's rushed Nashville sessions: "Reckless Love Affair" was a fifties-style cheatin' song caught out of time. "Tears Will Be the Chaser for Your Wine" has the wounded innocence of "Silver Threads and Golden Needles." Generally, though, the hurriedness took a toll.

If success in Japan was unanticipated, there were stranger times ahead. Electrola, the German affiliate of Capitol Records, had been successful with English-language artists like the Beatles and Cliff Richard singing in German. Somehow it was Wanda's turn. She wasn't Capitol's top-selling artist, but she might have been the only one who said Yes without thinking it through. "It was the first time I'd been to Europe," she said. "I didn't know what to expect. Electrola had asked if I'd do it. I said, 'Well, I guess.' Like an Okie, I could hardly speak English, but I told them if they had the patience to work with me, I'd try it. They had a vocal coach who went over every word with me very slowly and precisely, and I wrote it down phonetically in English, which they thought was very funny, and then I had to learn to form my mouth to say the words. And then I had to fit these words to the melody, and record in this new, strange way. The first song we cut was 'Morgen, Ja Morgen,' which didn't have a whole lot of lyrics, and then we came to 'Santo Domingo.' Not counting the time I spent learning the pronunciation, it took me another six hours in front of the microphone. I've never been a temperamental artist, but I'd run out of the studio crying, go to the ladies room, come back and start over."

"Santo Domingo" repaid the hard work. It was a hit, a by-God German hit, up there with the schlagers and the beer barrel polkas and the Beatles. Wanda was hauled back to Germany in October 1965 for some more sessions and television appearances, and again in October 1966 to complete an album. "It was hard enough to record these songs," says Wanda, "but you can't imagine what it was like to go on television when I had to memorize the lyrics and lip-sync." Wanda hadn't seen a major hit back home for four years; now she was at the top of the German charts with songs she didn't even understand. Had she been an existentialist, she would have reveled in the absurdity of it all.

Back home, Wanda was spending more of the year in Las Vegas and Reno. Notions of day and night were turned upside down. "I'd get off work at three in the morning, and we'd go out to some other places, catch some other lounge acts that were still on, party a little bit. Then we'd have something to eat, and it was eight in the morning before we got to bed. We did some drinking, some gambling. We'd go to movies every now and again." Without actually saying so, Wanda admits that these were her lost years. As of June 1968, Ken Nelson gave up producing her, passing her on to one producer, then another. This was a slap in the face, because he was still producing Buck 'n' Merle. To make matters worse, some of her singles now had the ghastly sixties poeticism that afflicted everyone in the wake of Kris Kristofferson. "Everything Is Leaving" was awash in minor chords and sophomoric wordplay ("old memories are flying, expanding pressures to my thinking").

A few songs broke out of the lower reaches of the country charts. "My Big Iron Skillet" was a feisty Loretta Lynn–styled number written by two friends of Wendell's. It reached Number 20. Then Wanda was handed to George Richey, later the fifth husband of Tammy Wynette. Richey pushed songs he owned, including one he'd written with two writers from

Wanda goes Vegas. Courtesy Colin Escott.

Tammy's camp, Norro Wilson and Glen Sutton. "A Woman Lives for Love" was so godawful that even Tammy might have rejected it, but it became Wanda's best-seller in several years, peaking at Number 17.

In March 1970, Wanda was whisked off on Capitol's European Country Caravan tour with Buck Owens and his son, Buddy Alan. Costars included the Hagers (who starred alongside Buck on *Hee Haw*); Tex Ritter (just a few years away from the Hillbilly Heaven he was always singing about); and Billie Jo Spears. The itinerary was punishing, and the combination of a heavy schedule, jet lag, foreign ways, and free drinks

from room service led inexorably to trouble. Ex-session pianist Earl Ball
was the road manager. "He tried to keep everyone sober and together,"
said Wendell, "but it was the blind leading the blind. In Amsterdam,
everyone had been up drinking heavy. We were out at the airport at 8:00 A.M.
and they had little scooters that you could use to get from gate to gate.
We were still drinking that strong beer and racing them things around
the airport."

The biggest change in Wanda's life, and the one she's most anxious to
talk about, came in June 1971 when she and Wendell rededicated themselves to Jesus. This is the way she tells it in her booklet, *Called Together*:
"My husband and I were living a lifestyle that I knew was not the best way
to live. We traveled all the time and half the time were absent from our
children. We sang in honky-tonks, nightclubs, and dance halls. This was
how we made our living: traveling with our band and entertaining in
places I was often not proud to be in. I also had become a problem drinker.
That was not something I wanted to have happen, but something I
allowed to happen. Every New Year I would decide to turn over a new leaf,
but that change would only last a few days. . . . I didn't know where I could
find real satisfaction and peace of mind. I was so confused. Real happiness
seemed beyond my reach."

"We thought we were Christians," said Wendell. "Then in the early
part of 1971, Wanda's church changed pastors. The new pastor was a
Wanda Jackson fan and got all excited, but we were never there. Then he
called us for a meal, and said some things that caused us to start looking
at ourselves. He said, 'You don't have to change or stop doing one thing to
come to God.' He knew we worked honky-tonks and were heavy drinkers.
If you just take the free drinks in a nightclub that people will buy for you,
you'll have eight or ten drinks a night. Brother Paul said, 'Give your heart
to Jesus, and then if there are changes to be made, God will reveal them
to you and give you the power to change them.' We thought we had to
clean up our act first. We left the next day on a three-week tour all the way
up to Alaska. We started thinking about what he'd said. We visited the
church after we got back and became born again. We raised up from our
knees praying as brand new people."

At first, Wanda continued working the same places she'd always
worked, but slowly realized that it didn't feel right. In October 1971,
Wendell cancelled their remaining dates. For three or four weeks, they did
nothing, then Wanda put together a gospel program and the invitations

started coming in to play churches and share their testimony. They cut taped background tracks and began working an entirely new set of venues.

Capitol took a jaded view of this. Wanda was now in the hands of Joe Allison, a songwriter, deejay, and man about the industry who'd written "He'll Have to Go" and "Live Fast, Love Hard, Die Young." He'd also managed Central Songs. "We were trying to look for material," said Wanda, "and my convictions had changed on the songs I wanted to do, and I remember Joe saying, 'When you take lyin', cheatin', cussin', and drinkin' out of a country song you ain't got much left.'" Wanda could see what was coming. "We asked for a release," said Wanda. "Ken Nelson said, 'Well, if your heart is really set on doing gospel, you ought to be with a gospel label.' We had three or four more years to go, but they let us out of the contract." Wanda was still charting regularly; no big hits, but charting nonetheless. "I didn't want to leave country music," said Wanda, "I just wanted to add country gospel to what I was doing, but the fans couldn't find the records anywhere. My career took a nosedive until Europe started opening up for us."

In 1984, Wanda recorded *Rockabilly Fever*, her first secular album in more than a decade. It was bankrolled by Tab Records in Sweden, then picked up in the United States by Varrick-Rounder Records. Wanda was more or less forgotten back home before a new generation of female country singers began citing her as an influence. Tanya Tucker's party girl image was a latter-day take on Wanda Jackson. Pam Tillis brought Wanda onto her TNN special, and Rosie Flores brought her onto a tour that took her back to the bar rooms for the first time in fifteen years.

Club world is better than it used to be. For most of her career, Wanda was a woman in a male environment. Songs were generally written from a male perspective; clubs very often didn't have women's dressing rooms; men would want to paw her, dance with her, or have her sign parts of their anatomy. Wanda learned to cope as well as anyone. Road stories would probably fill a volume if she cared to remember them. Things are better now.

Perhaps Wanda should have moved to Nashville. She gave it serious consideration after marrying Wendell. She knew you had to schmooze around town to get the first crack at the best songs, but she had family and friends back in Oklahoma City and decided to stay. Later, when the kids came along, she and Wendell wanted their parents to baby-sit when they were out on tour. Records weren't the be all and end all back then, but they're the most tangible artifacts left to us, so we inflate their importance.

At the time, they were only a sidebar. Sessions were squeezed among other commitments, and a hit was only an excuse to jack up personal appearance fees. Records meant less, so singers tended to be looser, more spontaneous, more willing to take risks or maybe bring in a technically inferior musician who might hit just the right lick. Perhaps the lower stakes account for the edginess of Wanda's best stuff. While other girl singers were simpering over "Where the Boys Are," Wanda sang as if they were in her hotel room. "When I start eruptin', ain't nobody gonna make me stop!" she sang on "Fujiyama Mama," and in those few moments pretty much invented the look and the sound of women in rock 'n' roll. She insists she wasn't *that* kind of girl, but the occasional glint in her eye seems to tell a different story.

Check It Out

Capitol's *Vintage Collection* is an excellent twenty-track overview of Wanda Jackson's career, both country and pop, while Ace Records's *Queen of Rockabilly* is a thirty-track import CD that concentrates on the hot stuff. For the deep-of-pocket, Bear Family has reissued all of the Decca and Capitol recordings in two boxed sets, *Right or Wrong 1954–1962* (four CDs) and *Tears Will Be The Chaser for Your Wine 1963–1973* (eight CDs, including all the foreign-language recordings).

CHAPTER 10

The Collins Kids

BROKENHEARTED RICKY

There has always been something a little perverse about a tot singing adult songs and mimicking adult emotions. Thirteen-year-old Brenda Lee singing "All the Way," for instance, is borderline sick when you think about it. The same can't really be said about the Collins Kids. Most of us have got stuff at the back of the fridge older than the Collins Kids when they started, but the whole point about rock 'n' roll was that it was *for* and *by* kids. No one made that point more explicit than they did.

Few child prodigies manage to sustain a career into adulthood. God knows how tough it must be when it's downhill from age eleven. The public loses interest at the first sign of facial hair. But the Collins Kids, Lawrence and Lawrencine (or Larry and Lorrie), made it into adulthood unscathed. Larry even found a little success in the music business after he quit jumping around onstage with his double-necked Mos-Rite guitar.

The Collins family lived in and around Tulsa, Oklahoma. Lorrie was born in Tahlequah on May 7, 1942; Larry was born in Tulsa on October 4, 1944. They grew up in a little town called Pretty Water. Lawrence Sr. was a dairy farmer for a while, then operated a crane in a steel mill. He truly had no interest in the entertainment business. His wife Hazel, on the other hand, had been an amateur singer and mandolin player, and became the prototypical stage mother. She and her sister had played school and church socials when they were in their early teens, and Hazel possibly wanted to experience success vicariously through her children.

Courtesy Bear Family Archive.

Lorrie was reckoned to be the talented one. In 1950, she won a talent contest hosted by Western Swing band leader Leon McAuliffe in a Tulsa ballroom. McAuliffe told Hazel Collins that California was where they needed to be, so in 1952, they made an exploratory trip. "We went to talent shows and agencies and they all thought they could do something with Lorrie if we lived in California," said Hazel. "At that time Jimmy Boyd was big, and a lot of kids were on television. In Oklahoma, there was nothing like that." Jimmy Boyd was thirteen when he hit Number 1 with "I Saw Mommy Kissing Santa Claus" in 1952; by age fourteen, he was washed up. God knows who would want that for their kid.

Hazel and Lorrie returned to Oklahoma. The next stop was a guest spot on the *Louisiana Hayride* in Shreveport alongside Hank Williams, Johnny Horton, and Jim Reeves. California, not Shreveport, was clearly the place to be. Hazel started pressuring Lawrence Sr. to move. Larry (then known as "Bubba") still didn't figure into Hazel's thinking. He had been given a guitar and a BB gun for Christmas 1952. "My mother showed me a G and D chord," he said, "and by the end of Christmas Day I was really whackin' that guitar. I played a song and jumped around like a fiend. They all laughed at me so I shot the guitar in the back with the BB gun. I thought I'd done something wrong."

Hazel and Lorrie got their way, and the Collins family moved to California in 1953. Lorrie started entering talent contests, like the Al Jarvis Show and the Hollywood Opportunity Show. There was Chef Lonnie's Lucky Strike contest in Redondo Beach. Larry entered that one, and placed first; Lorrie placed second. Separately, they contested on Squeakin' Deacon's Sunday talent show at the Riverside Rancho, broadcast over local radio. The idea that they should form a joint act came from Lawrence Sr. "One day," said Hazel, "he told them to go in the bedroom and practice together, and they came out an act. They said, 'Hey mom, dad, listen to us.' Larry carried the high tenor part and Lorrie took the lead. They played their guitars. Larry had already taught Lorrie some basic chords."

Hazel and Lawrence were thinking about heading back to Oklahoma, but the kids wanted to stay. It was Squeakin' Deacon (a transplanted Tennessean named Carl Moore) who told Hazel to take the kids to Bill Wagnon, who booked *Town Hall Party*. Larry and Lorrie entered a *Town Hall Party* talent search one Friday night in February 1954, and were hired to perform the following day. The show had started in Compton, California, in 1951; by 1954, when the Collins Kids joined, the regulars included music director Wesley Tuttle and his wife, Marilyn; Johnny Bond; Tex Ritter; Skeets McDonald; and Freddie Hart. The show was broadcast on clear channel KFI every Saturday night from 9:00 to 9:30 P.M., and on KTTV from 10:00 P.M. to 1:00 A.M. Starting in January 1955, NBC radio carried a portion. *Town Hall Party* later went into syndication as *Ranch Party*. Together and individually the Collins Kids were on every episode of the syndicated show.

Guitarist Joe Maphis had been on *Town Hall Party* almost from its inception. Maphis, the composer of the honky-tonk anthem "Dim Lights, Thick Smoke, and Loud, Loud Music," met the Collins Kids on the set of

Town Hall Party and began playing duets with Larry. It was Maphis's blindingly fast single-string runs that turned Larry's head around. Joe's wife, Rose Lee, remembers that her husband could be a stern taskmaster. "Larry wouldn't use his little finger to make chords," she said. "Then one night after the show, Joe went over to the Collins' house and told him that he wasn't doing it right. Larry started crying, but that's what it took because after that he started using his little finger. Larry was quick to learn. They never had to spend a whole lot of time rehearsing." For his part, Joe was a generous soul who never minded being upstaged by a kid. Rose Lee says he was as proud of Larry as he would have been of his own son.

Larry and Lorrie were still attending regular schools, but in 1956, after a few months on *Town Hall Party*, they transferred to Hollywood Professional School. Success already created problems; Larry couldn't participate in sports like baseball for fear of injuring his hands, and neither he nor Lorrie had regular peer friendships.

The Collins Kids were signed to Columbia Records in 1955. The label's country A&R man, Don Law, visited California regularly and, at the instigation of Johnny Bond, signed them on July 25, 1955. The terms of the contract suggested he was skeptical: a six-month deal at 2 percent. They signed in care of Johnny Bond, who fed them a steady diet of copyrights from Vidor Music, a company he co-owned with Tex Ritter. The first session was held in October 1955, and yielded the Kids' first single, "Hush Money." It must have sold well enough because Law renewed their deal in January 1956 and consistently thereafter until July 1963, despite the fact that they didn't score one hit in all that time.

"Rock 'n' roll was what we were doing," said Larry. "All the material was high energy. Our approach was always, 'Let's make this a little faster.' Maybe it came from the gospel churches we attended as children. I can't really say it was the influence of Elvis Presley or anyone else. Elvis really didn't figure in our thinking. We'd been on *Town Hall Party* a year or two before I ever heard him. It was on a jukebox in the McDonalds down the street from Town Hall that I first heard Elvis."

Larry believes that Columbia was scared of rock 'n' roll, and Don Law (who had the ultimate verdict on repertoire) seemed to prefer dumb preteen novelty songs like "Beetle Bug Bop," "Date Bait," and "Cuckoo Rock." But there was some good stuff sandwiched among the novelties: Clyde Stacy's "Hoy, Hoy," Ed Bruce's "Rock Boppin' Baby," and the Shelton Brothers' "Just Because" (someone dug deep to find those). "We

Mother Hazel, Larry, producer Don Law, Lorrie, and father Lawrence Collins. Courtesy Bear Family Archive.

were one of Columbia's pet acts," says Larry. "We played at their conventions. Goddard Leiberson, who was president then, was a very nice man, and he liked us a lot."

Columbia kept the faith. Some say that the Collins Kids gave it away for free on television every week, so no one needed to buy the records, but of course if that were the case Ricky Nelson wouldn't have sold half the records that he did. The Collins Kids were certainly visible. Aside from *Town Hall Party/Ranch Party,* they could be seen alongside Arthur Godfrey, Perry Como, Bob Crosby, Dinah Shore, and Steve Allen. They were also on the Opry and the *Ozark Jubilee,* and starred in a movie called *Music around the World.* Don Law was probably right when he said that the Collins Kids weren't too visible, but too visual. Larry also figures that the timbre of their voices didn't work on radio and records as well as on television. Hazel Collins believes that they should have stayed away from teen and preteen novelties and gone after regular material. By common consensus, their biggest-selling record was their version of Elvis's "Party," later revived by Wanda Jackson.

Shortly after the session that produced "Rock Boppin' Baby,*"* Larry's voice started changing, and little was heard from him for a while, except on guitar. "My voice actually changed on stage in Canada," he remembered. "We'd gone to eat and then started to do a show at an auditorium in Newfoundland. I began singing and this squeak came out. Everyone said, 'Uh-oh, time to do instrumentals.'" Larry's trademark was the double-necked guitar, the work of Semie Moseley, who originally designed it as a triple-neck monster that weighed over thirty pounds. Moseley, then in his late teens, brought the guitar to Joe Maphis in a club, and told him that he wanted to design a guitar for him. Joe threw in a few suggestions, and Moseley built a custom double-neck model with Maphis's name inlaid on both necks. The shorter neck was tuned an octave higher than the other neck so that it essentially functioned as a continuation of the regular one. There was an element of gimmickry, but the instrument had its advantages. On the soundtrack of the Robert Mitchum movie *Thunder Road*, for instance, Joe could do the chase parts quite effortlessly.

The double-necked Mos-Rite impressed the hell out of Larry Collins, who of course wanted one. "They presented it to me onstage," he remembered, "and gave me an hour of the show to play it." His original double-neck almost dwarfed him, but he became really very good. He was particularly fond of double-timed bass string runs with lashings of reverberation, and those runs influenced a generation of early 1960s pickers. Surf guitar pretty much began with Larry Collins and Joe Maphis. "I practiced a lot," said Larry, "maybe eight hours a day. But it was a gift. It was what I was supposed to be doing. I just can't believe I ever had that much energy. I look at those old videos, and I say, 'The kid's gone crazy.'" He really was able to hop, jump, jive, and duckwalk while barely missing a note.

For her part, Lorrie developed from a slightly gawky preteen into a beautiful young woman. Among those infatuated (and able to do something about it) was Ricky Nelson. He got her phone number, and persuaded Glen Larson of the Four Preps to call her on his behalf. They started dating. "We had a lot in common," she told Joel Selvin. "We really loved each other a lot. It was like being normal boyfriend and girlfriend. I think we both yearned for that." Lorrie even appeared on *The Adventures of Ozzie and Harriet*, and she and Ricky sang "Just Because." There were stories that Larry was sent out on dates to act as chaperon, but he denies it. He remembers Lorrie and Ricky coming in late and waking him up to play guitar with them. Rick and Lorrie were engaged when Lorrie and Larry went out on tour with Johnny Cash. Cash's road manager, Stew Carnall, developed a crush on Lorrie, despite the fact that he was nineteen years older. He persuaded her to elope

Bob Bregman, Larry, the double-neck Mos-Rite, and Lorrie. Courtesy Colin Escott.

with him to Vegas. Ricky Nelson found out about it in a Los Angeles morning paper. "It was the most devastating thing," says Larry. "Everybody thought I knew what was happening, but I didn't know a damn thing about it. She just went out the window. It put a damper on the act. We had movie deals lined up, and things were going well."

That was 1959. The Collins Kids split up for six months. When they regrouped, Carnall was their manager. They continued recording together until 1961. Lorrie had her first child in February of that year, and the Collins Kids essentially ground to a halt. Larry cut two solo sessions for Columbia in 1962 and 1963, and recorded for Monument before Mac Davis signed him as a writer to the Metric Music subsidiary of Liberty Records. When Liberty was bought out by United Artists, Larry started writing with one of UA's writers, Alex Harvey. Their first song, "Tulsa Turnaround," was recorded by Three Dog Night, and their first smash was "Delta Dawn." Ironically, the latter was the first hit for another child performer, Tanya Tucker. Larry and Lorrie premiered it at a Nashville deejay convention. They had briefly reunited for an appearance, and Columbia Records producer Billy Sherrill heard them perform it.

In 1981, Larry had his greatest success as a writer when David Frizzell and Shelly West recorded a song he'd written with Sandy Pinkard, "You're the Reason God Made Oklahoma." The success was tainted a little when Boudleaux Bryant claimed that they had stolen the melody from "Rocky Top," but the song was nominated for a Grammy. Larry attended the ceremony with Hazel. Lawrence Sr. had died a few months earlier. Together and separately Larry and Sandy Pinkard wrote several songs that ended up in classics of bubbadom like *Smokey and the Bandit* and *Any Which Way You Can*. Larry tried to use the renewed success as a springboard back into performing. He cut an album in Muscle Shoals, and performed in Vegas, but ultimately opted for the comparative security offered by his life as a golf pro.

"I wouldn't change a thing," said Larry, "except I wish Lorrie hadn't gone out the window and married Stew Carnall. We lost a lot of our childhoods, but we had some experiences I wouldn't trade for the world." In 1993, Larry and Lorrie reunited for a tour of Europe. They are, of course, still youthful performers compared with most rockabillies, most of whom now qualify for free bus passes and medicare. In fact, most of the Collins Kids' contemporaries are dead. The music they left is mixed. They underscored the fact that rock 'n' roll was teenage music, but perhaps their greatest triumph was that they managed to record at least some creditable rock 'n' roll, while everyone around them hated it.

Check It Out

At one time, Sony Music Special Products had a budget Collins Kids collection, *Introducing Larry and Lorrie—the Collins Kids*. Special Markets divisions bring items in and out of print, so it might still be available somewhere. Otherwise, it's down to Bear Family, which offers a single CD best-of, *The Rockin'est* (BCD 16250) and a two-CD boxed set, *Hop, Skip and Jump* (BCD 15537).

PART IV

Memphis

SUN RECORDS, JUNE 1957

Roland Janes, Magel Priesman, and Jerry Lee Lewis schmooze at Sun studios, June 1957. Courtesy Magel Priesman.

Magel Priesman: "In my biogbook of Elvis was a picture of Dewey Phillips, WHBQ, Memphis. My being a deejay might strike interest, if I could meet him. I hired a taxi at 9:00 P.M. to take me where he was doing his *Red, Hot, and Blue*, portfolio of demo tapes under my arm. Inside, I discovered that I was at the television studio where he did his day show. A secretary working late felt sorry I had come to the wrong place. She phoned Dewey and told him I had come all the way from Michigan. He told her to tell another taxi man to bring me to a certain door at WHBQ. I went up the elevator and met Dewey. He did much showing off, and I much giggling. He called Sam [Phillips] and told him about me. Sam said, 'Bring her round after your show,' which was midnight. One of Elvis's buddies came to the station, said there was a party at Elvis's place and invited me along. I thanked them and told them I was going to meet Sam that night.

"It was 2:00 A.M. when Sam told me, 'Come to Sun at 4:00 P.M. to meet Jack Clement the engineer and Bill Justis the arranger.' Jack was casual, with dark blond, deep wavy hair. Tallish and quiet. I noticed an affliction. He would blink his eyes, wrinkle his nose and distort his mouth with a twist, and jerk his head side to side. I mentioned to secretary Sally Wilbourn about how it was too bad a good-looking man like Jack had this affliction. She said, 'You noticed that too? He didn't do that when he first started working here.'

"Bill Justis was prematurely balding, round-faced and rosy color. His jive talk didn't fit his looks. Every sentence started with, 'Like, man. . . .'." His efficiency making arrangements was so speedy, my head was in a spin watching him. Jack said that they went out in a boat and Bill jumped into the water, down deep. Bill surfaced saying, 'Like, glub,' then he went down again. Coming up he said, 'Like, blub.' Third time down, then up, he yelled, 'Like, man, HELLLP!'

"I was staying at the Hotel Tennessee, across from the Peabody. I went into my room and a maid was changing the linen. I said, 'Go ahead, I have cards to buy and write home.' I went outside, and people were coming from all directions. I saw a man laying face up on the sidewalk, his head and neck sloping into the curb. I walked right up to him, my feet nearly touching his left shoulder. His dark brown glazed eyes were open, and he was wearing pajama bottoms only and a gold wristwatch. He had leaped from the sixth floor. I heard someone calling, 'Magel, Magel Priesman,' over and over, but I was completely transfixed by this dead man's eyes. Someone pulled on my right arm toward a car. Bill Justis, his left arm covering the steering wheel, body turned toward me, said, 'What in hell happened?' I said, 'I don't know.' Bill said, 'What the hell, it's probably just another hillbilly waiting for a release.'"

CHAPTER 11

Sonny Burgess

THE WILD MAN AT SEVENTY

Back in the mid-1960s, someone whose name I probably never knew made a good living importing records no one had heard of into England. He would fly to the United States, go to record warehouses, buy up box lots of discs, bring them back to England, rent an empty store for one Saturday, then advertise in the music weeklies. He'd sell his little stash by opening the boxes with a big flourish and playing the discs on a portable record player. That was how I, and twenty-four others, became proud owners of Sonny Burgess's "We Wanna Boogie."

The images conjured up by Sonny's record were of life lived on the edge: "Out to the dance hall, cut a little rug / We're runnin' like wildfire, and hittin' that jug." Wasn't this what it was all about: honky-tonk nights, drunken chases down dirt roads, bottle rockets fired through car windows, puking over the neighbor's car at dawn? We knew nothing about Sonny Burgess other than what was contained on that and two or three other Sun records. Here was total abandon: coarse, untutored singing, unintelligible lyrics; ragged drumming; distorted guitar, capped by a wildly bleating trumpet. Even Little Richard paled in comparison: his records were tightly marshalled; Sonny's had the unpredictability of jazz. Hearing King Oliver after a lifetime of Victorian parlor music must have been roughly comparable to hearing Sonny Burgess after a steady diet of 1950s pop.

When Martin Hawkins and I went to meet Roy Orbison in 1970, we asked about Sonny Burgess. They'd been on Sun Records at around the same time. Had they ever met? Indeed they had. Orbison told us a story

Courtesy Colin Escott.

that only enhanced Sonny's already high standing. Sonny had decided to dye his black hair blond, but black plus blond apparently equalled red, so he was left with a shock of flaming ginger hair. He and Orbison played Tucson, and were heading across the mountains toward Albuquerque. As Orbison told it, "We were driving two Cadillacs, and we had a blowout, so me and Sonny got in the car with [Johnny Cash's sidemen] Luther [Perkins] and Marshall [Grant], and headed on to Albuquerque without our equipment. We were heading down the highway at 120 miles an hour. Luther was driving. Then here comes this bunch of cattle across the highway. Luther headed off the road, through the brush, across the sand, circling the cows, and got back on the highway. Then we went on without our stage clothes. They had a Western Swing band back us. You never heard such a mess in your life. When we were leaving, I said, 'They'll always remember us in Albuquerque as the Wink Wildcat and the Red Clown.'"

Where was the Red Clown? Orbison had told us that Sonny was from Newport, Arkansas, and, as far as he knew, was still there. We called ahead from Memphis, found Sonny easily enough, and told him we'd like to come see him. He had no idea that foreigners were paying big bucks for his old records or that he was a legend to an admittedly small number of fans in countries he'd never thought about. French and German fans would call him "Soony Burr—Guess." "Come on, I'm here," he told us. The Memphis-to-Newport bus broke down somewhere in Arkansas. The Mississippi had risen over the levees that year, and floodwater surrounded us. A farmer circling what had once been his fields gave us a ride to Newport. There, in a faded storefront, we met Sonny Burgess. The shy, slightly pudgy, self-effacing family man was the last thing we expected. His life had clearly not been the stuff of our dreams.

When rockabilly died its swift commercial death and rockabillies wondered what came next, most got out of the business. Those that didn't usually reverted to their first passion: country music. Sonny reverted to his first love: rhythm and blues. He had a true R&B voice, short on subtlety and delicate shadings, but a magnificent instrument. Soon after he took the store job, he met an old black guy who'd bring in his guitar, and they'd jam for hours on Jimmy Reed songs. Oh, to have been there!

Born near Newport, Arkansas on May 28, 1931, Albert "Sonny" Burgess grew up on a farm, and listened to the Grand Ole Opry and R&B on Nashville's clear-channel megastation WLAC. He did his hitch in the army, and returned to Newport with the idea of trying for a career in baseball. He was working in a box factory when he joined his first band, the Moonlighters, and was back on the farm when, as he says, "farming started interfering with my music."

There was no shortage of venues because Newport was the seat of a wet county surrounded by dry counties; hence, there were more nightclubs

Workin' the clubs. Left to right: Johnny Ray Hubbard, Jack Nance, Sonny Burgess. Courtesy Colin Escott.

than the local population alone could support. The Moonlighters played area nightspots like the Silver Moon, Bob King's, and Mike's Club. King's, incidentally, is still in business and hosted Sonny's forty-year reunion in 1995. Back in 1955, Friday night at King's belonged to the Moonlighters, and Saturday night to saxophonist Punky Coldwell. According to Sonny, Coldwell led a racially mixed jazz dance band, and when Elvis came to the Silver Moon on Monday October 24, 1955, Sonny organized the supporting act. It was a Newport supergroup: some of Punky's men; some of Sonny's. "If you like GOOD western music (and who doesn't?)," said the advertisement, "you'll enjoy Elvis Presley and the Moonlighters playing your favorite western tunes. Showtime is 9 'til ?" By "?" according to Sonny, Elvis had tried to hire his pianist, Kern Kennedy, and Punky Coldwell. And by the time Elvis lit out for Memphis in the wee hours, he had implanted in Sonny the idea of recording for Sun. Ironically, Sonny got the idea to record for Sun on the very day that Colonel Parker secured Elvis's parents' permission to get Elvis off the label.

A few weeks after the Silver Moon gig, Sonny and the Moonlighters drove to Sun for an audition. Sam Phillips told them that they needed a fuller sound, so Sonny recruited Jack Nance and Joe Lewis from another local band. It was Lewis who came up with the name Pacers for the group, thinking of Pacer airplanes. Both Smith and Nance played drums so Nance (who had been a music major in college) switched to his other instrument, trumpet. Sonny had wanted a saxophonist to emulate Punky Coldwell, but figured that the trumpet gave the Pacers a little different sound.

On May 2, 1956, Sonny Burgess and the Pacers drove back to Memphis. Phillips liked what he heard, and cut their debut single that afternoon. These days lawyers talk to lawyers at $200 an hour, agreeing development budgets and publishing splits. There are meetings with prospective producers, and hours of preproduction before the first note is recorded. Sam Phillips just liked what he heard, adjusted the mic settings, and turned on the tape recorder. "We Wanna Boogie" backed with "Red Headed Woman" stemmed from that May afternoon and still ranks among the rawest records from rock 'n' roll's early days. You have to go to tiny no-hoper labels to find anything remotely comparable. It was punk before punk, thrash before thrash. It sounded as if gallon jars of Thunderbird wine littered the studio floor, although Sonny insists that everyone was stone cold sober, and nervous to the point of apprehension.

Nearly everyone who was on Sun bitches about no pay or low pay, and even at its height Sun was a shoestring operation run by a notorious cheapskate, but the fact remains that no major label would have touched "We Wanna Boogie"/"Red Headed Woman." Phillips was drawn to it for much the same reason he was drawn to Howlin' Wolf and Elvis. Sonny was raw and different: part Arkansas roadhouse music, part Louis Prima floorshow, part nothing he'd ever heard before. "We Wanna Boogie" was truly in its own category. Incredibly, it sold over 90,000 copies, doing especially well in Boston, although Sonny was unaware of that fact until Nance and Lewis toured there a few years later with Conway Twitty.

The Pacers were managed by Gerald Grojean, assistant manager at KNBY, Newport. On one of their early trips to Memphis, the Pacers went to see Elvis's manager, Bob Neal, who held the promise of broader horizons and promised to get them out on the road with Elvis. "We come back home," remembered Sonny, "and about a year later we hadn't heard nothing so we went back and saw him again. He said that Gerry Grojean had got on the phone crying, saying 'You can't take them away from me.' Bob said he didn't need all that crap and told Gerry he could keep us." Grojean, who knew little more about management than the group itself, had no idea how to get the Pacers outside northeast Arkansas. Neal, by then ousted from Elvis's camp and newly partnered with Sam Phillips in a booking agency called Stars Incorporated, eventually took over the group's bookings. He placed Sonny and the Pacers on interminable treks through the boonies, usually with Johnny Cash and Roy Orbison. Sonny used Orbison's amp on the road; built by Ray Butts in Cairo, Illinois, this very special, very heavy amp was equipped with a tape loop for built-in slap-back. Scotty Moore had one of the first, and Orbison had one too. They cost $600 apiece, but, according to Sonny, they were "the best-sounding amps I ever heard. I've used digital equipment that can't get anything close to that sound."

The Pacers had a fabulous stage act. They formed a pyramid on top of the bass player and jumped into the audience. "We were young, crazy and wild," recalled Jack Nance. "I remember one time we drunk more than we should have and woke up in our car in a field. A tractor had plowed all around us and the farmer charged us ten dollars to pull us out. Sonny never drank as much but he was a good athlete—an exceptional baseball player—so there was a lot of energy there that he used onstage." Sonny maintains that the original Pacers were the hottest working band in the mid-South. He says that the only acts to dwarf them onstage were Elvis Presley and the Collins Kids. "You can't upstage kids," he says. "Tougher'n appearing with dogs. We had a real good show, boy. Carl [Perkins] and Jerry Lee [Lewis] had nothing on us back then, visually or musically. We could go all night long. We'd sometimes play one song full blast for an hour at the end of the night."

Sonny believed that his second record, "Ain't Got a Thing," would be the one. The lyrics had the anarchic throwaway humor that Chuck Berry nabbed from Louis Jordan: "I got a check, but it won't cash / I got a woman, ain't got no class." It was catchy and tuneful, and there was a cute little modulation during the break, all to no avail. Still too raw, too rural. Sonny figured that it flopped because it was a little fast for dancing.

For their third shot, the Pacers revived Clarence Williams's jazz hokum novelty "My Bucket's Got a Hole in It." The song probably began life around the turn of the century in New Orleans as a hustler's lament: "Started out a racket, boy I done alright / Peddled moonshine by day, reefer

With the Pacers. Left to right: Johnny Ray Hubbard, Bobby Crafford, J. C. Caughron. Courtesy Colin Escott.

at night." Williams rewrote it and copyrighted it in 1933, but it lay unrecorded from 1938, when Washboard Sam cut it, until 1949 when Hank Williams and T. Texas Tyler recorded it. It's hard to know if Williams covered Tyler or vice versa. The references to pimping and hustling had gone by then, but the tag line, "My bucket's got a hole in it, can't buy no beer" remained. It was the Williams/Tyler version that Sonny remembered. Sonny was closer to R&B than any other white act at the time, and, in a swift kick of irony, suffered the fate of the R&B singer: scooped by a white pop act. Sonny's version was released in December 1957; Ricky Nelson covered it the following January. Sonny didn't even have the satisfaction of writing the song, thereby seeing some composer royalties. Nelson "Honey I'm homed" it: "My bucket's got a hole in it, won't hold no beer" became "My bucket's got a hole in it, won't work no more."

By this point, the Pacers had started to disintegrate; the two unmarried members, drummer Russ Smith and guitarist Joe Lewis, were let go. At roughly the same time, Jerry Lee Lewis's career was starting to explode and he was looking for a drummer. He called Jack Nance, who declined the job but recommended Russ Smith. A few months later, Nance quit the Pacers out of economic necessity, and joined Conway Twitty's band. Upstairs at the Flamingo Lounge in Hamilton, Ontario, Canada, Nance and Twitty wrote "It's Only Make Believe."

For a time, Sonny held down a day job with his brother-in-law in a sporting goods store, then reconstituted the Pacers with J. C. Caughron on guitar and Bobby Crafford on drums. They toured with Johnny Cash on the western country circuit. Sonny liked California, and was tempted to follow Cash there. After his fourth Sun single was released, he worked a tour with Cash, the Collins Kids, Joe Maphis, and Merle Travis that began in California and ended up in Memphis on November 14, 1958 at a benefit concert for Carl Perkins's brother, Jay. Cash's manager, Stew Carnall, gave Sonny $100 and told him to come to Los Angeles to join Cash on a television series. A few days later, Cash sent Sonny a telegram confirming the agreement. "We sat around for a few days, and got to thinking about it," said Sonny, "and decided we didn't want to go. So I sent Cash his $100 back."

On one of his swings out west, Burgess started looking for another recording deal. Bob Neal got him in the door at Challenge Records, and they went to Wynn Stewart's house to cut some more demos, but neither led anywhere. "Sam always said he didn't know what to do with us," said Sonny. "We didn't fit any category. We'd have made a few changes if we'd had any sense, but like most musicians. . . ."

There was one more Sun single, which appeared on Sun's Phillips International label. The sound was thin and poorly balanced, and the top side, "Sadie Brown," was ripped off from Yodelin' Jimmie Rodgers's "My Little Lady," but, flawed as it was, it was true to the Pacer credo. The single caught the attention of someone at Decca Records in England, and when it was released on Decca's London subsidiary it became the only Sonny Burgess Sun record released in Europe while he was under contract. These days, there are many more Sonny Burgess records available overseas than domestically.

Sonny never recaptured the Sun magic. His subsequent singles weren't that great. The fire had gone, and Sam Phillips had gone. Phillips knew how to capture Sonny's booming assertiveness and his raw-toned guitar. "There was no way Sonny was going to be a ballad singer," said Phillips. "His forte was rock 'n' roll. He could have been one of the greats but he never got the right break. I believed in the guy. We gave him what exposure we could but ultimately it's the deejays and the public who make the decision."

Sonny still can't quite unravel what happened at Sun. "Sam's secret," says Sonny, "was to get you to play like you'd play live. He'd just turn you loose. You'd play like you had a crowd watching—that's how come there's all the mistakes. It wasn't super good music, but it felt good to us. I was trying to play guitar and sing too, and that's tough to do. We should have brought in another picker." Then again, maybe not.

In 1959, Sonny joined Jack Nance and Joe Lewis in Conway Twitty's band, and Bobby Crafford took over the Pacers. Sonny stayed with Twitty until Twitty reverted to country music and moved to Oklahoma City. Sonny took a day job for a while before picking up the threads with a new band called the Kings IV (subsequently the Kings V). They played clubs in and around Newport, and on Sundays they'd drive to Memphis to check out the R&B bands at Sunbeam Mitchell's Paradise Club. "There was us and maybe a table of college kids," Sonny remembered, "and the rest of the room would be black. Willie Mitchell, Bowlegs Miller, and the musicians made us feel real welcome, but then toward the end the racial thing got real tense and we stopped going. We never saw R&B bands in the fifties, and that was the only chance we got to see the real good R&B acts." Around 1970, Sonny gave up music as his primary source of income.

When interviewed in 1971, Sonny could see no place for himself in the then-current music scene. He joined St. Louis Trimming, which made lace for bridal gowns and craft items, and traveled six states as a salesman. Shortly before retirement, he became one of the founding members of the Sun Rhythm Section band, touring far and wide and recording prolifically.

None of the original Pacers wanted to get back into it. Jack Nance worked for Dick Clark Productions, staging road shows, and making a living on the fringe of the music business until his death from lung cancer in 1999. Pianist Kern Kennedy worked for many years with the railroad and retired to a homestead near Little Rock, but played occasional Pacer reunion shows. Joe Lewis stayed with Conway Twitty after the switch to country, but was killed in a car wreck. Russell Smith stayed with Jerry Lee Lewis until the 1958 scandal. The subject of much rumor and speculation, he is believed to be living in New Orleans.

Sonny Burgess, meanwhile, went from strength to strength. His voice is marvelously intact, and he has finally found some of the acclaim denied him back in the 1950s. His 1980s and '90s records are generally excellent; he became a prophet with honor. He made an album with Dave Alvin of the Blasters in 1992, and another with former Bruce Springsteen sideman Garry Tallent in 1996 that featured an unrecorded Springsteen song. As his seventieth birthday loomed, he was still performing, and still in excellent voice. He's out there for the right reason: he loves it. "It's a young person's ballgame," he says. "Some guys my age, maybe a little younger, figure they're gonna grab the brass ring, but it ain't gonna happen." No it ain't, but Sonny has as many dates as he wants. These days, there's another Sonny Burgess making the rounds. He's a new country singer and apparently he's not bad. He's just not Sonny Burgess. There's talk of the two Sonnies playing some dates together. Sonny's all for it.

There's no escaping the fact that Sonny's entire career has been predicated by those few singles he made at Sun. His feelings about the label are understandably mixed. His original singles didn't sell, and the European Sun licensees issued material that he considered unworthy. He found it a struggle to liberate royalties, although he says the situation has improved. It still comes down to just three or four singles, though. Thirty years ago, they brought two pale Englishmen to Newport, Arkansas; now they take Sonny Burgess around the world.

Check It Out

Rounder Records has a best-of Sonny's Sun cuts (CDSS-36), and Bear Family has *everything* that Sonny recorded for Sun on a double-CD set, *The Classic Recordings* (BCD 15525). The CD with Dave Alvin, *Tennessee Border,* is highly recommended (Hightone HCD 8039).

CHAPTER 12

Ed Bruce

MAMMAS, DON'T LET YOUR ROCK BOPPIN' BABIES GROW UP TO BE COWBOYS

In the late 1970s, Ed Bruce was just about unavoidable. His song, "Mammas Don't Let Your Babies Grow Up to Be Cowboys," was a Number 1 hit for Waylon Jennings and Willie Nelson, and his records for MCA were on the radio. Meanwhile, his voice-overs were selling anything and everything from Hungry Jack Biscuits to Tennessee tourism. He was even on television as James Garner's sidekick in the beleagured 1982 revival of _Maverick_. By then, he'd perfected the grizzled look, like the Marlboro Man near retirement. But he didn't always look that way. In 1957, Ed Bruce was Edwin Bruce, a freshfaced seventeen-year-old rockabilly with a greasy kiss curl and a deal with Sun Records. He tried hard to become a teenage idol, but it didn't happen, and when the music changed he became one of the first, perhaps _the_ first, to revert back to country music.

William Edwin Bruce Jr. was born in Keiser, Arkansas, on December 29, 1939. His father, a car salesman, moved the family to Memphis when Ed was just a few years old. The Bruces lived on South Lauderdale, just across the street from Elvis's first manager, Bob Neal. A deejay and concert promoter, Neal did double duty as Uncle Piggly, hosting a kiddies show on WMPS where he plunked away on his ukelele. He showed Ed how to play a few chords.

Country music was Ed's first passion, which he was at pains to emphasize after he became a born-again hillbilly. "I remember going to a

185

Courtesy Colin Escott.

show at the Ellis Auditorium when I was twelve years old," he said. "I took my first true love, who was also twelve. Bob Neal presented the show and the headliner was Hank Thompson. After a while my date turned around to me, 'Do you really like this?' Just broke my heart, because of course I liked it." Ed went to Messick High School in Memphis and graduated in June 1957. That summer, he made his recording debut. He had gone to Sun to make a demo of a song called "Eight Wheel Driver," and engineer Jack Clement heard some promise in the kid. Clement brought in Sam Phillips, who gave Ed the usual Sam speech about how big Ed could be if he just believed in himself and let Sun take him there. The first record, "Rock Boppin' Baby," could so easily have made Sam's silvery words come true; it shuttled very effectively between moody minor key verses and a raging major key chorus. Ed was delivering papers for the *Memphis Press Scimitar* when it was released, which guaranteed a little local coverage, but not enough to make a hit. The Collins Kids covered it.

By the fall of 1957, Ed was at Memphis State University majoring in drama and speech, but went back to Sun to cut a second record in 1958. He also claims to have written part of "Guess Things Happen that Way" for the departing Johnny Cash. Bill Black was an early mentor, and Ed used both Black and Scotty Moore on club dates after they split from Elvis and needed some work. He sold used cars after graduation and worked a few lounges as a solo act, but didn't get another shot at recording until 1960. By this point, Jack Clement was working with Chet Atkins at RCA in Nashville, and brought Ed down to cut a single. One side was a sickie song, "Flight 303"; the other side, Ed's own "Spun Gold," was lovely and could surely have been a hit for someone. When Clement left, RCA lost no time cutting Ed loose, and there were no more records until 1962, when Bill Black got him a one-year deal with Scepter Records. Black also got one of Ed's songs, "Save Your Kisses," on the flip side of Tommy Roe's "Sheila," and with the money from that deal, Ed moved to Nashville for a year.

By the time Ed recorded for Sonic and Apt Records in 1964 and 1965, his career in pop music was just about over, inasmuch as it had ever started. The Beatles had changed everything, and Ed was thinking about getting out. Then he got some unexpected encouragement when Charlie Louvin scored a Top 5 country hit with a song he'd cut for Scepter, "See the Big Man Cry." In August 1966, with a BMI writers award under his belt, he moved back to Nashville and tried again. By September he was back on RCA. He had married for the first time while in Memphis (his son, Trey, has since become a very successful Nashville songwriter and producer). Ed met his second wife, Patsy, during his first year in Nashville, when they both lived in the same apartment building. They married in October 1964, and by the time they returned to Nashville they had a one-year-old daughter, Ginny. Later, Patsy took over Ed's management.

Ed was signed to RCA by Bob Ferguson, who signed Vernon Oxford and Connie Smith and produced Dolly Parton. Ferguson—who died in July 2001, just weeks after his former boss, Chet Atkins—favored stripped-down productions. In that regard, he and Atkins were very different. Under Ferguson's guidance, Ed cut "Walker's Woods," which broke into the country charts, peaking at Number 57, and created just enough interest to keep him on the label.

Some of the songs that Ed cut during his two years at RCA were in Kris Kristofferson's artfully poetic style, including two early numbers by Kristofferson himself. There was also a wonderfully spare and laid-back version of the Monkees' chart-topper, "Last Train to Clarksville." The first album, *If I Could Just Go Home*, is one of the era's underrated classics. Ed described its release as his proudest moment (with luck, his wife and kids took that the right way). Ferguson hit on ace songwriters Harlan Howard and Marijohn Wilkin, and Mister Rent-a-Quote, Ralph Emery, for little testimonials on the back liner.

All the while he was on RCA, Ed continued to write songs. "A Working Man's Prayer" was a country hit for Tex Ritter in 1967 and a minor pop hit for Arthur Prysock the following year. Jeannie C. Riley took "The Price I Pay to Stay" into the country Top 40 in 1969. Tanya Tucker took two more of Ed's songs into the charts, "The Man That Turned My Mama On" and "Texas When I Die." Ed never quite broke through, though. He paid the bills working with the Marijohn Wilkin Singers on WSM-TV and on the *Bobby Lord Show*, and did background vocals on commercials. As of July 1969, he was Pete Sayers's co-host on WSM-TV's *Morning Show*. A year or two later, Ed and Patsy bought a restaurant in the Biltmore Hotel on Eighth Avenue in Nashville. Then Ed discovered commercials. He sang and narrated spots for over 100 sponsors, Burger King, John Deere, United Airlines, McDonald's, and Maxwell House among them. "People in Nashville used to laugh at us," he said, "but they quit laughing when they found out how much money was in it."

An older, more weathered Ed Bruce, c. 1985. Courtesy Colin Escott.

The RCA deal was followed by a stint with Monument, and then a four-year layoff from recording. When Ed came back it was with United Artists, Epic, and MCA. Then his moment came. Waylon 'n' Willie hit the top with his urban cowboy anthem "Mammas Don't Let Your Babies Grow Up to Be Cowboys" in 1978. He'd started it during a moment of disillusionment as "Mammas, Don't Let Your Babies Grow Up to Be Guitar Players." Patsy finished it, and later took it all in their divorce settlement. While on MCA, Ed finally scored his first and only Number 1 hit as a singer, "You're the Best Break This Old Heart Ever Had." It had only taken twenty-four years. Then, in 1984 Ed quit MCA and went back to RCA for the second time (third, if you count the one-off single in 1961). In 1987, his chart career quietly died, but he was still visible for a while hosting lifestyle shows on the TNN television network.

Ed Bruce proves that good things can come just from hanging in. You try this, you try that. You show your face here, you show your face there. Maybe you'll come up with the record or the song that's just perfect for the time. You really never know.

Check It Out

The Sun and early RCA recordings are on *Puzzles* (Bear Family BCD 15830). There's nothing available domestically, except a greatest-hits package from the MCA years.

CHAPTER 13

Onie Wheeler

NO, I DON'T BELIEVE I WILL

There's never been an interview in which anyone has said, "Onie Wheeler was my main man." He influenced no one, and wasn't obviously influenced *by* anyone: a man apart. To those who live and die by *Billboard* statistics, he was a footnote: one record reached Number 53 early in 1973. To rockabilly fans, he was a minor celebrity by virtue of his solitary Sun record and some unissued cuts that he hated. To connoisseurs of bizarre musician deaths, he gets an honorable mention for dying onstage at the Grand Ole Opry house. But if you can find them, Onie Wheeler's small number of whimsical recordings are quite simply delightful—especially the earlier ones. He lived and died in almost total obscurity, but somehow managed to carve out a forty-year career in music. In the end, he was derailed by stubbornness, bad attitude, and bad luck.

There never was a comprehensive Onie Wheeler interview. We don't know who he listened to, whether he liked baseball or football, or how he came up with his stuff. We're left wondering about the missing years, wondering who Onie was. This is all the more galling because in 1971, Martin Hawkins and I met him backstage at the Grand Ole Opry, and moved on. We knew he'd cut one Sun record, but he told us right away that he didn't like it. We were pretty sure that he'd recorded before Sun, but had no idea how good those records were.

Here's what we now know about Onie Wheeler. He was born on the family farm near Senath, Missouri, on November 10, 1921. His mother

Courtesy Colin Escott.

died when he was four and his father, Daniel, remarried, eventually moving the family to Morley, Missouri, where Onie became one of thirteen kids. He played harmonica and guitar around the house, but didn't think about music as a career until he was in the service. He won a talent contest while on leave, and entered some other contests while serving in the Pacific during the Second World War. At war's end, music seemed a better bet than farming. He could do a great imitation of Ernest Tubb, but so could many others. He'd injured his hand in the war, so he concentrated on the harmonica.

Onie was on KWOC in Poplar Bluff, Missouri when he met Betty Jean Crowe, who was working as Little Jean with another band on the same station. They met in 1945, married in May 1946, and moved on to KBTM, Jonesboro, Arkansas. From there, they went to WKTM, Mayfield, Kentucky, then hit the Hillbilly Highway north to Flint, Michigan, around 1948. Onie worked in the auto plants during the day, and played at a club for homesick southerners across the street from the Buick plant on weekends. It was in Flint that Onie made his first recordings. Someone named Charlie Warson heard his show on WWOC and bankrolled the Agana label. Agana is a city in Guam; maybe Onie or Warson served there. Who knows? It looks like Agana Records begins and ends with Onie and Little Jean's version of "Shackles and Chains." It's a rare record alright, but not an especially good one.

Onie and Betty Jean left Flint and went back to Missouri, landing a gig on KSIM, Sikeston. The Nelson brothers, Doyal and A. J., were working factory jobs in St. Louis and playing local hillbilly bars at night. They were originally from Sikeston and went back often; one night, they met Onie Wheeler. Onie held out the promise of a career in music, so the Nelsons gave up their day jobs, moved back to Sikeston, and gave it a try. *Billboard* reported that Onie started on KSIM in May 1952; the Nelsons probably joined him soon afterward. They held down their radio job, and played the honky-tonks around northeast Arkansas, southern Illinois, and southeast Missouri.

After a while, Onie and the Nelsons decided that they had played out the area and should go to California. Every night they saved part of their earnings and put it into a California kitty. "We'd saved about fifty bucks," said A. J.,

> so we decided to leave, go as far as we could in one day then find a club, maybe even play for tips. We left the women at home, and started out. We stopped the first night in Texarkana, another few nights in Longview, Texas, and then we ended up outside of Odessa in a place called Monahans. There was a club with cars as far as you could see. Doc Bryant was running a remote broadcast out of there. I guess you could spot musicians back then 'cause Doc walked right up and started talking to us. He told us to get our instruments and play. He loved us 'cause we were different from that Texas stuff. He offered to book us, and he got us a gig in Odessa for six months or so before the place closed because of a liquor violation. Onie had a day job so he stayed in Odessa, and we headed off to Wichita, 'cause we heard it was wide open.

Onie and Betty Jean with daughter Karen, 1950. Courtesy Colin Escott.

On the way to Wichita we stopped off to see Doc Bryant, who'd gone home to Chickasaw, Oklahoma. He offered us a job with his band, so we stayed, working the clubs and playing TV and radio. One night they called me to the phone. It was Onie. We hadn't told him where we were, and he'd called clubs between Odessa and Wichita till he found us. He said the club in Odessa was open again and we should join him, so we went back.

One night Little Jimmy Dickens played there and told us we oughta be recording, so we headed back to Missouri, loaded down the car with tapes of all our songs, and went to Nashville. We tried everyone in town, then finally someone said, "Go see Troy Martin over at the Tulane Hotel." We went and played him "Mother Prays Loud in Her Sleep." Troy asked Onie what he wanted for the song, and Onie said he wanted a recording contract. Troy said, "You got it."

Troy Martin is a shadowy figure, one of the first operators on the Nashville music scene. He began back in the 1930s as a recording artist, and, as Dan Cooper observed, by the early 1950s he looked vaguely like Nikita Khrushchev. He worked under several aliases at several publishing companies, and drank with Don Law, another shadowy figure who ran

Columbia's Nashville operations between 1951 and 1967. "Troy was a big help to me," Law said later. "He'd make suggestions and bring people to me. He'd leave the impression that 'If you want to get to Don Law, you've got to go through me,' although I didn't find out about this until a lot later." Troy Martin later middlemanned Johnny Horton's Columbia contract, and had a role in bringing Lefty Frizzell to the label, too.

Landing Onie's deal with Columbia's OKeh subsidiary was not an act of altruism on Martin's part. He secured the publishing on Onie's material for Peer Music, whom he represented that month, and took half of the composer credits for himself under such pseudonyms as Tony Lee, George Sherry, and B. Strange. Don Law hardly mortgaged the farm to secure Onie, either; Onie was offered a two-year contract at 2 percent, to commence on August 28, 1953. That day, Onie cut four songs, including two that became closely associated with him, "Run 'em Off" and "Mother Prays Loud in Her Sleep." Martin had more faith in the songs than in Onie, because he persuaded Flatt and Scruggs to record "Mother Prays Loud in Her Sleep" the following day, and Lefty Frizzell to cut "Run 'em Off" a few months later. Both of these cover versions were on Onie's label, Columbia, which was hardly a resounding vote of confidence on Law's part, either. "Mother Prays Loud" has become a minor bluegrass gospel standard. Onie had written it with the three-part harmony of Doyal, A. J., and himself in mind, and it is Doyal's high tenor heard to great effect on the bridge.

Martin and Law chose "Run 'em Off" for the first single. It was the song that went over best on show dates, and although it didn't chart for Onie, it reportedly sold 250,000 copies. Back then, the *Billboard* country chart only had fifteen positions, and a record like "Run 'em Off" could sell well without ever showing up. Onie's version was subtly different from most country records of the time: the steel guitar (an instrument he personally disliked) was absent; drums (still no go on the Opry stage) were present and hustled the rhythm along; and solo honors were shared by the fiddle and harmonica.

Onie blurred the line between sacred and secular: honky-tonk numbers like "When We All Get There" and "Closing Time" sounded like gospel numbers by virtue of the three-part harmony on the chorus. "My Home Is Not a Home at All" sounded almost Celtic. The sacred songs had a sepulchral beauty, and the up-tempo numbers had a loose-jointed swing and quirky humor. Onie sang in his gentle bullfrog baritone, bending and breaking notes, his vocals complemented by A. J. Nelson's bass string runs and high tenor harmony. The endless nights on the bandstand had given them a telepathic ability to frame each others' work. "His mind worked overtime," said A. J. Nelson. "Different songs, arrangements, and he loved those screwy rhythms."

Onie's releases were moved from OKeh to the parent Columbia label in 1955. At the beginning of that year, one of his songs, "No, I Don't Guess I Will," became a hit for Carl Smith as "No, I Don't Believe I Will." Once again, Don Law showed a remarkable lack of faith in giving one of Onie's songs to another Columbia artist while holding back the original version. Meanwhile, Onie was getting his first taste of the changing times ahead: in May 1955, he went out on tour with Elvis Presley. Onie was managed by Charlie Terrell, who operated a trucking company from Sikeston. When he was short of money, Onie drove for Terrell. Bob Neal, then managing Elvis, contacted Terrell and placed Onie on several of Elvis's tours during the spring of 1955. In August of that year, Columbia picked up their option on Onie's contract, renewing it at 3 percent. When Onie returned to the studio in April 1956, he figured it was time to rock. "Onie's Bop" had two rockabilly guitar solos by Grady Martin and lots of Onie's gently self-mocking humor, but didn't stand a prayer.

The last Columbia single appeared in May 1957. It coupled a rockabilly number, "Goin' Back to the City," with a goosed-up version of Ernest Tubb's "Steppin' Out," one of the few nonoriginals that Onie ever recorded. The rockabilly recordings were fine in their way, but Onie functioned best at mellow midtempo. It was only then that the subtle shadings in his voice came to the fore. Somehow, there was a more compelling drive to the lilting "Run 'em Off" than to the faster numbers.

Onie had quit playing with the Nelson brothers at some point in 1956 because Charlie Terrell had landed him a gig with Flatt and Scruggs on the syndicated *Martha White Flour* television show. It was time to move to Nashville. Terrell lent Onie a truck and found him a house near the Cumberland River. Onie, as always, did his best to self-destruct. "He was getting calls from all kinds of places, wanting to book him," remembered Terrell, "and he thought he could move back to Sikeston and handle his career out of there. When he appeared at my door with all his stuff in a U-Haul, I gave up."

By the time the Columbia deal ended in 1957, Onie was working on Bob Neal's package shows. Starting in March that year, he was on the road

Mid-1955 tour. Left to right: Elvis, Bob Neal, Jimmie Work, and Onie. Courtesy Colin Escott.

with Jerry Lee Lewis, Billy Riley, Carl Perkins, and Johnny Cash. By the end of the year, he was pretty tight with the Memphis crowd, and, that November, went to Sun to cut a record. He considered Sun a bush-league operation, but nonetheless gave them one of his best songs, "Jump Right out of this Jukebox." It was a delightful record, and unlike most novelty records, had enough solid musicality to sustain repeated listening. If it's hard to know why Sun held off releasing Onie's single in 1957, it's even harder to know why they decided to release it over a year later. There were a few good reviews, then it disappeared.

By late 1958, Onie was working at a shoe factory in Sikeston. Trying to get his career up and running again, he moved to California. The following year, he and Betty Jean and the kids were in St. Louis, and Onie was working at Industrial Engineers. He recorded for K-Ark Records (run by the wonderfully wacky John Capps) between 1959 and 1961, and hosted a weekend country music jamboree in a park on South Broadway. (For years, the park was known as Onie Wheeler Park.) In 1962, he went back to see Don Law and got a joint Columbia session for himself and his daughter Karen. The result was "Sandyland Farmer," a not very good answer-disc to Frankie Miller's "Blackland Farmer."

Meanwhile, Bob Neal had moved to Nashville and landed Onie a slot on George Jones's package show, and Onie recorded for Jones's labels, United Artists (in 1964) and Musicor (in 1965). Then came the inevitable rift, and Onie went on to work for Roy Acuff while holding down a fairly steady day job with Sho-Bud guitars. One of Sho-Bud's owners, Shot Jackson, also worked for Acuff so no one lost their job for taking off work to play shows. In 1965, Onie persuaded Doyal and A. J. Nelson to rejoin him in Nashville. They quit Acuff and tried to make it on their own for a while, then Doyal became a preacher and A. J. went full-time with Sho-Bud. "At first," said A. J. with the regret shared by most journeyman musicians, "you're gung-ho, you'll break out your instrument and pick at the drop of a hat, you just love to do it. Then after years and years, you just lose that interest. I'd lost my weekends for too many years."

Onie was on his own again when he had a hit with "John's Been Shucking My Corn." It first appeared on Old Windmill Records in late 1971, and was then rereleased on Royal American in 1972. The latter label had enjoyed a huge hit two years earlier with Guy Drake's redneck classic "Welfare Cadillac." The success brought in a few show dates, but Onie couldn't find a follow-up. The releases became fewer and farther between, and less interesting. He operated a guitar repair shop from his home and made USO trips to Europe and Vietnam. Then came gigs set up by the American Federation of Musicians in nursing homes and other institutions.

"He had an unwillingness to do a lot of the things that were necessary to be successful," said A. J. Nelson. "He disliked going to radio stations and promoting his records. He thought it was a waste of time, and he certainly wouldn't leave a few bucks with the deejay. He was just too stubborn to do the things you had to do. Even little things, like after 'Run 'em Off' became a hit, the owner of KSIM wanted him to do a commercial that started, 'Hi, I'm Onie Wheeler . . . ,' and Onie wouldn't say it because he thought everyone knew his voice. Little things like that transferred to bigger things. The other side was that he wouldn't step on other people to get somewhere—and you have to do that in this business if you're going to get ahead. Onie just wouldn't, though. If he felt something was wrong, he wouldn't do it."

Charlie Terrell believed Onie was ahead of his time. "Sure, he certainly wasn't aggressive enough, but his songwriting was too far ahead. His best material was written ten years too soon. He could have been as big as Tom T. Hall became. Some of his material was *that* good. I thought so, and others did, too." For all that, Onie Wheeler was basically content. "He was off in his own little world," said Betty Jean. "His mind going a mile a minute on what he was working on—his songwriting or whatever. After we moved out to Mt. Juliet, he was real happy, he couldn't wait to get home. He had an acre of garden, and he loved to work in it."

Onie had an aneurysm removed in January 1984. It took him several months to get back on his feet, but he started working again. On Friday night, May 25, he walked out of the door, said "See you later" to Betty Jean, and drove to Opryland to fulfill a gig with the Reverend Jimmie Snow. "He'd turned into an old person since that operation," said A. J. Nelson, "but he was working Jimmie Snow's *Grand Ole Gospel Time,* and he wanted me to play it with him. We'd rehearsed a new song, 'Mother Rung the Dinner Bell and Sang,' as a trio with Doyal and me. We did a last-minute rehearsal in a side room, and I could see Onie wasn't feeling good. We were waiting for Jimmie's call, and Onie went back to a little bench and he sat down. Then Jimmie called him out, and everything was fine through the first number, then we got about halfway through 'Mother Rung the Dinner Bell,' and he just went down. He'd taken his mic off the stand and was standing next to Doyal. He fell with the microphone in his hand, attempting to sing. He didn't die right that minute. The medics got there and hooked him up to a monitor. There wasn't hardly any heartbeat, then there was just a straight line. They put the cups on and shocked him a couple of times, and the monitor hit a couple of licks then straightened out again. They took him to Memorial Hospital in Madison [Tennessee]. I called his wife and Karen."

The obituaries, few that they were, said "Rockabilly Pioneer Dies." If Onie appreciated irony, he might have enjoyed that.

Check It Out

It would be good to report that Onie Wheeler records are available everywhere, but that was never the case, and is less so now. The Sun recordings are scattered on various albums, but the only Onie Wheeler CD is *Onie's Bop,* released by Bear Family in 1991. It comprises all of his Columbia and Sun sides, which makes it pretty much essential.

PART V

Postscript

CHAPTER 14

Vernon Oxford

TOO COUNTRY FOR COUNTRY

Vernon Oxford looks through a box of photos. There are a lot of family shots: a few from back in Arkansas and some from Kansas, but most are from Nashville. There are many onstage shots, but surprisingly few with other country singers, emphasizing in a way that Vernon Oxford is something of a misfit. Too country for country music is a hell of a fate, but it is Vernon Oxford's fate. Country music has always paid lip service to its past, but it must be a past that fits into the country music theme park. It must be a past that can be captioned in that special kind of English reserved for Cracker Barrel menus. A past that never really existed. When country music is confronted with a living, breathing specimen who embodies the confrontational truculence of its past, then it doesn't know what to do with him.

Listen to the current crop of country music stars. They've been to media awareness classes, so they won't actually say this, but you're left with the feeling that country music is just a career option. If it doesn't work out, they'll be in software development or marketing next year. Country music wasn't a career option for Vernon Oxford; it was all he knew. Its bleak pathos was his life. He fought a one-man rearguard action on behalf of the music he loved. It wasn't a put-on. It wasn't a pose he copped to be cool. It wasn't an anti-Nashville stance. Vernon believed with all his heart that he belonged in Nashville. He had, after all, spent his last cent getting there.

Vernon can't understand why he wasn't more successful. Everywhere **203**

Courtesy Bear Family Archive.

he went, people loved his music; even overseas—the last place you'd expect hardcore hillbilly music to be accepted. Even now, he has a hard time comprehending music as business. Why can't they see the value in what he's doing? Why can't they appreciate the traditions he's carrying forward? From time to time, Vernon hints darkly at conspiracies, some involving the Mafia, that have kept him from being bigger than he was, but the truth is more prosaic. Country music has always relied on formats and formulas, and Vernon simply didn't fit. From the moment he left Arkansas, he didn't belong. That was as true in Nashville as anywhere else.

Through it all, Vernon Oxford's music has been remarkably sure footed. The most anomalous record he ever made, "Redneck," was his biggest hit. It was anomalous because it came close to lampooning his values, and Vernon is too serious about himself, his music, and his values to make light of them. Now he's past sixty, and his life is a glimpse of a lost world. Today's country stars will never grow up seeing all he saw. They'll never carry water up a mountainside or appreciate what the Grand Ole Opry once meant on a Saturday night. They'll certainly never experience a culture as regional or as isolated as the one in which he grew up.

Walter Oxford and his wife, Frankie, lived on a farm near a creek twenty miles east of Rogers, Arkansas, in a settlement called Larue. It's in the Ozarks, near the border with Oklahoma to the west, and Missouri to the north. Bentonville, where WalMart had its humble origins, is close by, as is Branson, Missouri, the headquarters of Not-So-New Country. At one time, the mountain communities around Rogers were as isolated as anywhere in the United States.

"We were way back in the hills," said Vernon, who was born on June 8, 1941, one of Frankie and Walter's seven children. "We didn't even have electricity. I was born under the hill where we ended up living. My mother had tuberculosis so my dad traded his creek farm for the one up on the hill 'cause that would be a little drier. The soil was real rich, and you could grow beautiful potatoes and corn. My oldest brother was in the army during the Second World War, and they had no other boys except me and I was real small so that throwed all the weight of the farming on dad, and all we had was a team and a plough. He couldn't keep it up and make a living out of it. There was a canning factory about ten miles from home, and mom and dad and my two sisters that lived at home worked at the canning factory. I'd go over there and I'd play outside all day until they got off work. Then we'd go home and pick enough tomatoes to load up the pickup to sell to the cannery the next day. They'd work for fifty cents an hour."

The Grand Ole Opry was Saturday night entertainment. "We had a big old battery radio," said Vernon. "Saturday nights, they'd always tune it into the Opry. Battery would be so weak, they'd sit it on the stove to heat it and charge it enough. Dad would bend his ear to the radio to hear it, but it'd be so weak comin' in. The kids had to be quiet. If someone was singing on the radio and you was making a noise, you'd get a knot on your head."

Sunday meant church. "They had an old country church that was three miles from the house. Dad had an old '32 Dodge pickup, but most times it wouldn't start and we'd have to walk. Mom made sure we went. That was every Sunday and every Wednesday night. One time they was having a revival and this preacher came in, and his favorite song was 'I've Been Waiting Lord To Go.' Everybody loved it, and I learned it by listening. I was maybe three or four. Mom had one of those old pedal organs, and she was sitting there playing that thing, and she asked me to get up and sing. I started singing 'I've Been Waiting,' and everybody got into crying. I went to crying." The preacher held Vernon up that day, anointing him as a singer.

The Oxfords hung on as long as they could. "In the winter there was nothing to make a living at," explained Vernon. "Dad tried to raise some chickens. There was this operation that would give you the chicks and the feed, and you'd raise 'em, and they'd buy them off you, but they'd falsify the amounts on the scale and you never would end up making any money. It got so bad in 1950 that dad finally went off to work in Kansas. Mom and me and my two sisters were still at home. We didn't have no electricity, no telephone. Nothing. Wood stove and kerosene lamps. You had to bring water up from the bottom of the holler, and the hills was real steep. You'd be carrying two buckets. We was so poor that mom made our clothes out of flour sacks. She made the sheets out of flour sacks. Twenty-five, fifty-pound bags of flour, they had prints on the outside of them, and that's what was on my shirt. Every year, just before school started, they'd go into town and get us a pair of used shoes to wear. You'd go barefoot in the summer. Everyone was that poor, and we had plenty to eat from the hogs and calves, squirrels and fish." Some country stars take an inverted pride in their poor upbringing, but there's a kind of hangdog shame in the way Vernon describes it. You almost want to reassure him that it's okay.

In 1951, Walter Oxford came back to Arkansas, collected his family and took them to Wichita, Kansas, about 200 miles northwest of Rogers. The family possessions were loaded into the back of a 1930 Chevy. The kids were perched high atop the bedding on the back seat. They ran into bad snow just outside Wichita, and had to spend almost all of their money on a hotel room. "Next day," remembered Vernon, "Dad got stopped going the wrong way down a one-way street. Never had seen one. Cop stopped us, and dad said, 'I was wondering why all them stupid fools was comin' right at me and honkin' at me.'" Walter eventually got a union job at the IGA food distribution terminal at $2.00 an hour. Frankie made paper roses, and Vernon sold them on the streets. The farm remained vacant until the Oxfords returned to it after Walter retired in 1963.

Vernon was ten or eleven when the family arrived in Wichita, but never truly left Arkansas. The kids in school laughed at him. "I was hard of hearing," he said.

> I had had some kind of disease that left holes in both eardrums, so I sung and talked real loud. After we went to Kansas, it was like going to jail. You had none of the freedom you had in the country schools. I was an outcast. They didn't like people from Arkansas anyway. I was a hick from the sticks. Biggest town I'd ever been in was Rogers, and that was only 3,200 people, and we'd only go there once or twice a year. I'd never seen an automatic door, or an elevator, or an escalator. Rogers had maybe one traffic light. I'd open my mouth to say something and people would snicker, you know. I couldn't hear what the teacher was saying half the time, so I didn't understand the lessons. The teacher would make me sit up front and by myself, kinda making a spectacle of me, and I had an infection in my right ear and it stunk so bad you couldn't get close to me. I'd go to doctors trying to get it cleared up, and it'd come right back. The only time I was popular was when I would open my mouth and sing. I'd been popular in Arkansas with a song.

Vernon badgered his mother into buying him a $16 guitar. He quit school halfway through the tenth grade, and, with a sense of timing that was always a little off, started playing country music around the time that rock 'n' roll hit. Most fifteen-year-olds with a guitar hurried to embrace rock 'n' roll; Vernon did not. "In '56, Elvis come out and that ended country music on the radio in Wichita," he explained. "That's the reason I hated Elvis, 'cause to me he killed country music. I took offense at it. When I was a teenager playing the bars, I'd throw in a fast one, like 'Jailhouse Rock,' have a little fun with it. You had to do 'em. I'd make up rock 'n' roll songs as I went along, and people would yell and ask for 'em again, and I couldn't remember what I'd sung."

Vernon joined a band with his sister and her husband, but eventually struck out on his own. He went to Utah and Arizona, then returned to Wichita. At some point in 1961, he met Loretta Robertson. They married on March 3, 1962, and Vernon insists that he has never been with another woman since. He tried some day jobs, but couldn't get the idea of Nashville out of his system. He needed to know whether he was good enough. In May 1964, Vernon and Loretta loaded everything into their car and headed for their celestial city. They stopped over in Arkansas to visit Vernon's parents, who had retired to the farm a year earlier, then drove on.

The first place they stopped in Nashville was Mack's on Broadway. It's emblematic of the changes overtaking the city that Mack's meat-and-three is now Ken's Sushi Bar. "We'd been lost," says Vernon. "I was tired of all the traffic. I said, 'I'll get me a beer.' Walked in Mack's. Loretta got her a coffee. I said, 'Where's Music Row?' Told the guy there that I come to get into the music business. He said, 'You any good?' I said, 'Durn right I'm good.' I started singing there. Told him I needed $10 a night, pass the kitty, give me a beer or two. Made $30 or $35 a night. Pretty good money then."

Vernon went up and down Music Row. One of the stops was RCA, where Chet Atkins was in charge. In early 1963, Atkins got approval to hire another A&R man. Bob Ferguson got the nod, and, without him, it's doubtful if we would ever have heard Vernon Oxford. Ferguson was from Willow Springs, Missouri, less than 200 miles from Rogers, Arkansas. He had managed Ferlin Husky, and written one of Husky's biggest hits, "Wings of a Dove." In 1961, Ferguson came to Nashville to start a publishing company. From time to time, Chet gave him tapes to check out. Ferguson had been with RCA a little more than a year when Vernon Oxford knocked and entered.

"I went to RCA," said Vernon, "and I said I wanted to see somebody about doing some recording. This woman looked at me kinda grand, went down the hall and said, 'Mr. Ferguson will be with you in a minute.' He looked round the corner, grinning. He said, 'We generally require a tape.' I said, 'If you really want to know what I sound like, you need to hear me in person. Tape don't do me justice.' He kinda grinned, cocked his feet up on his desk, and said, 'Sing to me.' I sung him four or five songs, and he said, 'Well, we're not signing anyone right now,' but he said I should come back if I didn't get a deal anywhere else. I checked around the rest of that week, and nobody wanted me, so the next week I went back. He said, 'I told you we wasn't signing nobody,' and I said, 'Yeah, but that was last week.' He asked me to come back at eight o'clock in the morning and do a tape in Studio B. He said he was going see what I sounded like. I said, 'Yes sir.'"

Vernon Oxford was very much in keeping with Bob Ferguson's vision of country music, but not Chet Atkins's. Ferguson took Vernon's tape to Atkins. "Here," he said. "I didn't know there was any of them left." Atkins had no interest. The reason, says Ferguson, was that Vernon sounded a little like Hank Williams. In the years immediately after Williams died, everyone who came to Nashville sounded like Hank Williams, but, by 1964, the pendulum had swung in the opposite direction. Ferguson gave Vernon the tape, telling him that it might help him land a deal elsewhere. Vernon played it to Harlan Howard, perhaps the most consistently successful songwriter in the history of country music. At one point, Harlan attracted a small cult who tried to figure out his secret from his mannerisms and his habits. Harlan's hits included Wynn Stewart's "Above and Beyond," Patsy Cline's "I Fall to Pieces," Johnny Cash's "Busted," and several Buck Owens hits.

Harlan Howard became a believer in Vernon Oxford, warning him off the sharks that hung around newly arrived hillbillies. He promised Vernon some songs from a publishing company, Wilderness Music, that he owned in conjunction with Don Davis. Vernon took that promise back to Bob Ferguson. "I called Bob and said, 'Would RCA be interested in me if Harlan Howard wrote me a song?'" remembered Vernon. "Bob says, 'Yeah, man, we'd be interested.' I said, 'Can I tell Harlan that?' He said, 'Sure.' So I called Harlan and he called Bob, and then Harlan called me back and said, 'How soon can you be over here?' I was at work, so I told the boss I had business, and thirty minutes later I was there. Harlan and his manager set up a session at one of the studios and hired the musicians. I went down and recorded three songs Harlan had written. On the session there was a guy who worked for United Artists, and he said, 'If RCA don't take him, I will.' Two weeks went by, and I don't know what went on. I guess Harlan took my tape up to RCA, and he called me and said to call Bob, and Bob

Vernon cradles his first RCA Victor Record, c. 1965. Courtesy Colin Escott.

said, 'Vernon, can you come over here right now? Chet wants to meet you.' Out I go again. Chet let me know they was gonna sign me. That was October of 1965."

When Vernon Oxford cut his first session on December 17, 1965, Eddy Arnold was atop the country charts with his revival of Jim Reeves's hit, "Make the World Go Away." Vernon was from the other end of the rainbow. The first single, "Watermelon Time in Georgia," tapped into a pretty familiar theme, the homesick southerner's lament. It got a fair amount of play, but didn't chart. Almost five years later, in May 1970, Lefty Frizzell cut the song and scored a middling hit with it. Vernon probably did his cause no good by coupling it with another equally strong Harlan Howard song, "Woman Let Me Sing You a Song." Before that first single came out in February 1966, Don Davis, Harlan Howard, and Bob Ferguson tried to get Vernon on the Opry. "Our idea was that if we could get the Opry to put him on then we could get RCA to spring for big trade ads," said Ferguson. "We went to the Opry to see Ott Devine and we played the session tapes for Ott. Ott said he was a little too country for the Opry. We were prepared for anything but that. It took the wind right out of our sails. We drove back to the office without saying anything. It was a sad day." Vernon got a guest spot on Porter Wagoner's portion of the show, and there was talk of him joining the cast of Porter's television show, but nothing happened.

The second session was, in some ways, Vernon's finest. Jeff Clay's "Move to Town in the Fall" could almost have been a page from Vernon's diary in its grim depiction of the empty promise of city life. Harlan Howard's "Goin' Home" took another stance on much the same theme. At that time, there was probably no commodity more precious in country music than a Harlan Howard song, and Vernon got more than anybody. The third session included a song from Howard's Wilderness Music, Shirl Milette's "Baby Sister." Milette went on to write some very mediocre songs for Elvis, but "Baby Sister" was a jewel. In the wrong hands, it could have been a joke, but in Vernon's hands it's heartrending: "I curse the man who made you what you are today / I hope he dies a thousand times, a thousand ways." Vernon takes baby sister's hand, leading her, her face daubed with rouge, from the honky-tonk. It was too bleak and unforgiving to stand much chance of airplay, but inasmuch as a song that never charted can be described as a classic, "Baby Sister" was one.

From the beginning, Vernon attracted a core of believers, but country radio wouldn't accept him. After two years, he was cut loose. Vernon had quit his day job in construction and had been picked up by the Buddy Lee Agency for bookings. When RCA dropped him, Buddy Lee dropped him too. Vernon went back to hanging drywall in the construction business, all the while looking for another record deal. The majors have always had a hammerlock on the country music business, so it was no surprise that Vernon's singles on Stop Records didn't get far. The next label, Omni, was even more of a commercial dead end.

Vernon didn't record again until 1974, and then it was for RCA. Something truly unusual had happened. "Around 1970," he remembered,

I started getting letters from overseas. I got some from a guy in Sweden and some from Mike Craig in Scotland. They was wondering why nothing new was coming, and I wrote back and told them I'd got dropped. They wrote back and asked if there was any unreleased material, and I wrote and said there was quite a bit. Mike Craig asked if there was something he could do to help me get back on the label, and I said he should write to the label. They wrote and got petitions from people all over England and Sweden to release the material and get me back on the label. I got people over here to organize petitions as well. Then in 1974, a guy came over to the house and asked if I'd do a tour of England. I didn't ask him how much or make any conditions, I just said yes. I just wanted to go. I paid my own airfare, and I got £80 a night and I had to sleep at people's homes.

Then they had a tour set for Patsy Montana over there, but they couldn't find her so they asked me if I'd do it. I said, "Sure." That was a six-week tour. Some people leased a coach and followed the whole tour. These people that booked me approached Mervyn Conn about getting me on Wembley [the International Festival of Country Music] the next year, and Conn's reply was, "Who's Vernon Oxford?" It wasn't long before Mervyn was calling me and said he wanted me on the next year. I was the first one on. I had twenty minutes. I gave it all I got, and they wouldn't let me go back and encore. People just kept hollerin'. It done me good to know that the people was lovin' me that much. When I come back to the United States, I got word that RCA was re-signing me.

In October 1973, RCA's British division issued everything Vernon had recorded for the label as a double album, and—incredibly—it sold well enough for RCA London to put some pressure on Nashville to generate some new product. Then word of Vernon's reception at the 1975 Wembley festival got back to Nashville. Bob Ferguson didn't need much encouragement to re-sign him.

On his second go-round, Vernon began showing up on the national country charts. Waylon Jennings and Willie Nelson had made stripped-down country music a little more fashionable, but Vernon was still countrier than anyone else. Despite the low chart placings, the cream of the Nashville songwriters wanted to get their material on Vernon's records.

"He caught the imagination of the writers," said Bob Ferguson. "They'd say, 'Bob, you've just got to cut one of my songs with Vernon.' Even Kris Kristofferson said that, though he never came up with anything." In the January 1975 issue of *Country Music* magazine, writer John Pugh painted a heartbreaking picture of Vernon going into RCA every day, sitting in the windowless conference room with a cup of coffee and a list of the 600 radio stations that programmed country music. He called them all, and time after time he was given the polite brush-off. "I try so hard," he told Pugh, "and I don't even get what I feel is an equal chance."

Success came from an unexpected place. Mitchell Torok had been hot in the 1950s when he'd written Jim Reeves's first hit, "Mexican Joe," then scored a Top 10 hit in England as an artist with "When Mexico Gave Up the Rhumba." By the mid-1960s, Torok's career had gone stone cold, and he was back in Texas. He and his wife planned to come to Nashville, and, just before they left, Torok was sitting in a nightclub watching the crowd. "These rednecks," he thought to himself, "are something else. Pinching the waitresses and so on." "Redneck (The Redneck National Anthem)," came to him in a flash, and, right after he moved, he went into the Fender Building in Nashville and cut a demo on which he played all the parts. Fender was across the street from RCA, so Torok took his tape, walked over to RCA, and asked for Bob Ferguson. After hearing half the song, Ferguson stopped the tape, picked up the phone, and called a session. He told Torok that it would be just right for Vernon Oxford. Torok had hardly heard of Vernon, but he was happy to get a song cut so soon after coming to Nashville. Vernon hee-hawed it up to perfection, and the result was a Top 20 country record.

"A company in Houston promised to make a sign for the record and put it around Houston on the interstates," said Vernon. "After we released the record, RCA flew me to Houston to pose with this sign, then somebody stole it. Sixty foot by forty foot. I'd have had a Number 1 record 'cept the big country stations in New York and Los Angeles wouldn't play it. RCA wouldn't buy me a full-page ad in *Billboard*. It was song of the year different places." The song was especially big in Texas. Vernon remembers people crossing their hearts when he sang it there.

The follow-ups sputtered in the lower reaches of the country charts. "Clean Your Own Tables" was by Chip Taylor, brother of actor Jon Voigt, sometime Buddah and Warner Bros. recording artist, and Polygram A&R man. Taylor had struck the motherlode in England with "Wild Thing" and "Angel of the Morning," but "Clean Your Own Tables" wasn't the smash everyone had hoped. RCA kept the faith for a few more singles. In an act of desperation, Vernon cut another Mitchell Torok song, "Redneck Roots," an appalling number that deserved the oblivion that enveloped it. Perhaps Vernon should have taken his last shot with Paul Craft's "Brother Jukebox." His version was the first, but it wasn't released. Later, in 1977, it became a minor hit for Don Everly, and then a Number 1 hit for Mark Chesnutt in 1990. Vernon can't listen to "Redneck Roots" objectively. He was so out of touch then that it amounted to a form of autism. "It should have been the biggest of all," he says, all evidence to the contrary. "They killed it. I knew right then I was out the door again. Why?"

Out the door he was. Bob Ferguson soon followed, quitting on January 1, 1978. "It was fun to be in Nashville when it was growing," Ferguson said, "but not then. It just wasn't exciting any more." While at RCA, Ferguson had studied anthropology at Vanderbilt University's graduate school, and married a Choctaw woman. They moved to Philadelphia, Mississippi, and Ferguson set up a video production unit for the Choctaw nation. He died on July 22, 2001, less than one month after Chet Atkins.

Vernon bottomed out at the end of his second RCA contract. He was drinking heavily, and the years of hanging drywall on construction sites had damaged his back to the point that it caused him incessant pain. Vernon's treatment at the hands of the music business compounded his bleak outlook on life. "I thought about killing myself sometimes," he said.

> It got to where I didn't care if I was alive or not. I couldn't see things coming together like I thought they should. I couldn't understand the business end of it. Why did they have to be so competitive and backstabbing? I was raised on handshake deals to be a man of your word, and I'd see people promise me something then go behind my back and laugh about it. My dad died in '76. I had been down there the week before, took them out to town. Dad was feeling good, but a week later he was sweeping the floor and fell over dead. That made me realize how close we are to Heaven or Hell. The next year my son was born, and we'd been married sixteen years with no children. I wasn't being the man I should have been in my marriage, drinkin' and so on. Through all the things I did, Loretta stayed with me. I don't know why. I wasn't worthy. I wasn't happy in anything. Being known as a singer, being married, having a son. I was just

miserable. Didn't want to live. Couldn't stand to be alone; had to be around people. I knew I was gonna have to do some changing. We'd bought a house, and I said, "We've got us a home now, and we've got us a child, let's start all over." My wife said, "What do you mean?" I said, "Let's go to church Sunday." I had been to church once since I was a teenager. My wife had said she would not go to church with a drunk. To me, the church was like the music business. No love there; just business. God wasn't in it. Anyway we went to church, and I think God said, "I've got to get him while I can." When it come to the altar call, God got me, and I went to cryin'. I went down front and committed myself to the Lord. I said to the Lord that I'd rather die and go to Hell than act the way I'd seen Christians act. He spoke to me loud and plain. He said, "Do you have to be that way? You can be a Christian and set an example." I made my mind up I was going to be for God, and wasn't going to be a hypocrite.

I quit the beer. I was drinking one time, and my son had just got to where he was toddlin', and he came up and said, "Me drink, daddy." I said, "No, this ain't for little children." When I said that, the Lord spoke to me again. He said, "Well, what are you doing drinking in front of him?" I got to cryin' again. I said, "Lord, I'll finish my six-pack and I'll quit." And I did. I had already quit smoking. I use to smoke three packs a day.

Vernon was still a star in Europe, and there were still a few believers back home. Ken Irwin at Rounder Records commissioned Bob Ferguson to produce two albums for the label. As before, Vernon attracted the cream of the songs and the cream of the pickers. The first album to be released, *His and Hers*, was tagged after a new song by Paul Craft, who, in addition to "Brother Jukebox," had written "Dropkick Me Jesus" for Bobby Bare. The jacket of *His and Hers* ranks among the all-time great country album sleeves. "Bob said, 'We want something to get the message across on the front of the album,'" remembered Vernon. "He had the license tags 'His' and 'Hers' made up, and they found a two-car garage out in Belle Meade somewhere. I'd just come in off the road, and I had that big Buick. The back end was filthy, and they said they wanted to get my car in the picture but we had to wash it first. I said, 'Sure, man, you want to wash my car, you're welcome.' We drove up around Highway 100, and there's a creek near the road with slabs so you can drive across it. We got it down there

"Hers." Courtesy Bear Family Archive.

and washed the back end off. In the picture you'll notice wet tire tracks."
Vernon, who has a hangdog face at the best of times, looks wonderfully
forlorn clutching the "Hers" plate. It belongs in the pantheon of great
country jacket art, dominated by Porter Wagoner and Mack Vickery's *Live
at the Alabama Women's Prison.*

The Rounder albums didn't sell, and there haven't been many releases
since. Unlike many country artists from earlier days who drifted into production, song publishing, management, or booking, Vernon has remained
a man apart. He still performs gospel music occasionally, but his biggest
following remains overseas. He still lives near Nashville, and works part-
time as a salesman. His radio is tuned to the country stations on the way
to work, and he tries to be positive about what he hears, but his lament is
a familiar one. "I like Vince Gill's way with a ballad," he said. "Randy
Travis, Alan Jackson. Different ones. My only gripe is that when Ernest
Tubb or Hank Williams kicked off, you knew it was them. They had that

distinct band, distinct voice. Now you listen to the radio and you can't hardly tell when one artist quits and the other one comes on. Same type song, same beat. There's no individuality. Thirty minutes, you're tired of it. There's no real feelin'. The person is killed out of it. Used to be you'd hear a sad song and bawl all over the place. The artist put his whole self in it."

The business has knocked him down once too often for Vernon to really cherish dreams of getting back into it. He once said that it was easier to become president of the United States than become a country music star. Inevitably, when the Branson scene opened up, Vernon thought of starting a theater there. It was so close to home. But financing fell through; then Branson fell through.

"I don't write songs anymore," said Vernon. "I can't get into it. Lost heart. You get discouraged, so many times you get passed by. You can only get knocked down so many times. People say, 'That should have been your break,' 'That should be you here.' People said, 'Boxcar Willie's opening should've been yours.' The timing was off. One thing a lot of them wish they had: I can go where I want to, and people don't pay attention to me. I have been big, travelled everywhere, seen a whole lots of places I never would have got to seen, made a whole lots of friends all over the world. Seen whole lots of walks of life. Seen people saved through the Lord through knowin' me. I've played with some of the best of them, the biggest. Even though I never got to be a millionaire, it was an experience you can't buy, an education you can't get in school."

Most of Vernon's venom is still reserved for the business, though. "I can't stand the lyin' and cheatin,'" he said. "When I was drinkin', I'd get my gun. I'd be likely to kill someone. I'd go down and get my money. Can't do that as a Christian, and I was lucky I got by with it as a drunk!"

Check It Out

The early RCA sides are complete on *Let Me Sing You A Song* (Westside WESA 849). All of Vernon's recordings from the 1960s to the '80s, are complete on *Keeper of the Flame*, a five-CD set from Bear Family (BCD 15774).

Index